Praise

"*Worthy*'s stories of resilience, grit and wit are funny, scathingly honest, and heartwarming. Showing that our success and worth are not defined by others, they are wisdom from the soul for women (and men)."

— Robbie Bach, former President of Microsoft, Author, Consultant, and Civic Engineer

"*Worthy*'s deeply honest and insightful stories of what it's like to be a rebel in work and in life prove why it pays to break the rules."

— Francesca Gino, Harvard Business School Professor and Best-selling Author of *Rebel Talent*

"Jane is a gifted storyteller. She shares what many have experienced and felt but are uncomfortable talking about. *Worthy* exposes harsh truths about life's challenges, both professional and personal, and does so with threads of courage, humor and vulnerability."

— Hedy Lukas, VP- Kimberly-Clark Corp, retired

"Jane's writing is raw and relatable. *Worthy* is an authentic look into the leadership mechanics of how resilience builds from failure and how success builds more confidence."

— Teri Citterman, Executive Coach and Author *From the CEO's Perspective*

"Jane's stories of overcoming are real and relevant to all. Her wit, vulnerability, and passion for life, people, and paying it forward—no matter what— shines through."

— Tim Motts, CEO, Boys & Girls Clubs of Bellevue

"A very honest, deeply moving book that connects smarts, hard work, and heart from an accomplished businesswoman. Inspirational and empowering!"

— Rafael Lisitsa, CEO, Affective Software

"Jane's book *Worthy* is an inspiration to all. Read this book!"

— John Gottman, PhD, world-renowned relationship expert, bestselling author

"Jane's achievements are far more than title and money, but resilience of the spirit in overcoming obstacles. Everyone can find themselves in her stories."

— Joanie Parsons, Founder, Revel 11 and Parsons and Co.

"Through countless fun stories that inspire because they come so close to our own, Jane shows us that our happiness and success starts with feeling worthy to unleash our human potential to drive sustainable positive impact for ourself, others and our world."

—Janneke Van Den Berkmortel, VDBCoach

"Jane's honesty about her inner struggles with guilt and self-worth while she outwardly soared is refreshing and compelling—making *Worthy* a very worthy read."

— Ingrid Ricks, NYT Best-Selling Author and Transformational Speaker

"A must-read for women stuck in career doldrums and questioning their worth. Jane's humorous, no-nonsense prose invites us to reflect on life's challenges and triumphs to find the courage to claim our seat at the table."

— Jan Hill, Author of *Smart Women, Smart Moves*

"*Worthy* will entertain, enable and encourage you to claim your worth."

— Lisa Hufford, Author of *Work, Your Way* and Founder, Simplicity Consulting

~~un~~Worthy

"scathingly honest and funny . . . wisdom from the soul"
— **Robbie Bach, former President, Microsoft**

"*Worthy* is an inspiration to all . . . Read this book!"
— **JOHN GOTTMAN, PhD, relationship expert**

~~un~~Worthy

From Cornfields to Corner Office of Microsoft

stories of overcoming

JANE BOULWARE

WORTHY:
From Corn Fields to Corner Office of Microsoft

Copyright @2024 by Jane Boulware

Published by Worthy Emprises LLC

www.JaneBoulware.com

All rights reserved. No part of this book may be reproduced in any manner whatsoever without the expressed written permission of the author.

Every attempt has been made to properly source all quotes and attribute all research.

Also available in e-book

Editor: Corbin Lewars
Author Photo: Keith Cockerham

Paperback ISBN: 979-8-9873419-4-0
Hardcover ISBN: 979-8-9873419-5-7
eBook ISBN: 979-8-9873419-6-4

Printed in the United States of America

First Edition

*For my family
by birth and by choice.*

Table of Contents

Introduction	11
The Pickle Bucket Years	
The Pickle Bucket	15
Me and Mine	17
Us Versus Them	23
Work Hard, ~~Play~~ Work Hard	27
On Being Catholic	33
The Magic Freezer	38
Buckle Up, Buster!	42
Busted But Not Broken	49
The Fields	54
Directions Not Included	63
For Sale: Used Carpet & Prayers	69
Learning to Laugh and Love	76
Beginnings	81
Lessons From the Forest	85
Purdue	87
Jane of All Trades	
Who's Kimberly-Clark?	93
Becoming a Cheesehead	98
Betterer	102
4 o'clock Friends	111
In the Black	116
Andy	119
I'm a Big Kid Now	126
La Gringa	131
Upside Down Worlds	139

From Stump to Rump	150
FUD (Fear, Uncertainty and Despair)	158
Jack	164
Perspective	171
The Only Constant is Change	175
Worth Beyond Wealth	
Lifting Up	183
Microsoft	186
The Battlefield	191
Out of the Frying Pan	202
Broken But Not Busted (again)	206
Choices	212
Legacy	216
Rebooting Jane	221
One Person Can ~~Only~~ Do So Much	229
Outside In	235
Doing What 'Can't' Be Done	240
Home	246
Enough	250
Correction of Errors	253
Time Out	260
From Boxes to Becoming	266
Retired to Inspired	269
Mom	272
Youth of the Year	276
It's Time	280
Epilogue	**285**
Acknowledgments	**289**

Introduction

Truth is, I was never meant to be successful and did so while no one was looking. Too scrappy to fail, too stubborn to give up and too scared to let others down, *Worthy* is a journey of grit, wit and learning self-worth is not defined by what others say, expect or have, but by what you make, claim and give of what you got. These stories are what I got to give.

Born the fourth kid in a one-bedroom house, my path was forged long before me: get married, make babies and stay on the good side of the church and the law, in that order. The law did me no favors, but a gnarly nun did, securing a $320 scholarship to a future I didn't know existed. I left for college before my folks knew I was gone, selling dad's used carpeting and mom's prayers to pay my way.

Penniless and married at 21 years old, I had an MBA at 24, first saw the ocean at 25, commuted to South America each week at 31, brought two sons into the world by 35, was a millionaire at 37, and was one of a select few Microsoft executives at 40.

Along the way to the corner office, I've been hit on, spit on, shot at, yelled at, a zero and a hero. I've been called a bulldog, a bitch, brilliant and inspiring all on the same day. Dismissed and underestimated by many, often myself, I sought relief through addiction, found support from the least expected, and hope when it mattered most.

I've learned on the journey I am worthy as I am. I didn't have to earn it or prove it. No one gave it to or took it from me. I didn't become it. Worth didn't come in a Tiffany's box, a graduate degree, a bank statement, or a title. I didn't lose it with failure or get more with success. I am worthy as I am. And so are you.

Part I

The Pickle Bucket Years

The Pickle Bucket

"He is rich or poor according to what he is, not what he has."
— Henry Ward Beecher

Highlights from the first 18 years of my life fit into a 5-gallon bucket. Literally. Each kid in my family had one. The buckets were lined up, five in a row, jammed under the rafters in the attic. Mine was white and originally stored pickles at Mac's Café until mom got ahold of it and scribbled JANE in bold magic marker across its white belly, making it mine. Five gallons worth of pickles is a lot of pickles. Five gallons worth of life isn't much, but it was mine. In that bucket was the time capsule of my life, where only the most important memories, photos, ribbons, and certificates of worth (birth, baptism, first communion etc.) were placed for safe keeping. The very proof of my existence was stored in that bucket. Some kids get scrapbooks and home movies; I got a pickle bucket.

What went into the bucket said a lot about me, my childhood value carefully tucked away among the ribbons and achievements, the vessel into which my pride was stored. Ours was a family where worth was defined by how hard you worked and I was determined to fill my bucket to the brim with what I'd done and achieved, the proof that I MATTERED. Only treasured items made the bucket. After all, treasures are not pickles.

Yet to this day when I smell pickles, I think of home and of Snorty, my stuffed hippopotamus and best friend into whose snout I whispered all my little girl hopes and fears. I carefully placed Snorty into my sacred pickle bucket for safekeeping after he became too fragile for the pragmatic world in which I lived, secure in knowing he was there, awaiting the day I should again seek his counsel, again stroke his thread-bare pink nose to find comfort among things scary and confusing. Until he was gone.

Gone with everything else dad deemed unworthy the weekend he cleaned the attic. Dad kept the scraps of carpet and barrels of moonshine lining the rafters but tossed the pickle bucket with JANE scribbled boldly on its belly and, with it, chucked Snorty and the assorted treasures preserving my dreams and proclaiming my achievements. Maybe he didn't think I'd notice or mind, for mine is a practical, hard-working family not one to dwell long on yesterday's achievement nor ponder dreams of tomorrow when there is plenty work to be done in the here and now. As I think back on my childhood in the here and now, some memories are sketchy and resist being brought back to life, some memories stay stuck in the bucket and are forever gone while others spring onto these pages, glad for the telling. Regardless, these are my stories as I remember them, even though most evidence was lost the day my bucket was chucked.

Me and Mine

Before you ask which way to go, remember where you've been.

— unknown author

For the first 18 years of my life, I thought Carroll, Iowa was the center of the universe. For me it was. For everyone else, Carroll is miles from anywhere and close to nowhere. The closest airport is nearly three hours and three decades away. You go back in time one decade for every hour you drive from the airport, eventually arriving in the mid-80s, where Carroll has remained pleasantly frozen in time. High-waisted jeans, *Reader's Digest, Catholic Digest*, parish cookbooks and pie have never gone out of style.

Everyone in Carroll was blonde-haired, blue-eyed and probably related somehow, if you looked close enough. Which you didn't. Everyone worked hard and lived modestly in well-kept tiny ranch homes with well-kept, tidy yards. Folks seldom traveled out of state except to Las Vegas and no one I knew belonged to the country club or drove new cars. The folks in Carroll look you in the eye when saying "hi" and mean it when saying "have a good day." Carroll is a strong, proud, hardworking community that smells of freshly cut hay in the summer, roast beef in the winter, and pigs throughout the year, depending on which direction the wind is blowing. There is a right and wrong way of doing things in Carroll, and folks are plenty willing to tell you which is which.

JCPenney anchored main street, providing both high fashion and function to generations long before me. It was the last stop mom made after scouring the county each autumn looking for used school clothes. Her quest ended at JCP, where she reluctantly bought the few necessities that couldn't be borrowed – knee high socks, undies and one new, good white blouse. The first 18 years of my life were spent wearing some other kid's clothes and for nine months of the year, a plaid Catholic school jumper. Onto the front of the jumper was sewn a well-worn patch (St. Lawrence Grade School, then Kuemper Catholic High School) and on the back label was a name carefully crossed out and replaced with Jane. My 'good' white blouse was starched until crispy and saved for 'good' occasions until all the good was gone and reluctantly replaced with an identical 'good' blouse in a larger size, thus renewing the good/gone clothing cycle. Such was and is the extent of my style savvy.

Mom always said, it matters less *what* you wear but *how* you wear it that counts; the people who matter will notice the smile on your face and the pride in your stance before noticing the label on your clothes. True or not, all I know is that we always held our heads high, because mom ensured we looked clean, pressed and proud, even when not wearing our 'good' clothes.

I was the fourth kid born in a one-bedroom house, the fourth of five Riesberg kids born within six years. Three of us (including me) were born within 26 months. Doug's 11 months older than me, making him my Irish twin. Doug and I were inseparable growing up, so tight that when Doug stubbed his toe I said "ouch." So it's not surprising that mom had a hard time keeping everything and everyone straight. For a long time, I thought my name was Juliejeffdougjanelinn because when mom called a kid, she just started at the top and stopped when she got to the name of the kid she wanted. You could tell by her tone when she was mad. When she was really wound up, she sometimes forgot to stop at the right kid's name and had to go around the horn and start at the top all over again. This could take a while and was a blessing for it gave enough time to make a getaway before mom landed on your name, like Russian roulette. I seldom heard the name Jane out of context of Juliejeffdougjanelinn, since like a small herd, we never strayed far from one another or the small world that was our home.

My mom's name is Madonna Bernadette. I think it goes without saying that there is a lot of pressure in being named after two power saints, two really big guns in the Catholic Saint Hierarchy. Maybe that's why mom avoided naming her own kids John, Joseph, Mary, etc. We were named after junior varsity saints, which fit us perfectly. We kids sometimes referred to mom as Madonna Bernadette. If you have a power name, you kinda have to use it. After all, you wouldn't call Mother Theresa of Calcutta by the name Terri or TC. Not that I'm comparing Madonna Bernadette to Mother Theresa.

Being Madonna Bernadette was a lot to live up to, yet by her own admission, it was sometimes all mom could do to make it through the day when I was growing up. When things got to be too much, mom would need time to regroup, refresh coping skills and renew prescriptions, all of which occurred during periodic stays at the state mental hospital in Sioux City. If someone had asked Madonna Bernadette as a 20-year-old, bright-eyed virgin bride if she expected to have five kids in the next six years she would have looked back horrified. And yet, all I need to do is look down and see Mom's 1956 Kuemper High School class ring on my right hand to remember we both graduated from Kuemper High exactly 25 years apart. At my five-year class reunion, I had an MBA and a career. At Mom's five-year class reunion, she had four kids with another on the way. Mom learned more in the five years after high school creating a family than I did creating a career. Only her education came without professors, books or curriculum. What can prepare you for five kids in six years? Nothing.

So it's not surprising that I have no memories of being tucked into bed at night, or being hugged or kissed as a child, although I suppose I was. Madonna Bernadette was not the mom who'd push us on a swing or utter the words, "let's go play" or even "I love you" although I suppose she did. If asked to name the color of my mom's eyes, I'd have said… sad. Although I'd never seen Mom cry. I didn't know the color of mom's eyes because I never saw them. They were focused elsewhere and always, understandably, busy.

Ours was a one-bedroom, one-bathroom house, located at the very bottom of Highland Drive. As far as I knew, our house wasn't small and we weren't poor, for we had what we needed and if not, borrowed it from the other families and houses just like ours up and down the block. Like everywhere, Carroll had a pecking order. In our neighborhood, worthiness and prestige weren't measured so much in what you had as in how clean and tidy you kept what you had, including your kids. That made my mom Queen Bee.

Mom would have made Mr. Clean feel dirty. Ammonia, vinegar and bleach were her good friends – branded cleaners were expensive and for the weak. Mere dusting and vacuuming were for amateurs. In our house, the walls were washed almost as often as the dishes. The windows sparkled. Beds were made with hospital corners and *everything* was ironed – with creases – with starch – even hankies. Mom believed *anything* could be born again with enough starch. Dirt wasn't welcome and crumbs weren't tolerated at the Riesberg home. The waffle iron was carefully vacuumed before being put away on carpet-lined shelves. The floors so spotless that feet became cleaner if you walked around barefoot. If cleanliness is next to godliness, Mom earned an express elevator to heaven.

When it came to cleanliness, Mom was a perpetual motion machine, like one of those perfectly weighted bobbing bird paperweights found in airplane magazines, constantly picking up lint here, wiping a counter there, never stopping. We didn't question her quest for the immaculate, didn't judge as she sought to create a household that was perfectly clean and tidy. She wielded her broom like a conductor wields a baton, sweeping us five kids in a symphony of vacuuming, dusting, washing, wiping. Having a spotless home and tidy children were as necessary as food and drink, requiring absolute focus and infinite energy. No matter how big or small your world, everyone needs a piece to master, to provide a sense of accomplishment, achievement and self-worth. Five kids were too unruly to manage, much less master, so mom looked right past us to the dirt around us. Dirt was one of the few things she could control and conquer in her never-ending attempt to receive respect and approval from my dad; no one banished dirt with more zeal or tenacity.

Mom learned the 'right way' to clean from her mom. Cleanliness was mom's inheritance, given to her then to us five children as surely as the gift of music from musicians or education from the educated. There was a lot to learn. For starters, there were special towels, good towels, drying towels, scrubbing towels, good rags, window-washing rags, old rags and regular rag rags. Each had a special place in the cabinet and woe to anyone caught using a good towel for an old rag job. Cries of "Don't use *that* towel for crying out loud!" happened so often that it no longer merited an eye roll. Dirt is cunning and clever, clinging to places and in ways only mom could see. It wasn't gray hair that signaled mom's aging, it was the realization that she'd stopped vacuuming the garage daily, moving to a more reasonable every other day schedule that signaled the perpetual motion machine was slowing a bob or two.

We hadn't a lot but took good care of what we had. If something broke, it was fixed or repurposed, not replaced. There was less pride in buying new than in making something work like new again. Plastic bags had nine lives, used and reused until finally knotted and woven into a durable rug that provided years of service. Even old bathtubs got a second life in the backyard as a shrine into which was placed a statue of the Blessed Virgin Mary (BVM) and some plastic flowers. Lutherans and other heathens referred to this as a BVM on the half shell.

While learning the 'right way' to earn, clean and care for my things, I inherited a strong work ethic and an absolute faith that all has value, even the things 'used' or discarded by others. All this was passed to me in moments spent washing, cleaning and repurposing the old until it was like new again. It seems to me most things of worth aren't inherited at life's end, they're taught and given during moments throughout a life. I'll inherit no money or land from my family, but instead was given the means to earn both.

Us Versus Them

You can't be bitter and expect your life to be sweet.
— unknown author

Dad was 'Ron' of Ron's Floor Service – it said so right on his shirt. He left the house well before 6:00 each morning to lay carpeting, climbing into an old white Dodge van which guzzled a quart of oil a day. His van had two front seats, tools carefully stored on racks dad designed and mounted on each side, and a metal floor with holes rusted clear through upon which were placed rolls of carpet and buckets of glue. Dad's hands and knees were thick and tough with calluses earned working long days to ensure we were fed and clothed. During family trips, all five kids and several coolers piled into dad's work van, each kid roosting on an empty glue bucket that generally covered any holes in the floor. It worked well until the van cornered too fast and five kids + five buckets went tumbling. Occasionally, Dad would have a large roll of carpet in the van and there was no room for the buckets. We straddled that roll of carpet and hung on for dear life, riding it like a bucking bronco, balancing to keep from getting thrown each time dad made a turn. We thought it was great fun; Mom did not.

But the long days of physical labor and responsibility took a toll on Dad. As a 26-year-old father of five, dad had exchanged the confidence and cockiness of high school for durable polyester work pants woven with stiff strands of exhaustion, worry, and regret. Just a kid himself really, doing his best to support a wife and five kids he didn't really want. His proud, broad back sagged as much from the weight of the chip on his shoulder as from the rolls of carpet he carried. It's difficult not to become bitter when there's so little to show for having worked so hard, and not to despair when you look into the future and see more of the same. How do you love and not resent the very family for whom you labor, in a job you hate, when everything within you is yearning to be free from the vows and responsibility you can never escape?

Most days, Dad drove an hour or more to the homes/offices where he laid carpet. He said he didn't like working locally, but I often wondered if each mile he drove away from us enabled him to exhale just a bit, to loosen the yoke of responsibility just a few notches. Sometimes the courage it required to return to us, to resume the role of husband and father, was too great. On those nights, Dad could be found elsewhere, pretending for just a while that he was someone he wasn't, until responsibility called, and he returned to the life and family to which he was bound.

Dad had an old motorcycle that he liked to ride, and occasionally he would give each kid a ride around the neighborhood. Those rides were magical, the wind gently lifting my pigtails then releasing them in a soft womp, womp, womp. There was no place I wanted more to be than sitting behind my dad, my fists clinging to his shirt, cheek pressed against his strong, bony back. I felt scared yet safe, my heart flooding with emotion during these rare, intimate moments when I had Dad all to myself. The rides seemed to end before they began. One beautiful summer evening I threw caution to the wind, so filled with joy that I mustered the courage to shout, "I love you, Dad!" as I clung tightly to his shirt, wind womp womp womping my hair just as I'd hoped it would. I'd never told Dad I loved him or heard it from him or another. I listened for his response but there was none. Instead, I felt his muscles tense as he rounded the corner and pulled slowly into the driveway. The look on his face told us there would be no more rides that day as dad lifted me to the ground and put away the motorcycle, leaving me standing silently on the sidewalk, wondering.

I used to wonder why I blurted my love despite my fear, for we weren't a family that made such declarations. Love was implied rather than said or expressed directly. But still, why didn't he respond at all? I've since come to understand that dad's love was never a question of 'why' but an answer of 'how' for sometimes love is spoken in actions, not words, in ways often overlooked, discounted or dismissed. Playing catch, finding and fixing old bikes, giving rides around the block on your motorcycle. Food. Clothes. Mortgage. Coming home. Yes, my dad said 'I love you' often although the actual words never left his lips. Still, it would have been nice to hear.

Dad wasn't big on reading or following others' directions. Fortunately, he didn't need manuals to figure out how things worked and to make something out of nothing. One summer, Dad and some buddies tore the roof off our one-bedroom house and added two bedrooms upstairs – one for the three girls and another for the two boys. Brilliant with a hammer, welder and spare parts, he converted pipes into a swing set, hammered spare plywood into a fort and even glued old carpet remnants to the basement walls to convert a dark, damp and cold concrete room into a relatively warm, fun "rec room." What dad lacked in income, he had in ingenuity and resourcefulness. A room with shag carpet scraps made us the envy of the neighborhood kids and made me understand that you don't need book smarts to be smart. With a little effort and creativity, like MacGyver, he could make pretty much anything from pretty much nothing. And did.

But having so much of nothing made dad bitter. His bitterness was aimed at people with money, whom he referred to as "they" and "them," usually with contempt. I never knew what "they" did to us, but I knew it was bad. And I learned early on that you can't trust "them." I didn't know for sure who "they" were, so I generally distrusted everyone who wore a tie or dress outside of church.

Over the years, I watched as the chip on dad's shoulder grew, tainting his relationships as the "them" came to include more and more people that were not like "us." This included, but was not limited to, anyone wearing a suit, college folks, and people who didn't do "real work" as revealed through their clean fingernails and lack of calluses. It was well known that people who didn't do "real work" got rich off the sweat of those who did. Just a fact, no exceptions, not even for his daughter.

Work Hard, ~~Play~~ Work Hard

"The harder I work, the luckier I get."

— Joe Ricketts

In the Riesberg house, hard work wasn't expected, it was a given. From a young age, everyone had a job and was expected to contribute and be productive. To reinforce a strong work ethic, Mom hung needlepoint propaganda throughout the house with catchy phrases like, "The harder I work, the luckier I get." Evidently, we were damn lucky.

There was always something to be done, something to do, so sitting wasn't done for long. Dad used to come home from work, walk in the house and feel the TV. If the TV felt warm and homework wasn't done, chores weren't finished, or dinner wasn't ready, there was hell to pay. Mr. Rogers would not have wanted to be our neighbor if we'd been caught watching TV rather than getting work done. Rules were clear and seldom broken – punishment was quick and decisive. The Stick saw to that.

Mom seldom used The Stick but you learned not to cross her. She was more creative and devious in her punishments. I was in the third grade when mom discovered Doug and I had been stealing and smoking her Kool cigarettes. Her punishment was simple and brilliant. She sat us at the kitchen table, put a few packs of cigarettes between us and told us to start smoking and not stop or get up until we'd smoked every cigarette. Ha! Little did mom know that I was already a pack-a-day girl and had been smoking for months by the time we were caught. I couldn't believe I was smoking in front of my mom, even using her lighter! I puffed smugly on my first cig, feeling pretty darn cool with her Kools. Smug turned to silence as Doug and I puffed away. Gone was the usual sense of adventure or snickering that occurred when doing something naughty. Smoking in front of your mom, at the kitchen table with a picture of Jesus hanging on the wall, was serious business. With every cigarette, I felt progressively less cool as the haze of blue cigarette smoke began to hang heavy and smug grin became grim determination. Doug and I turned as gray as the smoke we were choking on until, inevitably, we barfed. And barfed. Maybe Dr. Spock would not have approved of Mom's methods, but I haven't stolen or smoked a cigarette since.

I quickly learned how to stay on Mom's good side and push the rules enough to avoid big infractions. Like cussing. Using the Lord's name in vain was a clear commandment breaker, resulting in an automatic grounding. But a little creativity made a curse into a prayer, of sorts. By adding just a few clarifiers, I could invoke Jesus' name any time I wanted. JESUS! Mary and Joseph! Sweet JESUS!

Mom knew the key to keeping five kids out of trouble was to put us to work. Even our play modeled real work. Mom kept us busy for hours and hours, day after day, throughout the summer with just a bucket of water and a paintbrush. She'd line us up outside our stone house and we'd "paint the house" with water, delighting as the water turned the stone different colors. We painted and painted, faster and faster, racing to finish a section before it dried in the sun.

I sometimes still catch myself 'painting the house,' doing the same thing over and over, working harder and harder to achieve an impossible outcome, yet never stopping to change my approach despite the obvious, inevitable failure. I wasn't too bright back then; I didn't know better. Now I do. Mostly.

When we weren't busy painting the house, Doug and I trekked to the Carroll Lumber Company to fill our little red wagon with scraps of wood and nails we found on the ground. We'd spend days hammering nails into wood, competing to see who could get the nail all the way into the wood with the fewest whacks, skills that have come in handy during dozens of home renovations through the years. I strongly believe every girl should own a decent hammer, screwdriver, socket wrench, measuring tape, level, roll of duct tape and jar full of nails/screws/hooks. Despite what many might believe or have been taught, a penis isn't required to use any of these tools. In fact, I've created, fixed and mended far more swinging a hammer and wielding a screwdriver than any needle and thread.

Fortunately for me, work and play were blind to gender, age and size. I would do almost anything ethical (always) and legal (mostly) for a buck. I can't remember a time when I didn't have a job. Really. I've delivered newspapers, mucked sludge, washed cars, been a babysitter, house sitter, housecleaner, field laborer, librarian, personal assistant, tutor, teacher, coach, clerk, bartender, waitress, delivery person, park attendant, park ranger and have worked a lemonade stand or two. I've worked for the city, the county, the state, for mom-and-pops and big box, for fine dining and fast-food. I've tarred runways and am killer with a pressure sprayer. There was no thought of what was a good job or a bad job, or of what I should or could do. The only criterion was did it pay.

Newspapers were delivered before the sun rose. Darkness didn't scare me but the old apartment building on main street scared the heck out of me. The air in that building smelled as if it (and its inhabitants) had been trapped there for decades and were waiting to escape by entering the body of a little girl. The teeniest, tiniest sniff would kill me for sure. I would run down the halls flinging papers as I ran, lungs burning as I held my breath, narrowly cheating death with each step. But you already know this, because I'm not dead. Only one block away was Don's Bakery where warm donut holes were my reward for not dying. Unaware that I had just outrun the Grim Reaper, Mr. Don (or so I called him) always remarked, "You are always so happy!" when we exchanged my dime for his donuts.

I helped the boys deliver newspapers but was too small to strap a bag across my chest like my brothers, so I pulled newspapers in the wagon or sled, depending on the season. If the snow got too deep, Dad would sometimes hitch the toboggan behind the snowmobile to carry the papers while we trudged through the snow making deliveries.

I mowed lawns and shoveled snow until I figured out it was easier and more effective to be the front man, arranging the jobs and collecting payment, while the neighbor boys did most of the work. It was lucrative, except for Mrs. Osborne who paid us in coupons. Everyone knew Mrs. Osborne was the richest lady in the neighborhood, yet she was least likely to pay for any services, big or small, done on her behalf. Mom told us to 'offer it up' as if getting some cosmic, heavenly bonus points made up for her paying us in grocery coupons again.

Conversely, Mrs. Lloyd didn't have two spare cents to rub together yet was forever pressing coins into our reluctant hands. We tried mowing Mrs. Lloyd's lawn when she wasn't home, but still she'd be sure to pay us something. Despite being the same size, Mrs. Lloyd's yard felt effortless to mow while Mrs. Osborne's yard seemed endless. Mom said it wasn't right to hate people, so I "very strongly disliked" Mrs. Osborne not just because she didn't pay us, but because I hated the way she made me feel – unappreciated and unimportant. I swore to never ever become Mrs. Osborne.

By the fourth grade, it was my turn to work at Lou Walsh Motors hand washing and waxing cars, pressure washing floors and scraping gunk from places they weren't supposed to be. Jeff had worked for Mr. Walsh with our cousin, then Doug worked with Jeff and I worked with Doug. With so many cousins, finding work was kind of a family thing. I was small enough and cars were big enough that I had to stand on a stool to wash the middle of the hood. Luckily, I was just the right size for going down into the grease pits to muck out the gunk. The mechanics would occasionally buy me a soda during lunch breaks; they got a kick out of watching the little kid with blonde pigtails fill buckets of hot soapy water and drag them along the floor to wash cars. I could barely see over the steering wheel, but eventually became a whiz at pulling Oldsmobiles and Caddies in and out of the wash stall. Until then, touch-up paint was used to hide my many scrapes.

I tried babysitting but was terrible and refused to do it. Yet mom insisted and kept accepting jobs for me. So after putting the Koeking kids to bed and polishing off the ice cream in their freezer, I did the dishes and walked home…leaving behind the Koeking kids, probably/maybe sound asleep. Mom was fit to be tied. She insisted I return immediately but nothing she said could make me return. So she did. I don't know what mom said to Mr. and Mrs. Koeking, but requests for my babysitting services generally dried up after that night.

The problem with babysitting was that it required caring for and playing with little kids. How can you do what you don't know or give what you didn't get? It was much easier and more natural for me to muck and clean and mow and deliver than to babysit. Mom finally abandoned any hope that she could mold me into what she thought was acceptable work for girls to do. I was a hard clay to shape, impatient and unwilling to comply as she sought to push me in directions I didn't want to go.

At an early age, I branded myself 'not the nurturing type,' a label I mentally retained well into adulthood. It took me years to realize it wasn't true. But it was far easier to label myself not nurturing than to admit I was scared, inexperienced and unsure. Why is it so easy to assign and adhere labels to ourselves but so difficult to remove them? Even when I try, there remains a gummy, sticky residue of self-doubt.

On Being Catholic

"Don't waste your suffering."

— St. Pope John Paul II

"Hearing nuns' confessions is like being stoned to death with popcorn."

— Fulton J. Sheen

I am forever grateful that God rested on the seventh day! In Carroll, that meant no one worked on Sunday, stores were closed and everyone went to church. The one thing everyone in Carroll County had in common was being Catholic. Being Catholic was a given, not something you chose, defended or thought about. We weren't just Catholic; we were *Roman* Catholics. I'm still not sure what that means exactly, but *Roman* was always said with great emphasis so we knew we were special. Kids in Carroll knew how to say the Hail Mary before they could recite their ABCs. Attending Catholic schools was the norm, not a privilege, with attendance five times the public school. We went to mass on Tuesdays, Fridays, Sundays and 'holy days of obligation.' During the 40 days of Lent, we said the daily rosary with KCIM radio, gave up candy and abstained from eating meat on Fridays. Other than the parish Fish Fry, Lent was dreaded because, in Iowa, fish only comes one way – in a can – and is served using the same recipe found in every local parish cookbook as follows:

Tuna Burgers

> 1 can tuna
> 1/2 cup ketchup
> 1/4 cup diced dill pickles
> 1/4 cup salad dressing
> 1/2 lb Velveeta cheese
> 1/4 cup onion
>
> Mix ingredients together and spread on 12 buns buttered with oleo.
> Wrap separately in aluminum foil and cook in oven for 10 minutes. Can also be frozen.
> Yum.

I've got cookbooks from St. Mary, St. Lawrence, St. Gabriel, Holy Spirit, Holy Names, Immaculate Conception and Sacred Heart parishes. That's a lot of firepower sitting on a kitchen shelf. Each parish cookbook is basically the same and adheres to the same strict guidelines:

> Sanctioned ingredients: Velveeta, macaroni, oleo, butter, bacon, ketchup, canned soup, more butter
>
> Suspect ingredients: seasoning or spice except salt, pepper, onion powder, garlic salt or Lipton dried onion soup mix

Mom made us 'offer up' a lot during Lent and was forever lighting votive candles for 'special intentions' which were evidently further boosted by statues of the Blessed Virgin Mary and various saints which graced every room of our house. Mom still uses a 4" statue of St. Joseph in her purse to keep from misplacing it. But when she does lose her purse, a chorus of "Pray to St. Anthony!" is heard followed by, "Tony, Tony look around, something's lost and must be found." It always seemed to me that St. Anthony should have a little chat with St. Joseph about keeping better track of mom's purse because it was forever missing.

The thing about being Catholic is that there were a lot of us. We were everywhere. Week after week, you would see the same neighbors in the same pews at church. Every home I knew said the same prayers before meals and had the same crucifix of Jesus and statues of Mary in our homes. It was easy to be a slipstream Catholic in Carroll, yet most weren't. Most lived their faith earnestly, with every beat of their heart. I wasn't quite so sure. My Catholic heartbeat had arrhythmia. A rebel and tomboy at heart, I was bad at being a 'good Catholic.' For years I believed (and was taught) that heaven was earned by being and doing good, like the merits and demerits the teachers handed out for good behavior in class. Unfortunately, my 'good' balance sheet leaned badly under the weight of demerits. Talk in church? Demerit. Get in fights? Demerit. Pass notes in class? Demerit. Forget the words to prayers? Demerit and eternal damnation!

Yet when I felt lost and unsure, the words to prayers came effortlessly and into St. Lawrence Church I'd quietly slip to sit alone in silence, grateful the church was never locked. The after-hours God I found inside kept no tally of good or bad. I was surrounded by peace and compassion as I wordlessly shared my woes. Although the church was dark and empty, I never felt scared or alone. I was embraced by Spirit and the residual faith of my community. That's the great thing about being Catholic – it's a heritage, an anchor, a belonging, a community, a family. A big family. A very big, very loud family. Hell, my best friend was one of 14 kids. Sure, that's a lot, but not at all unheard of in Carroll.

Mom was one of 10 Ramaekers kids and all but one of her siblings lived within a days drive. Lots of aunts and uncles meant lots and lots of cousins. Ramaekers' family reunions were loud, fun, color coded and held every five years, come hell or high water. To keep track of who belonged to whom, each of the 10 siblings picked a different color for their kids to wear during the reunion.

Beginning Friday afternoon, Ramaekers kids and their kids and their kids were drawn to Swan Lake State Park outside Carroll as if it were Mecca. Swan Lake had no swans, few ducks and was so small you could wade from shore to shore and not get your hair wet. But like the ugly duckling, by Saturday morning, Swan Lake's transformation was a sight to behold, bursting with Ramaekers smiling, shouting greetings and enveloping one another in bear hugs. A typical greeting went something like this...

> "Well Julie! How are you?" asks Uncle Greg, despite the large JANE written on my nametag.
>
> "Hi Uncle Greg! I'm great, but my name is Jane, not Julie," I gasp while being smooshed in a bear hug.
>
> "That's wonderful, Linn! My goodness! You sure do look just like your sister, Jane," smiles Uncle Greg before he moves on to hug the next long-lost relative.

Because no one could tell my sisters Julie, Linn and I apart, we soon answered to any name, since our identical yellow t-shirts already designated us as Madonna's daughters, which was all that really mattered.

As the years passed, less time was spent playing softball and more time huddled around beer coolers in lawn chairs. Aunts and uncles told stories of ancestors, hardships and love, often stopping mid-story to wipe away tears or to burst out in laughter, depending on the memory. We heard how the bank foreclosed on the family farms during the Great Depression and how the ensuing poverty forced the family to split up – boys to work as farm hands and the girls as servants caring for others' homes/kids. No wonder they rejoiced each time they reunited!

It was just a matter of beer and time before the uncles would start singing songs they'd sung together as kids, from raucous (The Bear Went Over The Mountain) to raunchy (Lays On Ya) to religious (Amazing Grace). From a distance, aunts and uncles looked like a bunch of silver-haired cronies having epileptic fits with shoulders shaking and heads thrown back. But as you neared, the sound of laughter and singing reached your ears and your eyes understood they were seeing fits of something divine.

Time passed too quickly those weekends. Sunday morning, Father Tim (a cousin) said Mass as four generations of Ramaekers gathered, heads bowed and hands clasped, praying the same prayers as our parents' parents' parents before us. Although I no longer align with precepts of the Catholic religion, if ever I hear God's voice, I'll bet it sounds like Ramaekers singing hymns during mass on Sunday morning at Swan Lake State Park. Between reunions with Ramaekers and holidays with Riesbergs, I came to understand the strength of faith, the importance of family and the joy of belonging.

The Magic Freezer

"The scariest dragons and the fiercest giants usually turn out to be no more than windmills."

— Don Quixote

It didn't take many church potlucks to realize Madonna Bernadette's cooking wasn't divinely inspired. Yet like the loaves and fishes, she miraculously made meals appear from nothing three times a day, serving cookies that could chip your teeth in between. The source of Mom's magic resided in a huge white deepfreeze located in the darkest corner of our basement. Almost everything we ate came from the Freezer Beast. We might not like what was pulled from the bowels of the Beast, but that freezer always had something to offer when the lid was lifted.

There wasn't much we didn't feed the Beast – if it could be ingested, we stuck it in the freezer. Each fall during sweet corn season, we created an assembly line to shuck, boil, cut and convert 200+ ears of corn into enough baggies of corn to last the coming year. We fed our freezer every fall, and throughout the year it happily belched forth corn, apples, rhubarb, plums, walnuts, cookies, rolls, bread, beef, bacon, pork and chicken. Everything except fish. As I said, fish came out of a can.

During the fall, the freezer was a treasure chest so bursting with goodies you could barely shut the lid, but by late spring, it was a cavern whose riches had been plundered, reducing its foragers to meals of tongue sandwiches and gizzard dinners. There were just two crown jewels that the freezer was never without – dad's Blue Bunny ice cream and mom's diet aids. We knew better than to poach the Bunny, but ate mom's diet aids as if candy.

Like Santa's bag, lots more came out of the magic freezer than ever went in. Unlike Santa's bag, our freezer induced bone-chilling fear in me. It was a Beast. As a little girl, I'd stand paralyzed with eyes squeezed shut, trying to make myself invisible whenever Mom ordered me into the basement abyss to retrieve something from the jaws of the freezer Beast; moving only when Mom shouted "JANE! GO! NOW!!" enough times that my fear of Mom overcame my fear of the dreaded Beast below. Going into the dark, damp basement by myself was scary enough without that cold monster waiting to devour me. But down I'd go, creeping slowly, respectfully, with both awe and terror, knowing full well that I could be swallowed whole at any moment.

I stood in my thin cotton dress looking up, up, up at that old white Beast of a freezer, unable to actually see over the top without first climbing on a stool. My teeth chattered although I was not cold.

Attacking a Beast is all about grip. Grip is all about leverage. Leverage is all about stance. If you didn't have a good grip, leverage, and stance, you didn't stand a chance of overcoming the freakishly powerful suction that kept the jaws of our magic freezer Beast closed. Even then, it was a struggle, let me tell you.

A successful battle of Jane vs Freezer Beast looked something like this:

> **Round 1:** Stand with shoulders squared, feet slightly apart (but still firmly on the stool), both hands death-gripping the front edge, and then PUULLL with all your might until a soft 'pop' indicated the suction had given way.

Round 2: Push the lid up and back to open the freezer Beast's belly, exposing its frosty contents. This was tricky, but doable.

Round 3: Spy the frozen item Mom asked you to retrieve – was it corn or hamburger? Pray that you can find the item near the top and within easy reach – alleluia! Pray harder if whatever Mom wanted was lying beyond arm's length, deep in the belly of the Beast. Dangit!

Round 4: (I hated Round 4) Like a diver going beneath the surface for jewels, take a deep breath, then reach, reach, reeeeach with one anxious hand while the other hand hung on for dear life to the rim of the Beast's mouth. Inching carefully closer, I'd teeter over the edge, neither in nor out, legs dangling inches off the stool, terrified of losing my precarious balance and falling head-first into the Beast only to be found…too late…a frozen Janesicle, deep within the bowels of the Beast.

Round 5: (assumes successfully completing Round 4) Hamburger in hand, climb down the stool, scoot to the side of the freezer Beast. Reach up to grab the side of the open lid/mouth. Give it good yank, pulling the lid shut with sufficient force for the suction to resume its freakish grip.

Round 6: Back away slowly, keeping one eye on the Beast before bolting up the basement stairs. Exhale only after safely arriving upstairs with hamburger in hand.

Round 7: Do not pee your panties when Mom tells you she wanted a bag of corn, not hamburger and again shouts: "JANE! GO! NOW!!"

Repeat Round 1.

As I grew bigger and older, the freezer lost its power over me. No longer a Beast to be feared or bested, it became just a freezer. Which it always was, I suppose. How often in my life has my fear and anxiety created a Beast of something or someone in my mind? How much bigger and scarier do things/situations appear in the moment only to normalize once perspective is gained with time and distance? In time, I got much better at recognizing when a freezer was just a freezer. Yet, I sometimes felt like the little girl teetering on the edge, neither in nor out, gripping with all my might to hang onto something solid and sure with one hand while reaching with the other for what is just beyond my reach.

The little girl in me will probably always be scared by some things, but she reminds me to keep a good grip, maintain leverage, have a good stance and heed my inner voice when it says "JANE! GO! NOW!" for no treasure is beyond my reach.

Despite the magic freezer, with five hungry and growing kids, money was always tight, and tradeoffs were made. Eating out was a very rare and very BIG DEAL, reserved for major life events like First Communion or Confirmation. Such sacred events were usually commemorated and celebrated at the Big Dipper, where each kid got $2 – enough for a burger + fries + small pop OR a burger + milkshake with no fries. You could subsidize with your own money, but the key was to negotiate with a sibling to share both fries AND milkshake. Ideally, with someone who ate slower than me and who tended to get brain freeze from shakes. That was my little sister, Linn. Planning was critical. I planted the "let's share" seed days in advance so that none of my other sibs could swoop in and partner with Linn at the last minute. No negotiation seminar I ever attended could compare with skills learned bartering for French fries with my siblings. Between navigating the freezer beast and negotiating for French fries, my business and leadership skills were already being forged.

Buckle Up, Buster!

"Horses lend us the wings we lack."

— Pam Brown

For reasons I can't exactly remember, although I'm certain were valid, it seemed I was forever fighting – people, rules, requests, convention. Ignoring what was asked, testing limits, I wasn't a bad kid, just independent…less sweet than tart… not made of sugar and spice or anything nice, according to my sister, who was made of sparkles. A typical day might include carving arrows with a rusty pocket knife to shoot from my shitty bow onto the roof of the grouchy neighbor no one liked, starting small fires to see what would and would not burn/melt or shooting stuff – aluminum cans and birds mostly – with a bb gun. If that sounds criminal or cruel, you didn't grow up with empty pockets in a small, rural town.

Fall was the best time of the year because as soon as the air cooled, shoulder pads and helmets were yanked out of dark corners of basements and donned for neighborhood games. There was never enough to go around, so stuff was thrown in a pile, and everyone took turns wearing the mostly broken, mostly useless gear, more because it was fun than because it was safe. Mud, bruises, and scratches were displayed with pride. No one seemed to notice or mind that I was a girl so long as I was tough (I was), threw straight and strong (I did) and didn't cry (never!). I relied more on fists than tears to bring about justice.

My self-image didn't have room for Barbies, makeup, hair, beads or glitter, so Mom was surprised when I told her that I wanted to join the Girl Scouts. I wasn't allowed to join the Boy Scouts, so I figured I'd become a Brownie so that I could earn cool badges like my brothers and friends. It was not to be.

As I remember it, my demise happened early in second grade and was entirely Melanie Steven's fault. It was at one of our very first troop meetings and I was already nervous after having spotted bottles of glue, glitter and construction paper on tables. So when Melanie bullied my little sister and made her cry, I came out swinging. I walloped Melanie good. In hindsight, I probably shouldn't have thumped her in front of Mrs. Hurd, the troop leader. Melanie got a bloody nose; I got sent home and was kicked out of the Brownies. Before even getting a chance to earn my first badge. It wasn't my first or last fight, so I understood the consequences.

After dinner, Mom made me go apologize to Mrs. Hurd and the next day, walked with me to Melanie's house and waited on the sidewalk while I apologized to Melanie and her mom for the bloody nose. I wasn't sorry, but apologizing was needed to keep peace in the neighborhood and with Mom. I turned in my uniform, said a rosary and watched in envy as my friends wore their dumb Brownie uniforms with their stupid badges to school each week. Every Tuesday was agony as I watched the badges on Melanie Steven's sash multiply. I learned at an early age that championing others comes at a price. And that thumping people in general, although satisfying, was not always the best approach. Bullying, much less bullying a bully, never ends well.

As much as I wanted to fit in, color inside the lines and follow the rules, it was not within me to do so.

Because of my birth order and tomboy nature, I spent a lot more time with my brothers than my sisters. Julie was oldest and was the firstborn grandchild, a real beauty whom grandma doted on. Julie's golden hair retained lovely ribbons, her pretty dresses repelled dirt and her shoes remained sparkly and shiny, just like her. Julie was the princess who demanded others bow to her, although in the end, as the oldest of five, she became more like Cinderella as more and more of our childcare fell upon her pretty shoulders though we refused to bow. Jeff worked hard and did well at whatever he did – delivering papers, school, building/fixing/making things – not that anyone noticed because Doug and I came along pretty quick after Jeff was born. Only 11 months older than me, Doug and I were basically the same person, inseparable. He was my hero and I was his shadow. I was the fourth born, the last kid before the last kid, Linn. Linn was the baby of the family and different from the rest of us. She was content, gentle and kind, spending hours on a blanket playing with dolls in her make-believe world. She was seldom left behind when the car pulled away because, unlike me, she was always where she was supposed to be, quietly hugging her dolls, leaving us to wonder how/when she got there.

I found an outlet for my adventurous spirit in John Denver, whose music stoked my imagination, allowed my spirit to soar and put music to my dreams. For the first time I looked beyond the cornfields of Iowa and dreamed of mountains where John (I called him by his first name since we were such good friends) and I rode horseback for hours singing songs about Rocky Mountain High and Sunshine on My Shoulders. When I listened to his music, I felt safe and happy. Everyone needs that person and that safe place, whether real or imagined. To this day, when my heart feels tethered, and my soul needs to fly, you can find me in the woods singing with my buddy John. I've come to understand my inner child never grew up, she just got wrinkles.

I knew if John and I were going to be friends for real, I needed a horse. Besides, I desperately needed something real to love that loved me back. I'd been carefully saving money, quarters at a time, from mowing lawns, babysitting, washing cars, etc. and had saved enough money, or so I hoped, to buy myself a horse. I was ten years old when I let Dad know my plan. He just laughed. But a few weeks later, I came home to find an old saddle and bridle on the front porch.

That night Dad told me if I could pay and care for it myself, I could buy a horse. I wasn't exactly sure how one went about buying a horse, but sure enough, over the next few weeks, Dad, Grandpa Ted and I went around the county visiting farms with horses for sale, but all were either beyond my meager budget or were swayback nags whose giddyup was gone. Then one Saturday afternoon, Dad and Grandpa Ted drove me a few miles to the edge of town and pulled into a driveway that led to a house, barn and fenced field that would become my home away from home. I had no way of knowing that the kid who arrived that day scared and excited would be the same kid who pulled away years later confident and capable. "He's Buster. He's yours. Take care of him," said Dad, pointing to a huge quarter horse pacing the fence, seeking an exit. Even from a distance, I could tell this horse was nothing like the sweet horses named "Sugar" and "Dolly" that my friends had.

Buster was so big and I was so small that I couldn't reach the stirrups. Buster was proud and not too excited about being ridden by a little girl, but I was prouder and would not give up on my dream. By climbing the fence or standing on a stool, I learned to saddle him. All of this Buster found very demeaning and showed his displeasure by stepping on me, squishing me against the fence, or twisting about to make saddling him even more difficult, all while I said "Whoa! Ooph! Ouch! JESUS! Mary and Joseph!" about a hundred times. I didn't mind. I couldn't blame him for being pissed.

Luckily, Grandpa Ted knew his way around horses. Having trained horses in his youth, he saw something in Buster others didn't and somehow felt Buster was the horse for me. Grandpa taught me how to sit forward and stay centered in the saddle, using body movement to communicate with Buster. As he puffed on his pipe, he told me to be calm and confident in the saddle so that Buster could be calm and confident. Uhh…I was confident all right… confident Buster was going to kill me.

For the first few months, I could do no more than plead, "please don't let me die" as I clung to the saddle horn for dear life, praying not to fall off as Buster remained generally uncontrollable. No matter how I cajoled and sweet-talked him, it was clear that Buster was strong-willed and mean as hell. He didn't get along well with other horses or with people for that matter. Even John Denver would have been afraid. This wasn't what I'd dreamed of at all. But I followed Grandpa Ted's advice and tried to project calm and confidence, even if Buster wasn't paying attention.

Dad had a different philosophy and told me to take a firm hand and show Buster who was boss. He would punch Buster in the gut if he couldn't get the cinch tight and would kick Buster in the sides when he refused to go where he wanted, which happened a lot. I hated the way Dad sometimes treated my horse and silently cheered the day Buster revolted, throwing Dad off after one kick too many. After that, Dad never again rode Buster, which neither of us ever commented upon, but was more than fine by me.

I knew right away dad's 'show 'em who's boss' approach wasn't for me. Besides, it was clear who was boss and it wasn't me. Heck, I was still too short to even fully reach around his neck. I wasn't dumb or a coward. I was smart enough to know that Buster was big, unpredictable, and mean – he scared me. A lot. Mom didn't want me or anyone in the family around Buster, sure he was going to hurt someone. But as much as Buster scared me, my desire to love something that loved me back was stronger than my fear. Buster was my something. So I began the process of winning Buster over with care, kindness and corn. Lots and lots of corn.

I worked extra jobs to pay for his rent and feed. Dad created grain bins by cutting metal barrels in half and welding legs to the bottom. He kept one filled with oats and I was responsible for filling the other with corn. Each fall I'd take to the fields, gathering corn to feed Buster through the winter, filling and dragging gunny sacks with ears of corn that had dropped to the ground after harvest, not that my beloved Buster was grateful.

I spent all my spare time with Buster. Every day I walked or rode my bike to the barn at the edge of town to brush, talk and sing to him. Buster didn't mind that I didn't sing well and learned every John Denver song I knew, which was all of them. In return, Buster came to trust me and although he remained mean to others, permitted me to ride him, eventually carrying me with calm and confidence. In time, I grew enough to be able to reach the stirrups and to saddle him without the help of a stool or fence. And the day came when I was able to ride Buster bareback, racing through the field behind the barn, the wind whipping my pigtails, womp, womp, womp, just as they had behind dad's motorcycle.

Buster showed me that tenacious positivity and kindness achieves more than force and fear and that even when I'm unsure and vulnerable, others will support and carry me if they believe in me and I let them. Projecting calm and confidence makes others calm and confident. I fell off Buster many times, always because I was small and inexperienced, never because he threw me off. I was and am often afraid, but always got back on; you have to mount up to see the view from above.

Buster wasn't the horse I thought I wanted; he was the horse Grandpa Ted thought I needed. Like Buster, Grandpa Ted could be a gruff, hard man who scared many. But not all gruff things are scary. I didn't know it at the time, but both were shaping me, teaching me the importance of letting go, of working with, not against. Grandpa Ted had 10 children and 42 grandchildren, but I was one of the very few to whom he left an inheritance: a 6" plastic crucifix, warped and worn, and a tattered paperback book, *Never, Never, Never Give Up*. For a long time, I didn't see that the two are related, but now understand you can't have one without the other. Grandpa Ted wanted me to have the gifts of faith and perseverance. A more valuable inheritance there never was.

Busted But Not Broken

"It takes courage to heal."

— Anne Marie Lockney

At 11, my body was changing in ways awkward and awesome. I got pimples and glasses and sprouted boobs, which I didn't like but the boys did, which explained why boys no longer looked me in the eye, a theme that would last a lifetime. For the first time, I was being admired for more than my ability to throw a ball or climb trees.

The attention was nice so I was delighted when Robbie Feltman, arguably the most popular boy in the entire sixth grade, invited me to go skating on a patch of ice we used as a makeshift rink each winter. Well, technically Lori invited me. During school lunch that day, Robbie passed a note to Kelly to ask Lori to ask me if I would skate with him after school. Oh geez, this was big. Robbie was cute. My friends all said so. They also agreed that Robbie "liked me" and this was, most definitely, a "date." My first ever. I told Lori to tell Kelly to tell Robbie that I'd meet him at the park after school. Oh boy!

The park was only two blocks from my house. I knew the park like the back of my hand and had spent hours on the baseball diamond in the summer, which became the football field in the fall, then transformed into the ice rink in winter once the volunteer fire department flooded the field and the water froze solid enough to skate on. Robbie and I met at the park and sat awkwardly on the rocks next to the ice as we put on our skates, neither knowing for sure what to say. My awkwardness faded as soon as I hit the ice. I knew just what to do to impress. I skated forwards. I skated backwards. I twirled. I felt cool. I was confident. It was time to reveal my most daredevil move – a *backwards* twirl with a little hop. At the same time Robbie made his big move, an arm link intended to swing me toward him. It was a bad combo. We both went down. I was lying on the ice with my foot facing weirdly in the wrong direction. Unlike falling from Buster, I couldn't and didn't get up. The pain was incredible, but crying wasn't something I did, so it took a little while for Robbie and the other kids to realize I was really injured, and they needed to send for help.

A kid ran to my house and soon Dad was looking down at me. It didn't take him long to assess the situation. The pissed look on Dad's face and the soaring pain told me my leg was as bad as it felt. I tried to be brave, but tears leaked stubbornly from my eyes. I could not say which was worse, the pain of breaking my leg or seeing Dad's reaction and feeling I'd done something terribly wrong. Dad said nothing as I watched frustration and uncertainty cross his face as he scooped me into his strong arms, cradling my dangling leg. He said nothing as a few swear words leaked out with the leaked tears as we drove from Robbie Feltman to our local family doctor.

Leg screaming, I sat quietly while Dr. Fangman and Dad argued. Dr. Fangman insisted he could not set the break – it was way too severe. Dad wanted him to try, or to splint it up or whatever. I couldn't keep track of what was said, just how it was said. Loud. Angry. Firmly. "NO!" It couldn't wait until Monday, Dr Fangman insisted. "She needs to go to the hospital. Now!" Uh oh. This was bad. Dad didn't like to hear "NO" and he hated doctors and hospitals filled with lots of "them" people. This, I knew, was going to cost a fortune. Dad lifted me up and carried me back to the truck, less gently this time.

I was still wearing my snow pants and a skate when dad left me at St. Anthony hospital. I didn't hear or see him go and I wasn't sure when he'd return. No hugs or reassuring words were exchanged. Based on the set of his mouth and stony silence on the way to the hospital, I was guessing it might not be any time soon.

The nurse's hands that removed my wet clothes were gentle but unfamiliar. I was mortified and afraid to find myself alone in my underpants and a hospital gown as doctors went about the business of setting my broken bones. I had done a dandy job breaking my fibula, tibia, and ankle. After getting a cast from the tip of my toes to the top of my hip, I was put in a hospital room where I waited, unsure when I'd be reclaimed. I hoped Dad had gone to get Mom, some pajamas, my beloved stuffed animal Snorty, or some books. But he didn't return. No one did.

It was neither night nor day as fluorescent lights buzzed and equipment beeped, the antiseptic smells and scratchy sheets foreign and frightening. I remained awake, unwilling to close my eyes, not trusting what the dark would bring. It was not the pain of broken bones that made the minutes drag by, it was not knowing how many more minutes were yet to pass before I could go home. It was during this time that seeds of fear, uncertainty and despair began to germinate and worm their way into my mind and spirit.

I had seldom been away from home before, never by myself, never ever with no one I knew. Where were Mom and Dad? I felt jealous and lonely looking at the bedside statue of Mother Mary holding baby Jesus in her arms – where was *my* mom? I felt guilty being in the hospital, fearful of what it would cost, as I replayed the argument between Dad and Dr. Fangman over and over in my mind. Slowly, the fear that maybe I wasn't missed or wanted at home began to seep into my broken bones.

On the second night, 16-year-old Uncle Todd came to visit. He brought a personal pan pizza from Pizza Hut (my favorite) but no answers to the questions I asked. "I was just told to check on you and bring you a pizza. If you don't want it, can I eat it?" he asked, helping himself to a slice. I was relieved that someone knew I was there, but it wasn't long before he was gone. With the pizza. I wasn't hungry.

After Uncle Todd left, I stopped staring at the door and stopped waiting to be rescued by my parents. I began to see myself riding Buster in the sun — strong, confident, sure. John Denver sang and I hummed along, since there was no one to tell me to be quiet. A small pillow became a pretend Snorty to keep me company.

After work on Monday, Dad came to get me. He didn't offer a reason for his absence, and I didn't ask. He carried me to his work van, as he had only a few days earlier, only this time both my leg and heart were carefully encased to protect me from harm. Once home, dad set me on the sofa and handed me Snorty, then sat down to eat supper with the family.

I later learned Dad and Mom went snowmobiling out of state that weekend. The trip had been planned; my break had not. Dad never said why he didn't pick me up when they got home Sunday. Mom never said why she didn't come to see me on Monday. Nothing was said, which said everything. More than bones were broken that winter.

Okay, so maybe my first date with Robbie Feltman didn't go as planned, but I became a wiz on crutches and my cast soon filled with signatures. Robbie even drew a little heart next to his name, which was pretty cool. A few months later, Dr. Fangman removed the cast, revealing a puny, shriveled leg. I jumped enthusiastically from the doctor's table, anxious to be free of my crutches. I crumpled to the ground as my atrophied ankle and shriveled leg collapsed under my weight. Physical therapy was unknown to me or mine. I kept the crutches handy, because my leg never quite recovered its size or strength, alternating between sprained ankles and bonkered knees.

It would not be the last time I'd break that leg. Without proper care and therapy, the injuries of youth carry forward. The ache of broken bones eventually faded, but my heart retained a scar from which occasionally leaks the ache of that winter. I loved my parents. That would never change. But I would never again rely on others to be rescued. From then on, I lowered my expectations of them while increasing my expectations for myself.

The Fields

"My strength lies solely in my tenacity."

— Louis Pasteur

For every time, there is a season. In Carroll, summer began precisely at 3 o'clock on the second Friday in May. It's hard to say who was more eager for the bell to ring out the end of the school year, as both teachers and students willed the minute hand of the clock against the concrete wall to hurry toward the appointed hour. At precisely 3pm, school doors flew open and kids burst forth in freedom, the slow kids pushed from behind by their teachers. Teachers passed the chalk to Mother Nature, where life's lessons were taught in her outdoor classroom of corn and bean fields, beginning with roguing corn in May, then walking beans in June, July/August was spent detasseling corn and then back to walking beans then back to indoor school.

I would have loved to spend all summer goofing off, but there were only three months to earn enough money for the coming year, and a bit extra to put aside for tomorrow. And tomorrow didn't come cheap. Detasseling corn paid better than any other job available, with a 100% correlation between how hard you worked and how much you earned. The Riesberg family worked hard. I started getting up before the sun to work in the fields at eight years old. Mom packed coolers with sandwiches and stuck plastic milk jugs filled with water in the freezer each night before going to bed and somehow managed to load all this plus five kids into a station wagon and into the fields before most knew a new day had begun. Barely awake, mom, Julie, Jeff, Doug and I stepped up to the end of our respective rows, reluctant to take that first step, to make that first pull of what would be thousands of pulls that day, for it was detasseling season. Linn was too little to detassel corn and so was placed on a blanket with Barbie dolls, where she would remain at the edge of the field, waiting for us to reemerge from the rows of corn that had swallowed us.

Detasseling corn is insanely hard work, no matter how many snappy songs are sung while doing it. Even John Denver songs couldn't make it fun. At that time, corn was planted every 6 inches in rows up to a mile long. Each row was 18 inches apart. That's 10,560 stalks of corn per mile-long row, 21,120 stalks for a round trip, out and back. There are just over six mile-long rows to the acre. Each of us did three acres. So… one tassel per stalk of corn, 10,560 stalks per row x 6 rows per acre x 3 acres each = 190,080 tassels of corn per person, roughly a tassel every two seconds for three weeks… or four weeks if you stopped for lunch or breaks.

The corn was 3'-6' high, a lot taller than me. At the very top of every corn stalk was a tassel you pulled with a 'pop,' like pulling a cork out of a bottle. It took muscle. If you broke off the tassel instead of getting a clean pull, your pay got docked. The tassel was likely full of disgusting little brown bugs so that when you gripped it, your hand slid off. Gloves just slowed you down and got slippery once full of bug guts. You had to ignore the bugs, grip it and rip it, thousands and thousands of times each day. In the morning, the corn was covered in dew and the wet leaves cut your hands and legs. By noon, the sun would create steam and humidity, causing sweat to run into your eyes. The sweat stung, but there were too many squished bugs on your hands to wipe the sweat away. Besides, squished bugs stung more than sweat. By late afternoon, the corn had dried and the pollen exploded with each pull of the tassel so you had to cover your nose and mouth with a bandana.

By the time I was 10 years old, I had developed arm muscles any city boy would envy. Detasseling was tedious, grueling, exhausting work. When I felt too tired to go on, I'd count... 1,2,3,4,5 until I got to 100. Then I'd start counting all over again. And again. And again. Counting, pulling, counting, pulling. Perhaps today the repetition would be considered meditative; back then it was mind-numbing and exhausting. But if you needed money, you detasseled corn. I detasseled corn. There was no alternative.

We detasseled corn as a family for only a few years, until the older kids revolted and started working on crews that paid them. I was still too young to drive, so I boarded a bus that left the courthouse parking at 5am each morning. I hated taking the bus because I never knew where I was going or who I'd be working with. Eventually, I found work on an older friend's crew for better pay, until I finally turned 16 and was old enough to contract acres directly and hire a crew of my own. That's where the big bucks and hassles were.

I mostly hired my friends and their siblings who were either too young or unwilling/unmotivated to contract acres on their own. I quickly learned the difference between managing and leading. Managing was ensuring everyone knew when and where to show up and what was expected of them. Leading was getting them to do it. There's no better way to learn how to motivate others than to lead a team of friends and fellow teenagers at dawn into a corn field to do something they don't want to do all day in the sun. Just like Buster, the "show em who's boss" approach was a joke. I couldn't demand, intimidate or threaten anyone to do what they didn't want to do. These were kids and friends who could quit anytime, go home or join another crew. So I encouraged, reasoned, growled, laughed, bribed and cajoled, depending on the person, depending on the day.

Laughter motivated far better than fear. Even when everyone was pulling as fast and as well as they could, some kids just couldn't keep up. They knew it. Everyone knew it, so calling them out only made things tense and people defensive. Instead, we joked and sang to keep track of where everyone was while working our rows. No breaks were taken until everyone was finished with their rows. Rather than wait for folks to finish, people doubled back to help kids who had fallen behind. They didn't have to, but all it took was for me or someone else to start and before long, people naturally began supporting those doing their best, but who needed a little extra help. And thus, a team was formed, founded on a mutual goal, fueled by laughter.

Also, Twinkies. Celebrating even tiny milestones kept spirits high and people moving forward. Just the thought of Twinkies and a cold Pepsi was reward enough to help us power through the last hundred yards to the end of a row. Twinkies, HoHos, Ding Dongs, Nutty Buddies and Buns were eaten by the dozen to celebrate small wins like completing a row, or an acre, or anything really. These goodies had enough preservatives in them to be completely unaffected by the intense heat, regardless of how long they'd been sitting in the sun. We never worried the chocolatey icing on the HoHo would melt or the creamy filling in the Twinkie would curdle because there was no real chocolate or cream in either. It's impossible to care about eating healthy foods when you've just spent the past few hours amongst corn recently doused with RoundUp. It was a delicate ecosystem – the chemicals consumed via Twinkies balanced the pesticides absorbed via the corn. Or so we told ourselves. Whatever didn't get eaten was left in the fields, where I assume it remains today.

We sat on the dry, hot dirt joking and laughing when we'd finished our row, singing to a portable radio – Queen (We will, we will ROCK you!), The Eagles, Stones, John Denver… anything to lift spirits and feed the soul – until it was time for each to gather the will and resolve to step back into the corn and begin the next row, knowing the corn would soon swallow us whole as it reached high above and stretched endlessly before, any conversation gobbled by the rustle of leaves until there was just… pull, pull, pull, pull, pull, 1, 2, 3, 4, 5… thousands of times more until the row was done and we could reach for a jug of water instead of a tassel. As the leader, I couldn't make hard work easy. All I could do was create camaraderie and pride in doing the difficult, be the first to show up, the last to leave, and ensure there were Twinkies to celebrate and a portable radio tuned to a station that kept all moving forward in harmony.

Arriving home in the afternoon after a hot day in the fields was like arriving at the door of heaven. My feet ached to be freed of the sturdy shoes into which they'd been shoved hours earlier, toes delighting in the feel of cool concrete as I peeled the socks from my feet and emptied the dirt from each into a trash can Mom had placed against the wall for my use. If the garage was empty and dark, I could strip bare before coming into the house. Despite the dim light, the white, white skin of my belly, boobs and torso contrasted starkly with the grimy, burned skin of my shoulders, arms, and legs, making it appear as if I were still wearing clothes though I was naked. I gathered my things to launder, so I could wear the same clothes the following day. This was the moment. The cool, cool air inside the house greeted me like the whoosh of an angel's breath, making the hairs on my hot, bare body stand up as goosebumps briefly burst forth before disappearing as if embarrassed to have shown themselves. Heaven on earth lasted only a few seconds then was gone, easy to miss if hasty or distracted.

The shower's cold water washed over me, ending only when hunger or exhaustion could no longer be denied, but not before dousing myself with vinegar, mom's cure for all things burned. Often, I'd shower and get a quick nap before donning a McDonalds uniform for the supper shift, the tangy scent of vinegar mingling with the greasy residue of

French fries, both of which would be sweated off the next day in the fields. Some days, my arms lacked the oomph to lift and salt the french fries, so I'd ask to clean the lobby so my arms could dangle while wiping tables and mopping floors. On particularly tough evenings, Mom would pull cold towels from the magic freezer and lay them on my back, one after another, to soothe the heat radiating from my blistered shoulders. Bedtime and mornings came early on those days.

After a particularly scorching hot and humid day, my best friend Marita (aka Tweedle) stopped over just after supper to say she wasn't going back into the fields the next day. It sucked, she said. She was done. As she quietly said this, she rubbed an invisible spot on the counter with one of mom's good rags, over and over, eyes down, unwilling to meet mine. I knew how she felt. She was tired. No, exhausted. Mentally and physically drained. Tweedle was a vibrant, sturdy farm girl full of giddyup, but her giddyup was done and gone. I could see this from the way she stooped over the counter, her voice soft and low as she rubbed a stain that wasn't there.

Shit. I was screwed.

If she gave up, so would her sister, Theresa, and probably more. Many of my crew used the money to buy something they wanted. I used the money to buy things I needed – tuition, clothes, and a ticket to a different tomorrow. Tweedle wouldn't meet my eyes. She wanted me to say the words I couldn't. I couldn't tell her it was okay for her to quit. I needed the money, she didn't. Her folks had money for her tomorrow. I didn't have a tomorrow without detasseling today. Nothing moved her – not joking, bribing, persuading, reasoning. Finally, I stopped. I stopped telling her it wasn't that bad and why it was in her best interest to stay. I admitted the truth. It was that bad. Tweedle didn't need to stay for herself, I needed Tweedle to stay for me.

"Tweedle, don't quit. I need you."

"No." Rub, rub, rub. "I can't do it anymore."

"Yes you can, Tweedle. You have to."

"No I don't. I don't want to. I won't. I can't," her focus never shifting from the invisible speck.

"It's hard. It's really, really hard. But no matter how hard I work, I can't finish without you, Tweedle. Unless I finish the acres on time, there is no bonus. I need that bonus. I need you and Theresa and everyone on the crew to finish. Don't quit on me. Stay. Please. For me."

Long pause. More rubbing.

"Okay," she whispered as she stopped rubbing and looked me in the eye. The quiet resolve in her voice matched the determination on her face.

I slept little that night, afraid others would quit but all showed up. I asked the crew to stay strong with me until the end. They did. Because I asked, they answered by dragging out of bed the next morning and the next and the next, until we were done. The crew's loyalty fueled more than any Twinkie ever had. From then on, things felt different knowing we were working for the paycheck *and* for one another, that being there mattered. We finished together. On time. Bonus earned.

Detasseling completed, the crew shifted gears to walking beans which was relatively easy money, requiring no more than going up and down each row of beans with a machete and whacking out the weeds. I actually didn't mind walking beans. There's a quiet grace in rising before the sun, something sacred in witnessing the birth of a new day and with it the promise that anything is possible. Chin up and eyes open, I welcomed the cool early mornings and shorter days toward the end of the season, grateful to work hard with people I liked and enjoyed.

It was on such a morning, just before daybreak, that I left the machine shed with half a dozen freshly sharpened machetes wedged carefully between the two front seats of Tilly, our Volkswagen Bug. My mind was still half asleep and on autopilot as I drove the familiar gravel road to meet and lead the crew in the fields. Just as I came upon a hairpin turn, the sun peeked above the horizon, calling forth the day with all its brilliance. Too bright to see, too slow to react, too late to save myself, I swerved but missed my turn. Tilly's old tires tried but couldn't gain traction before surrendering their hold in the loose gravel as Tilly rolled down a steep ditch while I tumbled like a rag doll inside the car. I watched in slow motion as the windshield burst forth, taking with it the razor-sharp machetes. Tilly teetered with my leg dangling out the window. Just one more rotation, one more roll, and dangling would become crushed.

As if out of nowhere yet there all along, I felt a presence steadying Tilly and me, bringing both gently to rest as the sun lazily completed its ascent above the horizon. I sat uncrushed in the ditch's tall grass amongst the sharp machetes and shattered glass scattered about me, uncertain how I came to be there, certain it was not of my own doing. It was impossible that I would walk away from this. Thank You, I said aloud to no one there. I heard no angels singing, saw no bright lights and cussed no less afterwards. But my faith transformed from an ALL-POWERFUL GOD somewhere 'up there' to a personal, lower-case god beside me, with me, connected and protecting. Call it divine intervention, god, angels, saints or crazy, the Thank You spoken in the ditch became the first of thousands since.

When I first stepped into the fields, I believed if it was to be, it was all up to me. No one else, just me. That worked for a while. In time, reluctantly, I learned trusting and relying on others was the only way to be and achieve more – if it was to be, it was up to we, not me. Flying machetes provided the clear and obvious clue that I could rely on more – if it was to be, it was up to thee. Yes, in Mother Nature's classroom of corn and beans and ditches were taught the most important lessons of my life.

Directions Not Included

*"You have brains in your head. You have feet in your shoes.
You can steer yourself any direction you choose."*

— Dr. Seuss

Dr. Fangman tracked my age, weight and height during annual school checkups, but my emotional development could be tracked by the posters tacked over my twin bed. Posters of horses and John Denver were replaced by David Cassidy, then Rick Springfield, then airplanes, then nothing at all once I became too cool for posters. I outwardly adopted music by bands named after cities and states – Boston, Chicago and Kansas – but secretly remained true to John Denver, my clandestine love. I had no time or interest in finding real love. Sure, I kissed Scott Warnke in the second grade. Yes, I played spin the bottle with the Pudenz boys and looked at *Playboy* magazines with Danny Beidler in middle school. I figured out the mechanics of boys in grade school and the motivation of boys in high school. Though many of my friends were boys, I seldom dated. Unlike friends who dreamed of getting married and having a family, I figured I'd make a terrible wife and a worse mother. Heck, I didn't even like babysitting, much less want kids of my own.

Looking at the women up and down the block, there were none I aspired to be, including my mom. All were good women, but I could see little of me in the life they lived. But if not them, who *did* I want to be? I hadn't a clue. I didn't have any role models locally and had been out of Iowa only briefly during a family vacation to the Ozarks, which didn't raise the bar much. We didn't watch sports or the news on TV, didn't discuss politics or have a point of view on the world outside our house. There *wasn't* a view outside our house. I wasn't sure what was possible or what I wanted but was pretty sure it would be found outside Carroll County.

Mom and Dad weren't exactly the type to have heart-to-heart talks about life-changing events. Or any talk for that matter. My "sex talk" and my "what do you want to be when you grow up" conversations were pretty much identical and equally helpful. The sex talk consisted of Mom leaving a box of tampons on the lid of the toilet, signaling my passage from childhood. The "what do you want to be when you grow up" talk consisted of putting a red and gold "Class of 81" balloon and graduation cake on the picnic table, heralding my passage from financial dependence. Both gestures were appreciated, but neither provided much guidance on what to do next. At least the box of Kotex came with directions.

Maybe high school was simpler in the 80s. Helicopter parents hadn't yet taken to the sky – the term didn't exist because there was no such thing. Not that I knew of anyway. My folks weren't spectators, joiners, volunteers, or attenders although Dad sometimes watched me play tennis from the front seat of his work van, parking on the street away from the other parents. I lettered in sports, music and debate, but by the middle of my freshman year I stopped scanning the crowd to look for my parents.

Yet one of the greatest gifts I received from my parents was their absolute lack of expectations beyond "staying out of trouble." My parents taught me what they were taught – if you wanted something you needed to work for it. Period. No one, including them, was going to give you anything. But if you worked hard enough, you could get/achieve anything you wanted. They didn't realize it, but their Work Hard mantra, together with having no expectations, meant I also had no limitations. I was free to do and be anything, if only I was willing to work for it. And heck, I knew how to work.

But knowing I could do "anything" and achieve "something" was a bit daunting, let me tell you. Like the box of tampons Mom left on the toilet seat, it was the specifics that I found baffling. What was my "something" and where did I find it? What was the "anything" I wanted to achieve? Unfortunately, neither life nor my parents come with instructions and thus, I was left confused and conflicted.

The things I knew how to do – work hard, show up, clean, smile – suited me for a job flipping burgers at McDonalds. Until I got fired. Some kids snuck out the back door to smoke; I snuck into the walk-in cooler to steal cookies, ripping open the boxes and shoving Hamburglers two at a time into my mouth. After hurriedly wiping the crumbs from my face and tucking the cardboard box in my waistband to dispose of where no one would find it, I returned to flipping burgers, my anxiety sated. Until I did it all over again. And again. Soon I was taking milkshakes, fries, etc. into the freezer to inhale without chewing. It's not so easy to hide a melty milkshake in your waistband, which is probably how I got caught and fired. I never told anyone I was fired, nor did I tell anyone I had begun to binge and purge, a dangerous cycle that would take decades to end. The embarrassment of being fired was nothing compared to the shame, guilt, disgust, and self-criticism of shoving food, then fingers down my throat. But it was as close as I could come to purging the fear, uncertainty and doubt that sometimes overwhelmed me. Each time I swore to stop. Until I did it all over again. And again. As I said, I was confused and conflicted.

Remaining in Carroll was the easiest and expected path forward. I had a solid job, friends, family – a good and predictable life. Despite so many reasons to stay, something was tugging me out of my comfort zone to a life I couldn't predict. My senior year was flying by, but I had no idea what came next. I knew virtually nothing of the world outside of Carroll County, population 9,683. I had a pretty good idea of what I didn't want but hadn't a clue how to translate my interests or ambitions into action. Guidance ultimately came in the form of a person least expected – a nun. WTF? The Almighty works in mysterious ways, all righty. It must be true, "the hands that help are holier than the lips that pray" because it was my unholy lips that prayed for direction and it was into Sister Francis Xavier's holy hands that my hopes and dreams landed.

Sr. FX was old, shriveled and so stooped she could barely be seen at the front of the classroom in her black habit and robe. But Sister's eyes glowed with passion and her voice commanded attention as she brought concepts to life, situations to heel and made all things seem possible. I didn't think she even knew my name, yet she pulled me aside after class one random day to ask the question for which I had no answer – what was I doing after graduation? Who, me? Why was I worthy of her attention? What did she see in me that my parents didn't? I never learned the answer. I only knew her helping hands provided the answer to my prayers. I may not find help where I'm looking, but help is always found when and where I need it.

Sr. FX entered my life exactly when I needed her. She listened as I shared my love of the outdoors and my desire to live beyond Carroll. She proposed Forestry to leverage my interest in science and nature. She barely knew me, but after learning and embracing my dream, Sr. FX provided the spark that fueled my hope, translating my dream into something tangible. I competed for, and won, a $320 college scholarship. It wasn't much, but it was everything – validation that I was college worthy. The flame was lit. With her help, I applied to college.

Just one. It was enough. Iowa State University was two stop signs, 65 miles and a world away from my hometown.

I wasn't surprised that Dad snorted when I told him I wanted to go to college. For Forestry. Maybe it was because we grew corn, not trees, in Iowa. Maybe the snort acknowledged that I had never actually been in a forest. More likely, his snort reflected the reality that I had little money, already had a good job waitressing at Zeke's Place, so why would I go to college? For Forestry? College was for "them," not us.

I decided to interpret the snort as, "I won't pay for college, but I won't stop you either. If you want to go, figure it out." So I did. I was going to college. Buckle up, Buster.

With Sister Francis Xavier's words of encouragement ringing in my ears, I left for Iowa State University. No wistful goodbyes or hugs were exchanged. There were no tears, no hesitation, no backward glances. The ringing in my ears echoed the cheering of my heart as I leaned forward and urged the car faster, looking forward to what would be.

I arrived at Iowa State amongst 25,000 other students, mostly from small towns just like mine. I had traded my Catholic school uniform of plaid jumpers for a college wardrobe of plaid flannel shirts purchased from the Carroll Tractor Supply store, which looked remarkably like every other kid's flannel shirts from their local Tractor Supply store. Always the adaptable, ever-changing chameleon, it was easy to slipstream into college life. I could be anyone I wanted to be. For the first time, my identity was undefined by my name, family or uniform. I could be a good girl. I could be a bad girl. I tried a bit of both. Mostly, I decided I liked and had become pretty good at being the person I wanted to be, so I stayed the course.

I missed home and was surprised when other kids' parents showed up to visit on the weekends. Only 65 miles separated Carroll from ISU, but it wasn't the miles that kept my folks away. It was the reality that

I'd left 'us' to become a 'them,' a line Dad didn't cross, and Mom didn't consider crossing without Dad. They didn't hold me back, didn't push me onward, they let me be. I kept myself busy, busy, busy and was doing, doing, doing which generally kept fear and insecurity at bay. I aced most classes and was surprised to be voted Social Chairman of my dormitory, where my energy served the greater good, although probably not the greater good Sister Francis Xavier had in mind.

God had certainly packed some high-octane grace in the shriveled form of that gnarly old nun. Maybe that's why her eyes glowed. But by her grace, I was at college. I regret not slowing long enough to thank her for providing the direction and nudge I needed. Instead, I hurtled down the path upon which she launched me, which was, I suppose, the best way to express my gratitude and all the thanks she needed.

For Sale: Used Carpet & Prayers

"Ask and it shall be given. Seek and you ye shall find. Knock and it shall be opened unto you."

— Matthew 7:7

Being broke was nothing new. I swung between being almost broke and being completely broke, depending on when the next bill, tuition or rent was due. So before settling into the dorm, I set about finding a job. Working the concession stands at Stevens Auditorium paid minimum wage and provided a bottomless supply of leftover hot dogs and popcorn, which did far more to expand my bottom than improve my bottom line. So when my cousin Kelly told me about a job at Mr. Steak earning $2/hour plus tips, I grabbed it. The tips weren't great, but Mr. Steak upped the quality of my dining experience considerably, as patrons' leftovers soon rounded out my diet nicely.

Mr. Steak was an okay restaurant located on the edge of town, just after the fast-food, drive-through restaurants and before the hoity-toity dining establishments. It had cloth napkins, so that was pretty nice. But any restaurant with a buy-one-dinner-get-one-dinner free early bird special really isn't all that special. People who dined at Mr. Steak were budget conscious, which made the occasional $5 tip from a young couple or elderly patron a rare and precious gift that bolstered me spiritually and financially simply due to its generosity. Just like Mrs. Lloyd from my youth, it seemed that those who had the least to give, gave the most and were the best tippers.

Conversely, Mr. Steak was owned by a stingy woman who scheduled waitresses to come in early and leave late so we could vacuum, clean the bathrooms, prep the kitchen and do whatever else needed to be done for just $2 an hour. We knew she was taking advantage of us, but we needed the job and $2 meant a lot at the time. Being paid so little to do so much, we felt justified tipping ourselves with an occasional steak or two from the back freezer. Being stingy is expensive. It doesn't pay not to pay.

Money is one of those things you don't think anything of if you have it and think only of if you don't. I didn't have it, so thought carefully about how not to spend it. I bought nothing I didn't need and little that I did need. Things other students considered necessities were luxuries I couldn't afford. Like textbooks. My heart pounded the first time I stood in the campus bookstore looking in shock at the cost of the required textbooks. Are you kidding me? Even the grimiest used textbook cost a freakin' fortune. What a jam. I couldn't afford to flunk yet couldn't afford the required books not to flunk.

Instead, I discovered the Forestry Library where books and learning were free. The word 'library' is generous, because it was really just a large room down the hall from the forestry professor's offices. It had noisy fluorescent lights that buzzed, some shelves with books and a couple of tables. It was my refuge. I used the 'library' whenever I could beg one of the professors to unlock the door and let me in. Within a few weeks, I met kind Dr. Jungst, the Dean of our Forestry Department. Dr. Jungst said I was in the library so often that I might as well work there. He gave me keys enabling 24/7 access to the library, paid me $3.35/hour, PLUS (this was important) looked the other way each time the professor's break room was raided of snacks. Basically, he paid me for studying. Things were looking up, but I was still hovering in the red zone financially.

A solution came to me while sitting on some friends' beds in their dorm, careful to keep our feet off the freezing tile dormitory floor. I recalled the basement walls my dad carpeted to keep us warm. Wouldn't it be nice to have warm carpeting over this frosty floor, I lamented. Yes, Kim said, she'd pay a lot of money for that. Huh? Say what? Yes, everyone agreed, the floors felt like ice! Their feet were always cold, they grumbled, regardless of how many pairs of socks they wore. If only the floors were carpeted…Ding! Ding! Ding! Ca-ching!

Fast as a lightning bolt, my thoughts charged 65 miles due west and struck Dad's garage. For years, Dad had brought home the leftover carpet scraps from big jobs, temporarily storing the remnants in the garage until he had time to take a load to the dump. The garage always contained a smorgasbord of carpet scraps, some used and some new, usually in some combination of shag, tweed, cut-pile, level-cut, hi-lo cut, loop, and Saxony, a refined cut pile style of carpet that provides a velvety feel with a refined look, making it ideal for the more elegant dormitory room.

I was excited driving to Carroll that weekend but was hesitant about sharing my idea with Dad. I needed his help but was unsure how to ask for it. In my family, you could tell someone what to do, you could do something without asking, you could offer to help someone, but we seldom asked anyone for help. It just wasn't done. So Dad was surprised when I asked if he'd show me how to cut and glue together the carpet scraps. I told him about the ice-cold dorm floors and shared my idea to create and sell remnant rugs big enough to fit the various dorm rooms. I was shocked when he grinned and agreed to help me.

We moved piece after piece, turning each this way and that way to find the best fit, like a giant jigsaw puzzle. Each rug was a quiltwork of used and new carpet scraps, a unique combination of texture types, patterns, styles and colors, roughly the size of a dorm room. I felt like a pioneer, just like my great grandmother, as I knelt on the floor of the garage piecing scraps into something functional and beautiful. Okay, mostly functional.

Dad said he wouldn't pay for college and didn't, but he gave me something better. He helped me figure out how to help myself. I had never built or created anything with my dad but the weekends spent piecing together those stupid scraps created experiences and wonderful memories. We got to know one another, carefully piecing together a father-daughter relationship from the scraps of our life, tentatively selecting some, rejecting others, until we created something both functional and unique. Like the rugs, it seemed a little cobbled together, but for the first time in a very long time we both felt comfortable and even enjoyed being together. All he asked in return was that I make him pie.

I never pictured myself selling homemade stuff in a parking lot from the back of my car. But then, who does? It's not exactly something one writes on a 'to do' list, but something resorted to after everything else goes to crap. Yet, of all jobs and titles on my resume, Used Carpet Salesman is perhaps the most meaningful, for it is the role which best defines me: a self-made title for a self-made job for a self in the making.

And I made a killing. The rugs were a huge hit, with students shelling out up to $100 each, more for a luxurious Saxony rug. Even more if you wanted padding underneath. The crazier the carpet rugs looked, the better. Shag carpet was preferred amongst the guys, while girls were drawn to rugs with cut-pile or Saxony scraps. Sometimes the rugs were pre-ordered but mostly I just pulled into the dorm parking lot and sold them from the back of the car. The more kids in line to buy, the more I charged. I learned most people would rather pay too much and think they got something special than pay too little and think they got a bargain.

There was more demand than I could supply. I continued to make pilgrimages to Carroll to convert Dad's used and new carpet scraps into saleable rugs, loading so many rugs into and onto my poor Plymouth Ventura it's a wonder the wheels went around.

The skills developed and honed as a Used Carpet Salesman were more valuable and transferable than most things learned from the textbooks I never bought. I learned the path forward is never as expected or intended, but each time I successfully bypassed a block or breached a barrier, I got smarter and stronger. I came to believe there was nothing that couldn't be overcome, nothing I couldn't do, just things I hadn't done yet. No didn't mean no; no just meant *not yet*. The word Yet is what separates hope from despair, those who do from those who don't.

Sometimes the way is divinely inspired. Or at least that's what I told myself to feel better as I sold my mom's prayers. Yes. I sold my mom's prayers. Forgive me Lord, for I have sinned, although I'm hoping St. Peter will understand my good intentions when I get to the pearly gates and he gives me a thumbs up or down.

God knows (I hope) it seemed harmless and started innocently enough. My classmates had often heard me talk about my mom, Madonna Bernadette, and her direct hotline to God. They knew Madonna Bernadette prayed for people in need and lit votive candles on the stove for particularly desperate cases. So naturally, when a friend wasn't quite prepared for a quiz or had a big exam they needed to pass, they'd show up on my doorstep, frantically asking if Madonna Bernadette would pray for them. I'd give Mom a call and yes, of course she agreed to include my friend in her long list of prayer recipients.

Over time, word of Madonna Bernadette spread. The name Madonna Bernadette was spoken in hushed, reverent tones throughout the dorms. No one knew who she was for sure, only that she was powerful. Madonna Bernadette was said to make impossible tests easy. Essays practically wrote themselves, the words flowing as if coming from a Source greater than themselves. Just knowing Madonna was in your corner (or on her stove) brought hope and peace to despairing students. Many a passing grade was attributed to this mysterious person and her hotline to God. It was as if the flames of Madonna Bernadette's votive candle carried – no, fast-tracked – requests from weary students directly to the Almighty's waiting ears.

Students were desperate for divine intervention. I was desperate for cash. It was a match made in heaven. Friends were free. All others made a 'donation.' For $10, I promised Mom would include you in her prayers. For $20, she'd light a votive candle on the stove and mention you by name. Almost everyone went for the candle option; $20 was a small price to pay and quite a bargain if you had more than one exam that day.

I would track all the prayer requests and give Mom a call, mentioning that 'Katie' needed help with an upcoming exam and ask Mom to say a prayer for 'Katie' on a specific day. "Well, of course!" she always said. Madonna Bernadette faithfully woke every morning before 5am to begin praying, so surely a few more prayers wouldn't hurt. Finals weeks were especially busy. Prayer requests sometimes came in so fast that I needed to make several calls in one day, insisting Mom write the names down. After all, I was honest and didn't want to be responsible for flunking anyone.

Although there was no data to support any claims, many swore a positive correlation between their grades and Madonna Bernadette's prayers. I couldn't say for sure, and there were no guarantees or refunds of course, but I believe their claims were true. Who am I to doubt the power of Madonna Bernadette's votive candles? What I know for sure is that mom's prayers were a Godsend to me, heaven-sent during my darkest days of financial need. It's hard to say who was helped more, my classmates or my pocketbook. Sometimes the experiences that seem unremarkable in the moments are moments that change your life. I'm no angel, but God does work in mysterious ways and who am I to judge? I'll leave that up to St Peter.

Learning to Laugh and Love

"No. No. No. No. No. No. Yes. I will. I do."

— Jane Boulware

The event that forever changed my life began with the flip of a coin. Or more accurately, after seven flips of a quarter. That's how many times 17-year-old Scott Boulware tossed a quarter into the air to determine if he should ask me to the prom. Maybe the quarter knew something we didn't, the agent of a cosmic flip destined to bring us together. I'd like to think that the coin came up 'heads' with each toss, an undeniable sign from the heavens that we were meant for each other, but the odds of that happening are 1 in 128, which seems a lot to ask of the heavens for a prom date. More likely, Scott just kept flipping until he got the courage and answer he needed to give me a call. Either way, I wish I had that quarter – it's worth the world to me now.

On May 9, 1981, Scott arrived at my door, corsage in hand, wearing a white tux with a sexy seafoam green ruffled shirt to match my seafoam green prom dress. We were both 17. I didn't know Scott very well. He was the little brother of my friend MaryBeth, which placed Scott outside my circle of potential boyfriends. We agreed to go to the prom as 'just friends' but over the following weeks, I learned Scott was funny, smart, hard-working, motivated, kind, and tenacious. And cute. Perhaps most important at the time, Scott was both cute and managed the local Dairy Stripe, where he made magical ice cream concoctions that cast a spell on this girl's cold heart.

It seems preordained by prior generations that Scott and I come together – our grandparents had been friends and my mom and his mom had been friends since grade school with frequent sleepovers. My parents partied with his parents, before kids were born and partying receded to memory. So it seems inevitable that I became friends with his older sister, MaryBeth, and that I'd fall in love with her little brother Scott, who was the best of all before him. Except I wasn't planning on falling in love. Especially not with someone in Carroll.

Scott and I went different ways after highschool as Scott earned a scholarship to a college 200 miles from me. But our paths crossed again. As Scott's eyes met mine, he turned to his date, telling her that the girl he was going to marry had just arrived. She left with another boy, and I left with my future husband, the evening a surprise to us both.

For two years, we professed our love and lives to one another in letters that arrived almost daily. Slowly but surely, Scott wore down my defenses, expressing his love, hopes and fears, gently peeling away the layers that kept me from him. In the process, Scott taught me how to laugh and how to love, two gifts beyond treasure. Scott's laughter was distinct – quick, free, loud and abundant. I don't think you can love without laughter. Laughter is the lubricant that keeps the brain from getting constipated and the antifreeze that thaws a frozen heart. I know, for Scott's laughter freed my brain and warmed my heart until I was able to laugh, love and be loved. In Scott, I didn't have to be anything but myself, achieve anything to prove myself worthy. He saw me fully and loved me anyway. Well, almost fully, as my bulimia remained encased firmly in shame, shoved and buried into a deep, dark hole, a part of me I shared with no one, not even myself. The love I saw reflected in Scott's eyes was reflected back as I began to imagine a future with him, something I had resisted and thought impossible. Despite my best intentions, I had fallen madly for my high school sweetheart, the kid from Carroll. Carroll, the place I wanted to be from, not tethered to. Dammit anyway.

"Jane, I love you. I want to spend the rest of my life with you. Will you marry me?" Scott said as I snuggled more closely to his side, his voice filled with emotion.

"What? What did you just say?" I said, perking up. Alarm bells started ringing. "NO! #$%!@#" I shouted, although the specifics were garbled through tears of betrayal, anger, and fear as I flew from his side. Hadn't I been clear? Scott knew that I didn't want to get married. Couldn't he see I wasn't cut out to be marriedwifebabiesmiserable? These went together.

But Scott saw something in me and us that I didn't, and he kept asking.

I loved him but wasn't going to be anyone's wife…although I began to wonder that maybe, perhaps, it might not be so horrible. I couldn't see myself being miserable with Scott. We supported each other's dreams. We'd never limit one another, right? Yet being married, being a wife, was less a dream and more a limit, it seemed to me. No, I didn't want to be limited by marriage, but I did want to be with Scott. I wasn't sure what a happy marriage looked like, but I knew we were happy the way things were. Why ruin what we had?

Scott felt otherwise and kept asking...

Each of Scott's proposals chipped away at the protective barrier meant to shield me from hurt, fear and feelings of unworthiness. Fear I would eventually be abandoned and left behind like the little girl, alone in a hospital. But he never gave up, eventually creating a small crack through which the light of faith, hope and love entered.

And, I began to see the something special in us that Scott saw.

We married in the same church as my parents 25 years before. We exchanged our vows while standing on the tiles upon which I'd been baptized, confirmed and received First Communion. The vows said by millions before were as if new to us, as if spoken and heard for the first time, surging from our hearts, through our tears and past our lips, finally free to form the words 'I do.' Three letters, two words, one vow. Spoken between two, 'I do' seals a promise, a commitment of forever. Spoken before God, 'I do' forges a sacred covenant of eternity between three – we and Thee – promising we would never journey alone.

Surrounded by family and friends, we stood in the spiritual embrace of those seen and unseen, clear in the choice we were making. I whispered the two words I swore I'd never utter to anyone. I Do. Scott's faith in us and in God was the bedrock upon which our marriage was built. If ever that foundation should crack, I didn't know if I could support us. I committed to myself never to break the bedrock.

It was a beautiful wedding. I knew this because my favorite aunt told me so and she was known to be the honest aunt. A collective effort, mom's friend made the cake, another had silk flowers that became the bouquets. Scott rocked a white tux, swapping the sexy ruffled green shirt of prom for a smokin' hot white cummerbund and tails, which really stood out against the red shag carpet and shiny gold wallpaper of the local tavern, where we held our reception. We got the tavern rent-free so long as we shared food and cake with the bar's patrons. Our aunts made and served the food, uncles bought the booze and danced on tables. Scott's friends provided music and took photos. Almost 200 friends and relatives attended. With the dollar dance, we made slightly more than we spent, although most who attended were as broke as Scott and I and came for the free beer. All in all, the entire kit and kaboodle cost $500, the amount Dad gave us just after he recommended we elope and use the money to live on. Years passed before we got the wedding pictures printed. We didn't have the money and didn't need the proof. Besides, photos couldn't do justice to our memories of the day.

Sometimes we resist committing to someone or something not because it is wrong but because it challenges our deep-seated fears and assumptions. In marrying Scott, I left behind the 'go it alone' Jane. Saying Yes was my most difficult and best decision. We didn't care that we were broke; we were committed to growing old and growing up together. We'd figure the rest out along the way.

Beginnings

You know you're broke as hell when your bologna doesn't have a first name.

— unknown author

Two weeks after tying the knot Scott and I began classes at Iowa State University, otherwise known as Moo U. Scott was a junior majoring in communications; I was a senior in forestry. We worked half a dozen part-time jobs, were full-time students and were constipated. Being constipated was the hardest part, no pun intended.

Scott and I qualified for food stamps but refused, instead choosing to stand in line each month to receive a free allotment of surplus government cheese and butter. That's 5 pounds of cheese *and* 3 pounds of butter. Each. Every month. Cheese was featured in virtually all our meals – on toast for breakfast, in chunks with fruit and saltines for lunch and in grilled sandwiches for dinner, which is different from breakfast because the bread was grilled instead of toasted. On a good month, we could afford the raisins essential to keeping our plumbing flowing, but in tight months with no raisins, things tended to slow down with occasional stoppages. During those times, everything seemed difficult and we occasionally resorted to stealing roughage from neighborhood gardens.

Scott and I carried an empty cooler in the car whenever we visited Carroll, as inevitably, my dear Aunt Audrey would whisper that we should stop by her house on our way out of town. We'd have a beer with Aunt Audrey and Uncle Clete before they silently transferred packages of ham hocks from their plentiful freezer to our bare and grateful cooler. Ham hocks, as if you didn't know, are pig ankles. They have virtually no meat. We didn't have a cookbook or internet at this point so we learned through trial and error that ham hocks are absolutely NOT good grilled, BBQed, fried, broiled, breaded, baked or with cheese. They're not even good made with 3 pounds of butter. It would have been nice if Aunt Audrey had included a recipe with the hocks at some point, but I think we've already established that my family isn't good about providing directions. Instead, we spent two years trying to gnaw meat off pig ankles, which is even less pleasant than it sounds. Years later, we finally learned that ham hocks are delicious when combined with a bag of navy beans, onions, celery and carrots then cooked for 10 hours or so in a crockpot. Not that it mattered, since we couldn't have afforded the carrots, celery or crockpot.

We were lucky to rent a teeny, tiny house with three teeny, tiny rooms. The house was dilapidated and had been left to our neighbors after the old man who lived there died a few months earlier. The neighbors didn't know what to do with the house, so they let us rent it for $210/month plus a few hours of cleaning and babysitting each week, a good arrangement that worked out well for everyone but the old man.

Our life was good and today our memories are filled with what we had versus didn't have. We hadn't much but needed little. Through thick and thin, Scott's faith never wavered as he maintained enough faith for both of us. He kept saying, "don't worry, we're taken care of," whenever I looked at the empty jar that represented our savings. I felt the path forward was to try harder and work more; Scott believed it was to pray harder and believe more. We were both right.

We worked, played and prayed hard as a team. We lived day to day and like the loaves and fishes received all that we needed, just as Scott said we would. Our first winter was a doozy. We practically converted our teeny, tiny house into an igloo, covering the windows with plastic sheets and putting bales of straw around the house to keep the cold out. Yet our heating costs left little for anything else. I was losing faith in Scott's faith when, on a cold, dark night, the doorbell rang. We opened the door to find a small, Charlie Brownish Christmas tree, some ornaments and a grocery bag filled with canned food – the good stuff, with labels still on the cans. There was no note, no explanation, no credit or thanks to be given. Despite our inquiries, we never learned who was responsible. Instead, we assumed everyone was the gift bearer, which made us look at friends and neighbors in a new light. We saw generosity, kind-heartedness and compassion in all. It's curious how you find in others what you look for. All I know is the giver filled our home with faith and hope as well as food. Their act of kindness has been paid forward many times.

It was during this time that I realized a job in forestry probably wasn't a good fit for me. My summer as a ranger at Swan Lake State Park wasn't all it was cracked up to be. Leading buffalo chip throwing contests for campers wasn't the kind of leader I had in mind. I loved the outdoors, but forestry didn't pay much more than McDonalds and I wanted to earn enough to no longer qualify for government cheese and butter.

Unsure what to do, I sought help from Dr. Jungst, the head of the forestry department. He suggested getting a graduate degree. Who? Me? I'd mostly aced my college classes, but graduate school felt like the major leagues, and I was still playing T-ball. I'd gone to college hoping maybe to get a good *job*. But grad school seemed like something other people did; people I sure didn't know. Yet, my mind lit up as I considered words like *career* and *professional* for the first time.

Dr. Jungst connected me with colleagues around the US to discuss a graduate degree. Over the next few weeks, I was interviewed by the heads of colleges throughout the US. Each wanted to hear about managing four jobs, a marriage and being a full-time student with nearly perfect grades. I guess they figured I was a good bet because within a few weeks, I was offered full scholarships at Cornell for environmental law, University of Oregon for forestry and Purdue University for an MBA in Industrial Forestry. Everything happened so fast that Scott and I did our best to keep our footing as we were swept from our little stream into a rushing river.

We said yes to Purdue because 1) the head of the Forestry department had come all the way to Iowa State to meet me in person, 2) they offered a full scholarship, 3) the other colleges seemed really, really far away and 4) we didn't own a car that could go further than Indiana.

Lessons From the Forest

"And into the forest I go, to lose my mind and gain my soul."

— John Muir

Though off to earn an MBA, I retained the lessons learned as a forester from Mother Nature and remain a life-long student in her classroom:

<u>Dendrology 101</u> – Not all trees are alike. What makes one tree flourish causes another to wilt. In a final exam, I had to identify 256 different species of trees by any one of the following: leaves, wood, bark, shape & height, Latin name, smell, use, geography or color. Initially, I didn't know an oak from a maple tree. Much less red vs white vs burr oak or dozens of the other oak species. It was overwhelming at first. Most trees seemed the same – green. Grouping into big categories was deceptive. Each genus and species had both similarities and yet unique qualities that, once identified, became obvious and clearly differentiating once you knew what to look for. So it is with people. It's easy to put people into big categories – gender, age, education, race etc. But look closely and you will identify what makes each person unique, providing the key to what's needed for each to grow and flourish. Look closely and you will experience the forest and people with a new appreciation and awe.

<u>Forest Mensuration 101</u> – Jack pine's cones are sealed close with a sticky, resinous bond that requires fire to open and liberate the seeds.

There are lots of crusty people who, like jack pine trees, showcase their gifts only when under extreme conditions. It's easy to count people out, but their best stuff might be just what is needed when things heat up.

Biology 101 – During the late 1990s, a science experiment called Biosphere 2 (an enormous closed domed research facility designed to mimic Earth biomes) experienced an unanticipated problem: the trees were falling over. Everything else grew fine but one by one, the trees fell over. Perplexing until they realized that out in the real world, trees are exposed to wind from the time they are saplings. The wind pushes against the trunk and branches of the tree causing the tree to sway in the wind and the branches to move about. This movement changes the tree and creates what is known as stress/reaction wood. The stress wood strengthens the tree by changing the ratios of cellulose, lignin, and normal wood such that the tree can grow properly and stand strongly against the constant pull of gravity and the force of the wind. Without the stress of the wind during development, the trees could not support their mature mass. Like trees, it's the stresses endured that provide the strength to hold yourself up.

Forest Ecology 101 – Giant sequoias are the world's largest living organisms and among the oldest living things on Earth. Despite being nature's skyscrapers at around 30 stories high, their root system averages only 12-14' deep, roughly the depth of an average home's basement. To support its nearly two million pounds in weight, the sequoia tree entwines its roots with neighboring sequoias, providing the mutual support needed for sequoias to live thousands of years. Which is why giant sequoias are only found in groves – a sequoia on its own will fall, before achieving its full potential. Despite its massive size and stature, sequoia seeds weigh only 1/6000th of an ounce, are the size of a pinhead yet can remain green and viable for 20 years. Like jack pines, the seeds are liberated by fire. Moral of the story: to become a giant, you need to start small, give yourself time, endure some fire and work well with others.

Purdue

"If it doesn't challenge you, it doesn't change you."
— Fred DeVito

With a Forestry degree in hand and two years of marriage under our belt, Scott and I left for Purdue. Mom and Dad drove behind us, towing our life in a tiny trailer. I was in pursuit of an MBA; Scott again transferred colleges, never complaining despite adding yet another year to get his degree in communications. We qualified for subsidized housing and promptly took in a roommate, Russ, a fellow MBA student, to help pay the rent. Russ and Purdue changed Scott and me, exposing us to new ideas, experiences and people from around the world. They introduced us to food not served with ketchup, wine not served with ice, and perspectives not formed in the Midwest or forged from Catholicism. Slowly but surely, flannel shirts and hiking boots were replaced by ironed blouses and high heels.

Purdue was a top 10 MBA school that drew top talent from around the world. I was in over my head, having gotten into the MBA program through a back door, via the forestry department. I had taken none of the classes required for the MBA program and did not have the minimum 2 years' professional work experience required. I was 22 years old and felt completely overwhelmed and unqualified because I was. How could I contribute in a Global Economics class when I couldn't even balance my checkbook and eating Swiss cheese was the sum total of my global exposure? I'd not yet seen an ocean, much less a foreign country.

I called my parents and begged them to come get us and bring us back to Iowa. They refused. Thank God.

There was no choice but to dive in, learning calculus and the other prerequisites on the side. I listened to everyone and absorbed everything, eventually summoning enough courage to contribute ideas formed from what I'd heard, learned, and experienced. Fear eventually gave way to confidence.

My mind is a busy, noisy place, not unlike a pinball machine. On a good day, thoughts get launched like a steel ball in my brain, bouncing around from side to side, pinging and dinging as ideas take shape and gain momentum, fueled by the flippers of new information. After some random dinging, thoughts coalesce until my brain lights up like a scoreboard and my ears ring to signal that I've hit the jackpot of a big idea. Of course, I occasionally tilt, launching an idea like a lead weight that gutter-balls straight down the middle, draining without a single ping or ding. Kerplunk. At least that's how I see my mind working. As I said, it's a noisy place.

As I became more immersed in coursework, my mind tilted less and thoughts coalesced more. It turned out I was good at connecting the dots. My intuitive brain put together information in non-linear ways that were obvious to me but not to others, coming up with creative solutions and solid ideas to address the challenges posed by professors. However, my pinball thinking process was too ring-dingy intuitive versus the logical, linear thinking of most MBA students, many of whom were guys with engineering degrees. But different isn't wrong.

The more I began to trust myself, the less willing I was to be dismissed, talked over or she-peated. At first, I tried to get heard by talking louder. That just made me obnoxious and more easily dismissed. Instead, I realized that *I* was the outlier; it was *I* who needed to translate my thoughts, to communicate in a way linear thinkers could understand and embrace. Ideas or answers blurted without context, even if correct, would be dismissed or unheard. If I calmly, confidently walked others through the process... A, B, C... my ideas became more credible, accepted, and adopted. To get heard and have impact, I learned to express myself logically in the way others could hear. Linear thinkers tolerate passion but demand facts, so even though lights flashing 'BIG IDEA' were lighting up in my head, my external presence remained clear, logical, confident, and calm.

It was a delicate balance. How did I give my freewheeling mind room to connect the dots in a nonconventional way to come up with new approaches, then deconstruct the big idea so that I could logically sell it to others? This wasn't like used carpet sales where I could just come up with the idea for carpet quilts and create and sell them without caring if others thought I was crazy. Crazy is frowned upon in graduate school.

It didn't matter if my approach would work if I couldn't get others to buy in and support my ideas. Luckily, even though I lacked the work experience of most in my group, I had an abundance of common sense, and I was lightning fast connecting numbers and ideas so that my solutions, while not initially obvious to others, usually stood up to analysis and rebuttal. Not much different from convincing Linn to share her French fries with me when we were kids. Some call this skill persuasion. Some call this leadership. Some call it sales. Professor Moriarty called it marketing.

One day after class, Professor Moriarty asked why I was specializing in industrial forestry rather than marketing. I explained about my scholarship and how I had gotten into Purdue's MBA program through the side door via the Forestry department. We talked for a while and nothing more was said until he asked to see me in his office. I'm not sure why, but Professor Moriarty went out on a limb for me. He found a position doing statistical analysis of Purdue's Executive Education program. The position included a scholarship that would enable me to specialize in marketing rather than forestry.

"Are you experienced in statistical analysis?" he asked.

"Uh huh," I lied. Hmmm…I think I took a statistics class at some point but had blocked the memory.

"You'll be doing a multivariate discriminant analysis to determine which variables are the best predictors of success for candidates applying to the Executive Education program."

"Yes, of course. No problem." Holy Mother of God! There better be a saint for statistical analysis! What the !@#$ did this have to do with marketing?

With his encouragement, I applied for the job and got it, along with the scholarship. A door had opened and I ran through it. Never mind that I didn't have a clue how to do a multivariate discriminant analysis. Yet. I learned. Fast. After a few months, the analysis was finished and I was promoted to helping teach the Executive Education MBA classes. Me! A *Teacher!* If only Sr. FX could see me now! Whodda thunk? Like Sr FX, Professor Moriarty's help and encouragement had forever redirected the course of my life and career. A year later, I graduated in the top 5% of the class and took another step away from the forest and toward a corner office.

Part II

Jane of All Trades

Who's Kimberly-Clark?

"You're going to say 'yes.' You just don't know it yet."

— Jane Boulware

I started my professional career working in a job they said didn't exist, for which I was supposedly unqualified, for a company that didn't recruit me. An unconventional beginning to an unconventional career.

I'm a Taurus, the bull, headstrong and impatient. So they say. More likely to seek forgiveness than permission, I've experienced only two kinds of doors – the ones already open, through which you can charge with your head up, and the doors that aren't yet open, through which you must charge with your head down and shoulders square. Either way, it's best to get a good running start. Better yet, save yourself a concussion and splinters by persuading someone to open a door for you. So it was with my first job as an entry-level brand marketer at Kimberly-Clark Corp (K-C), the makers of global brands Huggies, Scott, Kleenex, Kotex, Depend, etc. The job almost didn't happen. It shouldn't have happened. But it did. I made it so, without getting a single splinter.

Since my days as a forester at ISU, I'd been interested in K-C, which is a weird thing to say about a company that makes toilet paper and feminine hygiene products. As a marketer, I loved the idea of going to work for a company whose brands were globally recognized and used daily around the world. As a forester, I loved that K-C grew and sustainably managed thousands of acres of timber. K-C was as close as I was going to get to working in marketing *and* forestry. The only slight problem was that K-C recruited engineers, not MBAs from Purdue University. At least that's what I was told when seeking an interview. Undeterred, I figured they'd feel differently if they met me in person.

My plan was simple: crash K-C's engineering recruiting reception. I put on my 'good' starched white blouse, which turned out to be a mistake because it was clear none of the other undergraduate engineering students owned an iron. I helped myself to the free beer and tortilla chips while waiting patiently for the engineering students to scram so I could talk uninterrupted with Dave, the K-C recruiter. When my time finally came, I confessed that I wasn't an engineer, but I did want to work for K-C in marketing. Dave quickly dismissed me, saying that wasn't possible. K-C didn't hire MBAs from Purdue and besides had already fully hired their marketing class for the coming year. Sorry, he said, there were no openings. Hmmm – Dave didn't yet see what was going to happen. After another beer and badgering, he agreed to meet me for coffee the following morning. One cup of coffee proved long enough to yield a follow-up phone interview, which yielded an official on-site interview for a position they said they didn't have. Crrrreak – the door had opened. Barely, but enough. I got my foot in the door. The rest of me soon followed.

Scott wasn't so sure. When I initially told Scott I wanted to work for Kimberly-Clark, he asked, "who's she?" I had already interviewed with Clorox, P&G, Unilever, etc., global brand marketing powerhouses offering jobs for more money in more "desirable locations." Yes, a more "desirable location" sounded great, but everything about K-C felt right. The people were genuine, smart and open, took a lot of pride in what they did, and worked hard but did not take themselves too seriously.

One of the guys even flew a bi-wing airplane, which I felt was clearly a sign.

When K-C learned I was considering other offers, they flew both Scott and me to Neenah, Wisconsin to wine/dine us and to introduce us to 'Happy Valley' as the area was called by locals.

K-C could not have known that the trek to Neenah, Wisconsin was our first (and nearly last) flight together. Scott and I were excited when we arrived at Purdue University Airport on Sunday afternoon, but less excited when we saw our tiny airplane and realized there were only 10 of us boarding the flight, and two of us were the pilots. Scott was quick to note that the guy who took our ticket also loaded bags onto the airplane (the plane was too small for overhead compartments), did the pre-flight check and the safety announcement...and was our pilot. Once buckled into the cockpit, he looked over his shoulder and began to point. "You! Move there. You! Move here. Put that bag on that side. No, the other bag. Yes. There. That should do it," the pilot said, scooting us around like pieces on a checkerboard, until he had the weight distribution just right. Scott and I later learned these tiny planes were affectionately called 'puddle jumpers,' a term that would later become very familiar, but today was terrifying. I think Scott and I would have bailed but the pilot taxied down a short runway and we were airborne before we had time to open the bag of peanuts the pilot had tossed to us prior to takeoff.

When we landed at the Outagamie County Airport (the airport closest to Neenah, WI) it was Sunday night and already dark outside. Everything in the airport was closed, including the rental car counter. It was only 7pm. Unsure what to do, Scott and I looked around and spied a white envelope sitting on the Hertz counter, with my name written in pencil. The envelope wasn't even licked shut. Inside the envelope were car keys, directions and our hotel key along with a handwritten note welcoming us to Happy Valley and a reminder to meet in the lobby for breakfast at 7:30 the next morning. I thought that was pretty cool, but Scott was wondering what kind of hick town we'd just landed.

He soon found out. The following morning, I was preparing for the day's interviews as Scott sat on our hotel bed reading the local paper.

"We can't live here!" he said with conviction, looking up from the paper.

"Why not?" I asked.

"Because stupid people live here," he said, showing me a picture on the front page of a car being pulled out of the local lake. "There are two things wrong with this picture. First, that someone drove across a lake and fell in."

"Yes...." I said, curious where this conversation was going.

"And second, the tow truck says Joe's Towing and Ice Recovery... Recovery? Recovery? That implies that this kind of thing happens often here."

"Hmmm," I said, wanting to keep the door open.

"Jane, we can't live in a place where people are that stupid!" he repeated.

"Hmmm," I said again as I finished getting ready for my final interviews, hoping the day would go better from there.

Scott spent the day touring the area while I met with marketing teams across K-C brands. I had a great day, but Scott remained skeptical, to put it kindly. That night we were scheduled to go to dinner with Tom and Linda, whose mission was to persuade Scott and me to join K-C. Tom was the Brand Manager of Kotex. He spent the night extolling the wonders of marketing feminine hygiene products, which might have been tolerable with a few stiff drinks, but Tom and Linda were Mormons. They didn't drink. Not one drop. So neither did we. I think the waiter sensed our desperation because he kept asking if we wanted a drink. Or maybe he just got a kick out of seeing us cringe every time we said, "no thank you."

My heart sank as we returned to our hotel room. My interviews had gone well that day but couldn't compete with how many times the words "menstrual flow" were spoken during dinner. But again Scott surprised me, saying something about if K-C could make a guy that excited about Kotex it had to be a pretty amazing place to work. Despite having offers for more money from other companies, Scott and I decided to make our new home in Neenah, WI. We never once regretted not going to a more "desirable location," not even when the lake thawed and cars fell in.

Becoming a Cheesehead

"There's no season like deer season."

— Said by every Wisconsin resident

Scott and I were almost 24 when we moved to Neenah, WI, where being a Green Bay Packer fan, a Cheesehead and a homeowner were mandatory. We were told there were virtually no apartments for rent and that houses in Happy Valley were bought, not rented. Really? The thought of buying a house seemed ridiculous considering all our things fit easily into a tiny trailer and we still considered Domino's Pizza a luxury. Buying a house was something our parents did and not something we'd even considered, much less discussed. And yet, there we were having breakfast with a realtor - 4 eggs, 2 sausage, 2 bacon, hash browns, toast and a sweet roll the size of a plate – all for 8 bucks. In a food coma with syrup running through our veins, we waddled from the café to begin our quest to find a house within our meager budget. In minutes, we had viewed everything our realtor said we could afford. Fortunately, we'd found a small, two-story beauty for sale for less than the amount we owed on student loans.

When we'd mentioned to my brother, Jeff, that we were considering buying a house, he asked me something completely inconceivable:

"Have you talked to Dad?" Jeff wanted to know.

"No. Why?"

"Because Dad lent us the money for our house." WTF?

I said nothing as this comment sank in. According to Scott, my head spun around three times as if possessed. Maybe it was the syrup in my veins. It spun further upon hearing Dad loaned Julie the money for her house as well. What?!? Impossible!! Scott and I talked it over and decided to learn more.

"Hello, Dad?"

"Yes."

"Scott and I are considering buying a home in Happy Valley."

"Uh hum."

"Jeff and Leslie said you might be able and willing to give us money to buy a house."

"You mean *loan* you money, not *give* you money."

"Yes, of course. Loan us money. At a competitive rate."

"Maybe. We'll see."

My head did another rotation or two as I processed this.

Two days later Dad drove up from Iowa to inspect the property we wanted to buy. After Scott and Dad walked through the house giving it a soup to nuts inspection, Dad proclaimed it worthy, and whipped out a rusted Maxwell House coffee can from under the front seat of his unlocked van. The can was filled with moldy money, cash he had kept buried only God knows where.

I had always suspected that Dad had squirreled money away through the years and while it would have been nice to receive $20 every now and then, I was grateful for his can-o-cash. We'll never know how many or where Dad's coffee cans are buried, but my siblings half-joke that when Dad passes, we're digging up his back yard. The next day, Scott and Dad peeled the damp, musty money from the rusty coffee can, counting moldy $20s, $50s, and $100s. Shortly afterwards, Scott and I moved into our new home. Sort of. In reality, it was Dad's home and we owed him $55,000 at 10% interest for 30 years, all of which was clearly outlined in the payment plan he'd drawn up and we'd signed. Which just goes to show that not all bankers and people with money wear suits with silk ties; some have their names stitched onto polyester work shirts and carry starched cotton hankies.

Not long after moving in, I was having a Norman Rockwell moment standing in my robe on the little second story balcony, overlooking my lovely little backyard. It was a crisp, calm morning, the steam from my coffee mug swirling lazily into the air, its scent assuring me all was well with the world. Ahhhh, this was the American dream. It was then I first encountered my new neighbor, Terry.

It was the flash of orange that caught my eye, yanking me from my placid reverie. Yes, there it was again, a big orange blob coming out of my neighbor's garage. Forcing my reluctant eyes into focus, I turned to see my new neighbor, a large man clad head to foot in an orange coverall, standing beside something hanging from a tree in his backyard. "Hmmm…what is he doing?" I pondered, still nurturing my morning Zen. He looked up as I looked over, making eye contact for the first time. I waved my steaming coffee mug in greeting, my smile turning to shock as I saw a bloody hand wave back – Norman Rockwell meets Norman Bates.

I stood dumbfounded as all remaining traces of Zen gave way to horror and panic. My new neighbor had a deer carcass, bound from the hoofs, hanging from his tree. I watched in shock and awe as he finished, wiped his hands, stepped back, and carefully unzipped and stepped out of his orange coverall, revealing dress slacks and shirt underneath. He stepped into his garage and emerged wearing a tie and jacket. Surveying the deer in satisfaction, my new neighbor left for work a few minutes later, leaving the deer hanging and leaving me speechless.

Blood drained from my face as coffee spilled from the mug, my hand as slack and lifeless as the deer. After a few minutes and deep breaths, I went inside, poured another cup of coffee and casually asked Scott if he knew how to hunt. When I explained why, Scott merely nodded his head and smiled as if he'd been expecting this moment, as if my exchange with Terry was the most natural thing in the world. Which I later realized, living in Neenah next door to Terry, it was.

Betterer

"It isn't the ups and downs that make life difficult; it's the jerks."

— Charlie Chaplin

Diploma in one hand, student loans in the other, it was time to enter the world of corporate America. I was dressed for success, having swapped my park ranger's tan shirt for a killer blue pin-striped power suit, my hiking boots for high heels and my ranger name tag for a goofy flower-shaped bow tie thingy. Yet, I was feeling anything but powerful. I was scared. Scared that everyone would see past my kick-ass power suit, beyond the bow tie thingy and through the confident facade to the scared kid that was me. What if I didn't belong, wasn't wanted or wasn't good enough? It felt like the first day of kindergarten, me with my new clothes, two sharpened pencils and a full box of markers. Except there would be no naptime, no cookies and milk.

I'm happy to clap and cheer at others' successes but slow to recognize my own. Probably because I'm seldom satisfied with my performance, focused on what I'm not versus what I am. Constantly seeing the ways I can improve, be better and do betterer. Which, I suppose, makes me a competitive person. Competition motivates me to be a better version of myself, to be betterer. Maybe I'm competitive because I often played sports with boys growing up; maybe I played sports growing up because I'm competitive. Either way, I've always preferred activities where scores were kept. Stanford University documented that women often respond less favorably to competition than men, and that fewer women enter and win competitions. All I know is that women lose every competition we don't enter. I was determined to enter, compete, and win.

Yet, I fundamentally do not believe that for me to do well, you need to do poorly. I have no time to be threatened by your performance or success; I'm way too wound up in my own fear of failure, thank you very much. Within my first week in corporate America, I realized not everyone felt that way.

Kent and I started K-C on the same day. We were peers in the same hiring class and position, but Kent made it clear that I should never have been hired because *I* had only a second-tier MBA (at best) and no prior work experience. *He*, on the other hand, had graduated from 'the top' MBA school and had 'extensive' work experience. (I didn't see the need to share my work pedigree, including my stint as a used carpet salesman.)

I was already anxious and feeling unsure of myself while driving Kent and me to our orientation in Chicago, my rental car dying and having to pull over during rush-hour traffic on I-90 didn't help my nerves. I was horrified to realize that the car was out of gas – I'd been so nervous driving to Chicago that I hadn't kept track of the gas gauge. Kent began berating me in earnest, verbalizing all the negative things that I was already thinking about myself.

"How can we be out of gas? Didn't you look? Have you never driven before? You picked a helluva place to screw up. How are we going to get to the training on time? We're going to be late for orientation. It's all your fault. What a mess. I should never have let you drive." Then Kent just sat there, pouting in silence, waiting for me to say and do something, having already placed all responsibility and blame squarely in my lap.

What to do? No cellphone. Rush hour. In a city I didn't know. DON'T PANIC JANE! My heart pounded as the realization that I was in a jam...a big jam... hit me. Kent shrugged. I could expect no help from him.

I looked around and made out what I hoped was a gas station down the freeway, up an embankment of the ramp we had just passed. Taking a deep breath, I quickly told Kent my plan, adding "just sit tight" in response to his smug smirk. I marched down the interstate, scaled the wall, forged a trail up the embankment through the weeds. Thank God I wasn't wearing a skirt, although it wouldn't have changed my plan or slowed me one little bit.

At last I trudged over the railing and arrived at the gas station only to realize the flaw in my plan – I had no way to get gas to my car; the station didn't sell gas cans. Dejected but determined, I summarized my situation to John, the service manager...ran out of gas...late for my second day in a new job... Kent giving me grief. John looked at the interstate, then at me, then at the burrs stuck to my new dress slacks. John walked over to his pick-up truck and smiled as he handed me his gas can, saying I needed it more than him. In John's smile, I felt my confidence return. His act of kindness changed everything, dislodging my fear and anxiety. I filled the can with gas and courage.

Gas can in hand, down the slope I schlepped, through the grass, over the wall, down the interstate to the car. Kent and I were on the road in time to make the start of training, having missed only the coffee and donuts.

Kent told everyone about how I'd screwed up but people only nodded, mentally labeling Kent as 'that guy.' I felt mortified, mentally whipping myself for being the loser-screw-up Kent described. I *had* screwed up but wasn't *a* screw up. In fact, my screw-up was something other new hires could relate to. They shared their own sticky situation stories, expressing empathy. Yes, I'd gotten us into a bad situation, but I'd also found a way out. They were focusing on how I had addressed the situation, impressed by my take-charge approach to solving the problem so quickly. Huh. Kent and I were the only people berating me for getting us into the mess in the first place.

By lunch, I was able to see the humor in the situation and even chuckled while picking clumps of dried mud and grass off my shoes. Why was I berating myself when others weren't? Maybe I handled it better than I thought. Maybe I couldn't have done betterer. The experience had created a human connection, providing cracks in my armor for people to see the real me. Despite making a pretty stupid mistake, no one thought I was stupid. Or unworthy. It looked like Kent was wrong. I did deserve to be there after all.

But Kent never let up. He wasn't just good at self-promotion; he was a master at lifting himself up by subtly tearing others down. Kent was fond of cigars, whiskey, and all things found in the kind of bar where girls dance on a stage. In Kent's world, bonding with the guys was forged over experiences created in dark places, with stories that couldn't be told in mixed company. Dammit. My boobs were a dead giveaway. There was no hiding the fact that I was 'mixed company.'

There have been a lot of Kents in my career. I'm not talking about the guys trying to jockey for position by being better and smarter in their quest for success. That's honest competition, which fuels my fire. To them, I say "Game on!"

Nor is it the men who remark how well I've done "for a woman" or comment on my appearance in ways meant to flatter. I know the difference between a comment said with positive intent that's meant to lift me up, versus mean-spirited comments meant to tear me down.

The Kents are dangerous. The Kents are not about outdoing/outperforming people, they're about *un*doing them. The Kents massage their poison into your psyche subtly, over time, one jab, one cut at a time, preying on your fears and creating the doubt that replaces your confident "I can" voice with a fearful "I'm not worthy" whisper. Kents are truly dangerous because they seem one thing but are another. You don't realize they're sapping your strength, sucking your sparkle, robbing you of trust as well as confidence, until you're lying in a fetal position in your closet howling of a hurt that no Band-Aid can heal, trying but failing, to summon the will to get up. Been there, done that. Fuckers.

There will always be Kents in the world. Sometimes, Kent will be wearing a skirt, which hurts even worse. The thing about Kent is that he/she's been tearing people down their entire life. It's not personal, it's second nature. Kents put both men and women in the crosshairs, shooting down anyone who threatens his/her precarious self-worth. I've yet to find a man who is a pig or saboteur to women who isn't also a bully and ass to men. Kents tend to hang in packs, members of a nudge-nudge, wink-wink club that build up and feed off one another with insider jokes, buddy outings and anything that keeps 'us' on the outside and 'them' on the inside track. When confronted, Kents dive undercover or behind others. Eventually, most Kents find out their track only goes around so often before they derail or run out of gas and their buddies are nowhere to be found.

Fortunately, I met Dudley, the anti-Kent, soon thereafter. Dudley had superpowers Kent could never fathom. He could bring diverse people together and bring out the best in each so that the sum was greater than the parts. He was smart and experienced and willing to share both, yet taught us how to make and admit mistakes, humbly revealing lessons he'd learned with a wry smile. He set the business and the people up for success – to him, they were one and the same. And he did it all with a hot dog in one hand and a cigarette in the other. Although he was a top executive at K-C, I kept forgetting to be intimidated by Dudley.

Of course, I didn't recognize Dudley's superpowers right away. It never works like that, as Clark Kent will tell you. Dudley hid his powers behind scruffy shoes, baggy trousers, and loose-fitting polo shirts that afforded a little extra room for his belly, where excess hot dogs and HoHos were stored. Dudley drove a dilapidated Toyota Tercel hatchback because his dog, Deke, liked it and that meant more to him than what others thought.

I met Dudley after returning to Neenah from my orientation with Kent in Chicago, shortly after locating my new office but before finding out where the coffee machine and bathrooms were located. Uh, who was this guy eating a lollipop, nonchalantly folding his lanky frame into the tiny chair in my tiny office? The guy informally introduced himself, welcomed me and asked how I was doing, what did I need? He listened to my answers. For real. He asked about my family, later remembering Scott's name. He told me he was glad I was there, then left as casually as he had come.

I watched him walk to his office. His corner office. Oh. Crap. The guy with the lollipop was my boss's boss's boss. How was I to know? The guy hadn't made an official entrance, didn't lead with his title nor imply title was important to him because it wasn't. Foul! I had been given no indication that Dudley was *the dude*. I hadn't been given the chance to make a good first impression. No matter. Dudley never looked down on anyone; everyone looked up to Dudley. He didn't *make* people feel important; they *were* important to him. Before long, I knew Dudley was the kind of leader I wanted to be, with superpowers I wanted to emulate.

I was fortunate to land in Dudley's organization, where I remained for the next five years. I was 24 years old and working as a Marketing Assistant on Huggies diapers, where I learned:

- Baby poop comes in all colors and shapes. Keeping poop inside the diaper is important and harder than it seems.

- Babies don't pee or poop in their diapers, they 'insult' them. Knowing how 'insulted' a diaper can get before having a 'critical failure' is critically important and harder than it seems.

- Huggies babies are happy babies. If the diaper doesn't work, baby isn't happy, and mommy isn't happy. Unhappy mommies are scary. Ergo, keeping babies happy is important and harder than it seems.

- There are over 10,000 babies born each day in the US. As a consumer marketer, this means the opportunity to gain 10,000 new Huggies users each day… and the risk of losing 10,000 each day as children become toilet trained. Keeping track of these babies was a full-time job (mine) and harder than it seems, at least for me.

I did all the relatively unimportant, unremarkable work you'd expect of a new hire. Maybe my work wasn't super significant but I *felt* important and *that* was significant. I knew my work mattered because that's what I was told by people I liked and respected.

Asked what I thought, what I'd do, what I recommended and why, Dudley taught me to be clear and concise, honing my pitch to cover K-C's preferred framework – background, recommendation, rationale, cost, timing and next steps – in as little time as possible. The better command I got of the business, the more freedom I was given to make and own decisions, right or wrong. There was too much to do to wallow in worry so we learned as we went and we went fast. Title and tenure were important but didn't make you important. That, in itself, made the work and its people quite remarkable.

Competing against Pampers and Luvs (Proctor and Gamble) was like David vs Goliath. No one expected Huggies to put up a serious fight – our team and budget were half the size of P&G's Pampers. We didn't have the muscle with retailers that P&G flexed. But P&G underestimated the underdogs from the frozen tundra who took great pride in doing more with less, analyzing each market to capitalize on Huggies' strengths and exploit P&G's weaknesses. We challenged each other to work smarter, to translate knowledge of our consumers and customers into better products and marketing. We were scrappy. Bit by bit, we nibbled away at P&G's lead, never letting up until we finally achieved #1 national share. Nobody beat P&G's Pampers multi-billion-dollar brands! It just wasn't done. Especially not a bunch of cheeseheads from Wisconsin.

But we did it, beating P&G in what the *Wall Street Journal* dubbed the Diaper Wars. Billions of dollars were at stake. The *WSJ, Forbes,* etc. wrote articles about the Diaper Wars while Harvard scholars flew to Neenah to interview us. For years to come, students on college campuses around the US conducted Harvard Business Review case studies on how Huggies overtook P&G's Pampers. Despite the achievement, the company remained below the radar so that most people knew our brands but continued to ask, "who's she?" when I said I worked for Kimberly-Clark.

When we finally achieved #1 national share, there were no big bonuses, no exclusive trips to exotic locations, no lavish parties. No chest thumping or fist pumping. We got a personal note and a heartfelt thank you from our CEO, who knew each on the team by name. Everyone tacked their note where it could be seen easily, a daily reminder that they were valued and appreciated. Dudley bought pizza and pitchers of beer at

Cranky Pat's Pizzeria. It was Wisconsin, after all, where big celebrations were reserved for Green Bay Packers victories.

I'm convinced that remaining humble and scrappy was the secret to continued success. There were no streamers or confetti because winning wasn't a one-time occasion to be cheered. Achievement was expected every day by everyone. Dudley and his leadership team taught me the value of keeping folks focused on the competitor *outside* the walls of K-C, so that we could celebrate and build on one another's successes *inside* the walls of our K-C family. I've never regretted my decision to join the underdogs at K-C rather than the 'top dogs' at P&G. Better to be a mutt that can bite than a pedigree that's all bark.

4 o'clock Friends

"Friends are the family you choose."

— Jess C. Scott

While I was knee deep in Huggies spreadsheets, budgets and marketing programs, I was learning something vastly more important for which I was initially unaware. Being raised in Carroll meant Scott and I never had to search for a community, we were born into one, a member through birth of the Carroll collective. When we went to college at ISU and Purdue, we met lots of great people and friends, but looked no further than each other in times of need. It was in Wisconsin that we discovered the concept and importance of 4 o'clock friends.

A 4 o'clock friend is someone who, when you call at 4am for help, asks only where and when. A 4 o'clock friend is there for you in your time of need without hesitation, question, or judgment. Sometimes to lend an ear, sometimes to lend a hand; always with a compassionate, open heart. A trusty 4 o'clock friend will help push you out of a snowbank and not tell your husband because she knows that he had just warned you to "drive slower or you'll slide into a snowbank someday." A special 4 o' clock friend knows just when to nudge, wink or whisper encouragement before an important presentation and is there for you with a glass of wine to celebrate… or commiserate afterwards. A 4 o'clock friendship can sneak up on you and often goes unspoken and sometimes unappreciated, as evenings together pass so quickly.

Our 4 o'clock friendships began simply, somewhat reluctantly if the truth be told, when Scott and I were asked by three other couples to play bridge one snowy Wisconsin Sunday afternoon. Bridge? Really? Didn't you need to be at least 70 years old to play bridge? We felt like we were the last kids picked on the playground, but a fourth couple was needed, and we were available. We knew nothing of how to play bridge, and only mildly knew the other three couples, but dinner and wine were involved, so we said yes before they could rescind the offer.

I knew I was in trouble when not one, but two decks of cards were placed on the table and the words trump, rubber, opening count and vulnerable were used in the same sentence. The rules were explained. Many times. Many, many times. Patti created a cheat sheet to help me remember the rules. God bless her. Then Keith came up with a second cheat sheet. Wonderful. Then Connie created a cheat sheet to explain Patti and Keith's cheat sheets. Oh boy. Soon staples were necessary to contain the cheat sheets. About this time, I discovered I'm competitive about everything but card games. My philosophy of 'a card played is a card forgotten' didn't work well for a card game dependent on counting points and tracking all 52 cards played. I began studying the cheat sheets to focus and to refresh my memory, but there was no memory to refresh, my mind a sieve through which the rules of bridge flowed straight through.

Fortunately for me, I was always partnered with Scott, who became as awesome at bridge as I remained awful. Scott generally constrained his disdain to eye rolling and deep sighing whenever I made a bonehead move, of which there were many. Many. I felt bad for a while, but eventually redirected my focus to appetizers and dessert. Ah yes, better. Unlike my mind, my body was not a sieve through which appetizers and desserts flowed, my hips retaining each calorie consumed as steadfastly as my brain rejected every bridge rule studied. I soon dedicated a portion of my wardrobe to bridge attire – stretchy pants and fleece.

As winter set in and the piles of snow became higher than the snowblower could blow, we hunkered down and got organized, rotating host homes alphabetically. The hosting couple provided a main dish while everyone else signed up to bring either an appetizer, the bread, or a dessert. All brought wine, the lubricant that kept the bridge wheel turning, the stories flowing and the laughter plentiful.

We weren't very creative, referring to our get-togethers as Bridge Club, although over time, Bridge Club became less about bridge and more about eating and drinking. Creativity was saved for cooking. It turns out there are more seasonings than Lipton soup mix and more spices than garlic salt. Tom and Patti were gourmets. I knew Scott and I were out of our league when Tom served hamburgers with blue cheese and Patti served bruschetta with fresh garlic and basil. I didn't know garlic was a real thing. It is. I had always assumed garlic was something invented (like Cheetos) by McCormick and available only two ways – garlic salt or garlic powder. Likewise, who knew basil is a real plant, also not invented by McCormick? I assumed both were sold at specialty stores but was assured that most grocery stores sold both fresh garlic and basil. Bridge Club opened a whole new world of culinary capabilities for Scott and me, although Campbell's cream of mushroom soup remained the cornerstone of our dishes for a long time.

Over more time still, our gatherings became less about eating and drinking and more about fellowship. Bridge Club came to mean the place you go, the people you see, who know and keep your story, who teach you without knowing it how to be a good spouse, parent and friend. Year after year, we played the literal and figurative hands we were dealt. Fifty-two cards dealt in thousands of combinations that echoed the good and bad hands we were dealt in our work, health, marriages, families, children, fears, hopes and dreams.

We met at least monthly, often weekly, for 17 years. Initially, different couples rotated in and out until we settled into a cadence with the same four couples, eight people who came together as casual friends, then good friends, then family. The family we chose. We were all different – two lawyers, one engineer, two salesmen, two marketers, two lefties, three musicians, one composer, one mathematician, four introverts, four extroverts, four men, four women, all shapes and sizes, religious and not, different on the surface yet the same underneath. The two things universally shared were our commitment to one another and our annual New Year's resolution to lose the weight we'd gained playing bridge together over the prior year. We encouraged one another through weight loss programs, exercise plans, 5ks and marathons, only to find ourselves on the slippery slope of weight gain until it was time once again to renew our annual New Year's resolutions over a few glasses of wine.

I watched and learned as couples came to the card table with either light, carefree hearts or with hearts heavy and aching for the camaraderie, love and fellowship that would renew their spirits. We knew by the way someone walked into the room and said hello whether they were in a good mood or not, getting along with their spouse or not. It became an unspoken signal that any couple not getting along would sign up to bring the bread because bread was the one item that wasn't home cooked and could be easily bought en route to the host's house, without a word spoken. The way the bread was delivered usually left little room for doubt – the room cooled a degree or two as a discordant couple entered the house in single file, neither touching nor talking to one another, tendrils of tension their only connection as the bread was unceremoniously plopped upon the counter. Eyebrows rose slightly to acknowledge the plop, its message clear to everyone in the unspoken language of longtime friendship, the conversation barely skipping a beat. Eventually the warm balm of friendship worked its magic, loosening knots of discord until the banter flowed as effortlessly and generously as the wine poured.

Week by week, month by month, year by year, I learned more from Bridge Club about being a good partner, friend, wife and mother than could be learned from any marriage counselor, Oprah magazine or Dr. Spock book. Only John Gottman knew more about marriage. What I lacked in learning the rules of bridge I learned playing the game of life with my 4 o'clock bridge friends. If you want to stay happily married, have friends who are happily married. For real. When marriage was difficult and I felt wobbly and unsure, it was my bridge family whose arms reached out to support and strengthen us with laughter and tears, helping us regain perspective until Scott and I stood surely beside one another once more and it was another couple's turn to bring the bread. Because at some point in all marriages, every couple ends up bringing the bread.

In the Black

*"It's not about the goal.
It's about growing to become the person that can accomplish that goal."*

— Tony Robbins

I was thrown into the deep end of the pool, but soon took to K-C like a duck to water. For the first time ever, I had a job that didn't involve punching a clock, waiting tables or cleaning anything. My salary was $36k/yr. We were *rich!* I hadn't felt this affluent since working at Lou Walsh Motors as a little girl. Puffed up by our newfound wealth and giddy at the thought of actually *buying* stuff versus dreaming about buying stuff, Scott and I beelined to the mall. Yes, today was the someday we had dreamed about. Finally, we could afford to buy the good stuff, not just the stuff on clearance, returned or previously owned. We located the closest JCPenney and splurged on brand new, never used curtains, bedding and lamps that were still in their original packaging and boxes. Wow! Lucky for us, there was a furniture store in the mall where we found two lovely seafoam green chairs that reminded us of the ruffles from Scott's prom tux. Evidently no one else appreciated the color because the chairs were on clearance. We swooped in and bought both chairs to replace our threadbare gold chairs whose seat cushions had long since smooshed flat and lost most of the stuffing through fabric worn thin on the arms. Despite being "rich," we didn't go completely crazy and continued to shop second-hand stores and drive around town on garbage days to salvage things from curbs.

Scott and I had always been poor but never in debt. We learned too late that it's not how much you earn, it's how much you spend. Between the student loans, Dad's loan and newly acquired credit cards, we were soon living beyond our means. I found dad's words constantly ringing in my ears…

> "If you can't pay for it, don't buy it…"
> "Never live beyond your means…"
> "Pay cash or spend nothing…"

We'd never had finances to manage before. There was more to it than shaking the piggy bank and checking under cushions hoping there was something there to pay for groceries. Not that we put the pig away… but now that we had more than pennies in the piggy, it was time to diversify our financial planning.

It was hard to do at first, but we contributed the max allowable into K-C's 401k program from the start, so we never missed what we never had. We lived below our means, saving as much as was reasonably possible. We created a "fuckit" fund that would enable us to quit work or cover emergency expenses if needed. We didn't buy new cars, boats or branded clothes. Our vacations involved a car and bug spray, not airplanes and sunscreen. Date nights were spent in the plumbing and paint departments at Home Depot. We didn't join clubs – athletic, country or otherwise – unless they were free. We were in it together, shared a common vision and grew more financially stable, project by project, month by month. Our finances were mutually known, discussed and agreed. I vowed never to be surprised or uninformed about something so important ever again. Money gives choices and voices. It's too important to be clueless or quiet about.

Eventually, we were back in the black and able to sink into our seafoam green chairs, financially secure and content. Over the years, we'd kept track of all the bills we'd paid off until the night finally came when we built a fire in the fireplace, unscrewed the cap on a bottle of wine, and fed page after page of paid-off student loans and credit card bills into the roaring fire.

We maintained our modest lifestyle and were millionaires within a decade of leaving Purdue. Not that it mattered. Nothing changed. Sadly, we didn't become smarter, worthier, funnier, or better looking as our bank balance grew. Our big splurge was buying wine with corks. The millionaire milestone quietly came and went without celebration, although I'd be lying not to admit we felt proud of the achievement and how much we had grown and achieved together, hopeful we'd be forever free from financial anxiety, debt collectors and bounced checks. If only.

Andy

"I don't know why they say "You have a baby." The baby has you."
— Gallagher

Scott and I were only twenty years old when we got married. We were stupid enough to believe we were mature enough to get married, yet smart enough to realize we were too immature to have children right away. We agreed to have fun, graduate college, and grow up a bit before becoming parents, in that order. So I went to Planned Parenthood and got on the pill, secretly unsure when or if I'd ever go off. Ours was the fourth of five weddings in 18 months across my and Scott's family. Our newly married brothers and sisters popped out kids right away. Naturally, our parents expected to hear similar 'good news' from us any day. The first year passed. No good news. Then the second, third, fourth and fifth. By the sixth year, our Catholic parents assumed we were desperately trying to conceive, but sadly, one of us was obviously 'broken' and unable to produce a child. They told us they were praying for us and not to give up hope that someday we'd have 'good news' too.

In reality, I wasn't sure I wanted 'good news' and panicked each time I thought someday had come. At first I thought it was because we were so broke that good news would be bad. But after we got financially secure, I felt no different. While others embraced motherhood and welcomed children with a normal combination of joy and fear, I was terrified. Scott was a baby whisperer who transformed screaming babies into cooing bundles nestled in his arms. I was a baby terrorist who elicited primordial screams as other's babies attempted to dive out of my arms as if I was pinching them, which I wasn't, just for the record. I was doing well in my career and had only to look back upon my failed attempts at babysitting to know I just wasn't cut out for kids. I wanted to sell Huggies, not buy them. But Scott had no doubt or hesitation and his reassurance eroded my reluctance. Besides, I'd been on the pill for almost 10 years and wasn't even sure we could get pregnant. So we agreed to perhaps go off the pill for just a bit.

I was pregnant within a month. Not that I'd noticed. Not until a friend at work stared cockeyed after I'd complained of being tired and queasy and announced it. Oh. I left work immediately and went to Shopko to buy a pregnancy test, grabbing a pair of baby Nike sneakers displayed on an endcap, just in case it was true. It was. I was pregnant. With a baby. A baby. The pinball machine in my head began lighting up, up, up, metal ball rolling from emotion to emotion, slowly at first then faster as awareness grew, gaining momentum – thrilled (PING!) terrified (PING!) joy (PING!) uncertainty (PING!) fear (PING!) O!M!G! (PING! PING! PING!) – on the edge of tilting as the cacophony of pings crescendo – then slowly, a gentle hand took over and new emotions overwhelmed me – wonder (ping!) acceptance (Ping!) happy! (PING!) as the pinball's scoreboard goes from 'GAME OVER' to a 'BONUS – NEW GAME.'

I was ready but scared. Breathe, Jane. Which emotion would I feed my child during pregnancy? Fear? NO! Breathe, Jane. That night in the family room, Scott unwrapped the pair of teeny-weeny baby Nikes. His face reflected no fear, no uncertainty or doubt. Only pure joy – PING! Scott was thrilled, alternating between laughing and crying as he enveloped me in his arms, lifted me from the ground and twirled me around. Any uncertainty I felt about being a capable mother was overcome by certainty that Scott would be an amazing father. Love. Love flowed from Scott through me and into our child. Ping.

And so, after ten years of marriage, we finally announced the 'good news' to our family. The news was greeted with shock, alleluias and thanksgiving for what was, in their minds, clearly a miracle. Which, for me, it was.

The story of my pregnancy is as old as humanity, shared and sacred, told and retold through the ages by women to women, unremarkable to all who aren't living it. As my belly grew bigger and my ability to belly up to the conference table grew physically more difficult, it seemed men found it harder to relate to me professionally. Perhaps they saw in me their own wives, round with child. Maybe they thought my IQ was flowing to the child I was carrying. But I worked the same as always, undeterred by the body that had become unrecognizable to me. Mine was not a delicate or subtle baby bump, having gained far more than the 25 pounds suggested in most baby books I never read. I was nervous and big as a house as I stood on stage before our sales organization, unable to understand why the audience was laughing. Since when were product launch plans funny? Looking down, I understood. My maternity dress was moving as if it had a life of its own – which it did. Fueled by my adrenaline, the child within was kicking up a storm, adding exclamation points to my presentation, my dress a canvas for its expressions of joy. Even in the womb, the baby would make itself heard. Like mother, like child.

It was impossible to ignore that there were two of us going to work each day. I gave up trying to pretend otherwise and appreciated the little kindnesses humans do for others carrying little humans within their womb. Of course things were changing and going to be different. Pretending otherwise was to suggest I was no different than the men around the table, that the pregnancy was a temporary thing, the baby a product to be launched, then I'd resume focus on the business at hand.

Things *were* different. *I* was different. My capability, passion and drive were unchanged, but I had begun driving on a more complicated road that few women in my position had navigated.

Overall, my pregnancy went just as expected according to the *What To Expect When You're Expecting* book. But the book doesn't have a chapter called "what to do when your dumbass doctor doesn't notice that your baby is breech during delivery." By the time a nurse recognized that my baby was trying to cannonball out of me, both baby and I were exhausted by our efforts and in distress. Yup, the doctor agreed, I needed an emergency C-section. I responded logically. I fired him.

The doctor thought I was kidding but Scott knew I was deadly serious and quickly took control of the situation, persuading another obstetrician on call to perform the surgery. Okay, so this wasn't going according to the book, but when I heard Scott joyfully shout "It's an Andy!" I knew we had a son, and I knew his name, both of which were surprises.

Although Andy hadn't been on the pre-agreed list of names when we'd arrived at the hospital, it was my son's name when we left. The 'and' in Andy implied a bounty of blessings, which seemed to fit our son perfectly from the start.

There were no primordial screams, no fear as Andy was placed in my arms. Our souls embraced as if they'd been waiting a long time to meet, as he gently nestled into my heart, where he will, forever, remain.

There must be a special place in heaven for parents of colicky babies. I'll never know. God knew I'd go off the deep end with a colicky child, so instead was blessed with a mellow, happy baby who cried so infrequently that our parents worried he "wasn't quite right." We took him to the doctor, several times, for confirmation that he was in fact, 'quite right.' We began calling Andy our Joy Boy the day he gave us his first smile and we gave him our hearts. Andy was so easygoing that he went everywhere with us – on walks, to movies, dinner, etc. He became a community baby during weekly Mass, passing into the arms of person after person, a vessel into which everyone poured their love and blessings. A holy exchange was made, as Andy bestowed hope and happiness upon those in whose arms he was held. Andy had an old soul that seemed to beckon the best within others.

For six weeks, Andy was the center of my universe, as 4 o'clock friends provided crash courses in all the things that seemed to come naturally and joyfully to them, but seemed a struggle for me – feeding, diapering, burping, diapering, bathing, diapering, sleeping, diapering. Scott was a natural, spending hours with Andy cradled in his arms or sleeping contentedly on his chest, watching football together. Scott knew just how to swaddle Andy so he felt safe and content. Friends and family came and went to coo and cuddle, but my favorite moments were sitting quietly under a tree in the sun, babe in arms, singing. It's never too early to teach your child John Denver.

I loved my son, but needed to work, both mentally and financially. I wasn't confused or conflicted. I was a better mom because I worked full time, not because I stayed home full time. At the time, it was common for women to quit work after starting a family and I was often asked if I was *really* going to return after maternity leave. Yes, yes I was. No apology. No explanation. No guilt. Everyone would have lost if I had stayed home full time.

Scott and I had found a loving, responsible caretaker into whose hands we entrusted our son. I could never decide whether Andy's guardian angel was just lazy or was overworked because Andy was forever climbing and leaping over, into, off, or through things. We came to know the folks at Child Protective Services, having been interrogated whenever we brought Andy to the hospital. We no longer panicked at the words associated with Andy… broken, torn, concussion, contusion, under observation, emergency room. Accidents happen in the blink of an eye. Andy blinked a lot. As Andy grew, he began to look more and more like Scott and behave more and more like me. As much as I would have liked to encircle Andy in bubble wrap, there was no protecting him from himself, for the internal fire that fueled his happy and adventurous spirit was the same one that occasionally caused his pain. The best I could do was keep a well-stocked first aid kit on hand and know that Andy's bumps, cuts and scrapes would have happened had I been a stay-home or working mom.

I didn't ever feel as if I entirely fit in at childcare, school or other places where children clung to their moms as tears were shed by both. I told Andy, "I get to go to work with my friends now, and you get to go to school with your friends. I can't wait to hear about your day when I see you tonight. Bye Andy. See you soon. I love you." After a big hug and kiss, he was gone. No clinging, no tears. I would sometimes sit in my car afterwards and try to summon a tear or two. Nope, nothing. I was happy and not saddened by Andy's milestones.

In these moments, I wanted to fit in and be like all the other moms. I wanted to join the other moms for coffee and talk about how fast our kids were growing up. But it was not to be. In truth, I was still learning how to be an engaged mom, having never had one. I sometimes called my brothers and sisters for guidance on how to play and care for Andy, but really, I just liked being reassured that they were equally baffled and struggling with how to go about playing with their kids. All but baby sister Linn, who had grown up playing with dolls and instinctively knew the secrets of motherhood. Understandably, Linn was shunned although we secretly were in awe of her capabilities.

In truth, I felt more comfortable in the office than in the schoolroom, far more intimidated by other moms than by other corporate executives. I chose to stay on the sidelines, learning from the master moms who could get 20 children to make cool stuff out of macaroni, pipe cleaners and paper plates. No, I wasn't up to being a classroom mom;

sensing my weakness, the kids pounced on me like a pack of wolves taking down a frightened doe.

I was usually okay not being and having it all – trying to do so would make me and others crazy. In the end, I did exactly what I told Andy to do – I went to work with my friends, and he went to school with his friends, and we talked all about our day over the dinner table. No one can be good at every job, but everyone is good at some jobs. I knew which jobs I was good at and was grateful to leave Andy in the more capable hands of teachers and volunteer moms who made it possible for him to come home from school each day with a smile and something wonderful to share.

I'm a Big Kid Now

"Alone we can do so little; together we can do so much."

— Helen Keller

After a few years of cutting my teeth on Huggies, Dudley decided I was ready to become a Big Kid and made me Brand Manager responsible for introducing Pull-Ups Training Pants nationally. The job had a big marketing budget, and was responsible for coordinating sales and operations to ensure the launch went smoothly and that we hit budgeted profitability. For the first time, I'd have others reporting to me. It was a plum job everyone had thought Kent was going to get, at least according to Kent. After my promotion, Kent insisted he chose to remain in the Kotex business. Sure, Kent.

Pull-Ups became a huge success. Sales exceeded our initial expectations by so much that it took two years for us to build enough capacity to make Pull-Ups national. In the meantime, moms road-tripped to buy cases of Pull-Ups the way college kids used to road trip for Coors beer. Enterprising moms would buy and send or sell cases of Pull-Ups to friends/others where Pull-Ups weren't available. Who knew disposable underwear could turn ordinary moms into modern-day smugglers?

Pull-Ups was awarded Best New Product and lots of awards by the grocery and advertising industries. Which sounds great until you sit across the desk from a buyer at Ralph's grocery who threatens to discontinue Kotex and Kleenex if you don't "get me some Pull-Ups dammit" because his customers, including his wife, were furious about having to buy pirated Pull-Ups from smugglers on the other coast. My plum new job turned into a prune as I sought to sell *less* until we could make more.

All success comes with a price tag. For every get is a give. As days flew by in a blur of production schedules, sales forecasts and roll-out plans, I soon forgot to make time to celebrate and listen to the people who had made success possible. I had begun filling my calendar with reviews and meetings, was focused on spreadsheets and plans, not people. No longer taking time to ask people how *they* were doing, I was interested only in *what* they did. Once my calendar began leading me, I became too busy to lead. When everything seems urgent, nothing important gets done. Celebrating, connecting, and listening to people is what feeds my spirit and fuels my enthusiasm, yet I started deeming them 'soft stuff' and relegated them to the category of important-but-not-urgent. How very Kent of me.

Arriving before dawn and leaving after sunset each day, my team began looking as pale and dull as we felt. This wasn't success, this was insanity. I regained control of my calendar, stopped attending most meetings, canceled others, and focused on fewer priorities. I was VERY IMPORTANT, so I expected push-back. There wasn't any. Oh. Dammit. *I* was the cause of my own insanity. I had allowed my workload and perfectionism to escalate so that people were no longer coming to me. Colin Powell says that the day people stop bringing you their problems is the day you have stopped leading them. They have either lost confidence that you can help them or concluded that you do not care. Either case is a failure of leadership. When I finally redirected my calendar to make myself accessible and available, the people and problems returned and I began leading again. I did care and I could help.

One Friday night, alone in the office and anxious to go home, I reached for a stack of letters from our Consumer Services department expecting to read positive Pull-Ups feedback, a nice way to end a difficult week. Instead, I read of a problem I didn't know existed. Heartfelt letters from parents, children, and grandparents explained the shame and alienation experienced by the young child in the family who had never spent a night away from home, never been on a sleepover, never spent the weekend at grandma's or at camp, who hid their 'problem' in fear and shame. What problem? Bedwetting? Really? Is this really such a big deal? I read on. Children wrote of dread and fear upon waking to a wet bed. I learned that bedwetting is a leading trigger for child abuse by those who believe it's done purposefully because the child is 'willful and naughty' and 'old enough to know better.' The lump in my throat finally released the torrent of tears as I read letter after letter. It was late and I just wanted to go home to my own family. But the letters could not be unread or ignored. What to do? Who could help? I looked out the window to see my own face reflected back with the answer. I knew who could help, or at least try.

The following week, I shared the letters with some friends on the team. They got it, some sharing deeply personal stories of similar experiences. We began outlining a business plan. Armed with the letters, it wasn't hard to recruit people in research, operations, finance and sales. My boss was understandably skeptical – we didn't even have the manufacturing capacity to meet Pull-Ups demand, much less introduce a new, larger size to help a handful of kids. The numbers simply didn't add up to a viable business. We were not deterred. We dug deeper. It turns out there are lots and lots of older kids who experience bedwetting for lots and lots of reasons, many having to do with lengthier normal development, often inherited from a parent, some due to illness or ability, none having to do with willpower. The more we learned, the more committed people became. Plans gained structure, suggestions became possibilities, which became probabilities, then became reality.

We were sitting in my office brainstorming names, all agreeing we shouldn't just launch an XXL, XXXL size Pull-Ups. After all, these kids were not potty training and did not fit the jaunty "I'm a Big Kid Now" positioning of Pull-Ups. We needed to create a new brand. Something neither negative nor insulting. Potential brand names were swatted around the room like a beach ball tossed into a crowd. The words GoodNites were uttered and there was no need for further brainstorming, for the name landed squarely into our waiting arms. The tagline "GoodNites mean good mornings" soon followed.

Everything came together quickly. Within just one year of reading the letters, on a tiny budget, using a prototype machine that had been mothballed in storage two years prior, a small group of people brought GoodNites to market. The GoodNites team worked with a sense of passion and urgency not driven by deadlines, but motivated by the will to make a positive impact on the lives of kids.

We weren't prepared for the overwhelming response as demand quickly outstripped production. We maxed out shifts and capacity, applying all we'd learned from the Pull-Ups rollout to get GoodNites into national distribution as quickly as possible. Even so, it was clear GoodNites was addressing a much bigger need than we knew, as sales far exceeded even our high-side forecast. GoodNites had been a relatively small side bet that was paying off in a big, big way. Despite reining in marketing, national rollout took much longer than initially expected as production caught up with demand. It was a happy problem to manage.

GoodNites won even more awards than Pull-Ups. The plaques, awards and industry recognitions were showcased inside a glass display case outside the cafeteria. People often paused and smiled as they passed the case, paying little attention to the awards, mostly hidden behind what really mattered to the team. Scotch taped to the outside of the display case were dozens of letters from kids, parents and grandparents expressing how GoodNites had impacted their lives. No longer haunting, their stories were filled with happiness and hope. Only a year earlier, I sat crying while reading letters of despair, wondering who could help. I need not to have worried about who would help, I needed only to ask help from a few, who became a few more, who became many. Over the year, countless people stepped forward to help, my face but one amongst many reflected in the window.

I think if I'd have asked people to help create a new, billion-dollar business, people would have sighed and told me how overworked they already were. When a busy person thinks of all they have to do in a day, they picture tasks to be done and hours on a clock. Their hands are already full, you'll hear. If you appeal only to the head and not the heart, people will think much, care little and do less. But offer someone an opportunity to contribute their time and talent toward removing someone's pain and suffering and suddenly tasks become meaningful while hours lose their meaning. Motivating the heart to care and the hands to act makes anything possible.

La Gringa

"If you risk nothing, you risk everything."
— Geena Davis

"Never use someone else's yardstick to measure your life."
— Jane Boulware

I've never had a personal 5-year plan or anything close to it. Hell, I didn't even know what a 5-year plan was. People who had such a plan for their lives were like exotic animals to me, both wonderful and yet curious to behold. I wasn't intentional about what I wanted to be, perhaps because I didn't really know what was possible. Like I said, my parents had set the bar low for me and never expected me to 'be somebody' which gave me the freedom to be anything I wanted. More and more, I wanted to be more, do more. I wanted to stretch, to take risks and put myself in a position to learn and grow, which often meant I was in over my head. I rather think growing is more about being willing and courageous enough to knock on doors and to say 'yes' when an unexpected door opens, rather than creating a plan that optimizes the best doors to open and the timing thereof.

So it's not surprising that my resume doesn't make a lot of logical sense – it looks more like a game of tic-tac-toe than a game of chess. That's because I kept seeking, getting offered and accepting jobs for which I felt unqualified. It turns out that I rather like taking on challenges and roles that others think are too risky, shitty or likely to fail. All I know is that there is something in me that says "hell yes" when others say "oh no." I wasn't usually the first person offered a role, but I was always the first to accept.

But really, how risky could saying "Yes" be? Neenah, Wisconsin isn't exactly the epicenter of danger and adventure. It's the kind of place where neighbors wave as you walk by, windows go dark shortly after the 10 o'clock news, and folks make sure to bake enough cookies to share. If something out of the ordinary happens, people call to offer help not to notify the police.

My detour to the danger zone started innocently enough on a Friday afternoon, shortly after the launch of GoodNites. Tom Falk, then COO of Kimberly-Clark, stopped by my office to check on me. It was a casual chat. He asked how I was doing, to which I replied, "Fine." Then like an idiot, I casually told him the three things I look for in a job:

1. Am I making a contribution – does my work make a meaningful difference?

2. Am I learning something new – does my work stretch and grow me in ways that make me better professionally and personally?

3. Am I working with people I like and respect?

I then went on to casually say I felt I was making a contribution, I liked and respected my team, and was finally feeling comfortable in my role. In the next year or so, I'd probably like to be considered for another opportunity. Nothing definite, just casual conversation. That was Friday.

A few days later, Tom again stopped by my office. He talked to me about taking the lead marketing role in our Latin American region, comprising 16 countries south of Mexico. Estas loco? This is what happens when you have a casual conversation with a COO on a Friday afternoon. After picking my jaw up off the ground, I pointed out just a few of the obvious reasons this was a bad idea…

- I'd be a white woman, el gringa, in a notoriously machismo culture
- I didn't know how to say more than gracias and burrito in Spanish
- I was only 31 years old, had a 1 ½ year old child and a husband whose job was not in Latin America
- And… I was pretty sure I wasn't qualified.

Tom pointed out that the job fulfilled all three of my criteria, that I *was* qualified, and he knew I could do it. He was taking a chance on me. I'd never traveled, much less worked overseas. I had a passport, but had only dreamed about using it. I agreed to think about it, already knowing what my answer would be. No. Não. Nada. Nope. No way.

Later that night, I started the conversation with Scott something like, "You'll never guess what happened at the office today," thinking we'd both have a chuckle then move on to eating supper. I wasn't expecting Scott to take Tom's discussion seriously, but after dinner, we loaded Andy into the stroller to go for a walk, a sure sign that a 'serious conversation' was about to ensue.

Scott asked question after question, for which I had few answers. He began filling in the blanks himself, asking "what if" then "how could," slowly creating a picture of what might be possible. As we walked, Scott began to find solutions to problems I hadn't even considered, eliminating stoppers to blockers until I too began to imagine 'what if' instead of 'why not.' Scott had no doubt that I was capable and would thrive in the job. He saw through all my reasons not to go and saw only that I should and would go. He would do whatever it took to make it so, which he began outlining to himself while thinking out loud. "We will have to move to Atlanta, which means I'll have to quit my job at Sound World. I love managing that place and hate to leave it, especially now that I've hired and trained such a great team. We're doing so well. I'll miss my friends there. But it can't be helped. I'll have to get our house ready to sell and buy a new house in Atlanta. I can't expect much help from Jane since she'll be working day and night 5,000 miles away in South America. And what about Andy? I don't trust putting Andy in childcare with people I don't know. That means I'll need to care for him which means I can't work, which means…."

"Hello? Hello?" I interrupted. I had been listening to Scott noodle the situation and could see it becoming real to him. We had already walked miles and were at Leon's, where the world's greatest frozen custard was sold. By the time we finished our cones and returned home we had decided. When we left the house, I saw all the reasons the job clearly wasn't a viable option. While Scott and I walked and talked he knocked down all the barriers, one by one. I wasn't expecting to take a 5-mile walk to discuss the possibility. I wasn't expecting to become excited by the possibility. I didn't see a Yes coming. But Scott did.

On Wednesday, I accepted the position. On Sunday, I was on a flight to Buenos Aires, frantically listening to "How to Speak Basic Spanish" cassette tapes while reading business plans for our Latin American Operations.

Within weeks, our worlds turned upside down, me landing in the southern hemisphere and Scott (with Andy in arms) arriving a thousand miles south of Neenah in Atlanta. Scott was the gravity that anchored our home and the tether that enabled me to both fly away and return safely each week. But in many ways, Scott's new world was far more foreign and difficult to traverse.

In Neenah, Scott was Master of His Domain. He managed a high-end electronics business and had become the go-to guy, known and respected by audiophiles and high-end sound innovators nationally. Scott was a Dude. The transition to Andy's stay-home dad in Atlanta was brutal. Scott's domain shrunk to a 1 ½-year-old, 24-pound little old boy just 31 inches high who refused to be mastered and had no idea his dad was a dude.

Scott was a pioneer, among the first men who left the workplace to care for their families full time while their wives worked. There is no good title for these guys. Mr. Mom, stay-at-home-dad, professional dad. None of these capture the courage and strength required for the job, for they did the work of traditional stay-at-home moms without the support of other women…or men, for that matter. He didn't fit in anywhere, really. When the neighborhood stay-at-home mom brigade in our Atlanta subdivision came knocking on our door carrying a homemade welcome-to-the-neighborhood cake, they weren't prepared to be greeted by Scott sporting a ponytail down his back and Andy on his hip. They didn't stay long. Once they realized I wasn't home, they promptly left. With the cake. The welcome wagon didn't welcome dudes in their circle.

Being acknowledged and included in the moms' club was just as tricky and unlikely for Scott as infiltrating the boys' club was for me. At that time, it was rare for a man to be the primary caregiver. Scott wasn't welcomed at Mommy & Me classes or asked to join any neighborhood play groups. He didn't fit in among those who menstruated. Men responded to Scott and his new role in one of two ways – with jealousy or bewilderment.

During this time, we heard it all. Words of judgment were offered more freely than the hand of friendship. I often heard other women (always women, never men) say some variation of, "Oh, I could *never* do what you do! I could *never* leave my baby and husband!" ...which really meant *What kind of mother/wife does that? Don't you care?* For a while, these comments really stung. I felt defensive and guilty. Was something wrong with me/us? Why were we happy with our unconventional life? The truth settled in my soul, becoming a personal mantra I repeated to myself often through the years: *Jane, don't use someone else's yardstick to measure your success/life.* Scott and I had forged a path that others judged inappropriate, but we were happy and committed to each other and our family, which became our measure of success. Within a few months, we established an unconventional but comfortable stride, me traveling to South America to build our LATAM business and Scott traveling to Home Depot to renovate our Atlanta home.

I often flew through the night to arrive in a country (Argentina, Brazil, Columbia, etc.) in the early morning hours. There was always someone I may or may not know to greet me at the airport and take me to my hotel. The drive gave me time to shake off residual fuzzies from any sleeping pills I'd taken, as I focused on the city passing by my window, seeking clues about where I was and what I was supposed to do that day. It wasn't long before the car pulled up to a beautiful hotel, which was wasted on me, for I was there for only long enough to shower and caffeinate before heading to the K-C office. On a particularly grueling trip, I was gone for 10 days but expensed only a few nights in a hotel. The other nights I spent in the air. Fly, work, repeat. New day, new country, new team.

In Neenah, the greatest risk while going to work was icy roads. In South America, the greatest risk going to work was being kidnapped. One of my guys, George, was kidnapped outside of Lima, Peru. George's driver ultimately convinced the thugs that George had no money and wasn't worth kidnapping. The kidnappers released George but not before beating his driver so badly he had to be hospitalized.

My boss, Juan Ernesto, was from a prominent Colombian family and was extremely paranoid, or wisely careful, depending on who you asked. Juan Ernesto insisted on using code names for cities and countries when we traveled. Our itinerary didn't even use our real names, making it hard to keep track of where, when and with whom we were going. I felt like Waldo in a *Where's Waldo* book. I once called Scott in a panic after waking in the middle of the night unsure where I was – my itinerary was written in code, and I couldn't figure out which country I was in. I wrote "student" as my occupation to minimize the likelihood of being kidnapped. I dressed and looked inconspicuous, exchanging my diamond wedding ring for a plain gold (or no) band. I sprinkled tampons and maxi pads liberally throughout my bags and kept pamphlets on menstruation in my briefcase. There's nothing better than a few tampons and vagina illustrations to deter airport security guards from ransacking your luggage, taking the 'care' in Feminine Care to a whole new level.

Sleep came in rare and precious moments, stolen minutes spent in car rides between the airport and hotel, in flights between countries, in shuttles between factories. Like Pavlov's dog, when I heard the sound of an engine, I fell asleep. But just to be sure, I often took a sleeping pill before boarding an airplane to help me sleep through anything that might occur in flight. By the time the airplane's engines roared, I was already fast asleep, dreaming of home.

I threw the sleeping pills away, however, after a dicey flight on Aero Peru from Lima to Buenos Aires, Argentina, when shortly after securing my seatbelt and already nodding off, I noticed passengers filing past me in the wrong direction, descending a roll-up staircase. A flight attendant tapped my shoulder and pointed to the stairs, where, in a haze, I joined my fellow passengers on the tarmac. Our luggage was pulled from the plane and laid out as dogs sniffed and security teams looked for a suspected bomb. Finding no bomb, we and our luggage reboarded the plane, only to deboard again 15 minutes later for another round of the sniff and search exercise.

I was so tired and groggy that the entire experience seemed surreal. Until I saw it – the plane at the opposite end of the runway began burning brightly in the fading light of day. Holy $@#! It was very real. They'd searched the wrong plane. The security team and dogs quickly made their way down the runway, declaring our plane safe.

We could reboard if we wanted. Some did not. I thought about Scott and Andy, wanting desperately to share my experience with Scott, but knew I couldn't and wouldn't. He would have wanted to protect me, which he couldn't ... and I didn't want. Scott wanted to keep me safe, but to keep me, I couldn't be kept safe. It takes faith and courage to see the one you love leaning into experiences you can't share. It wasn't the miles apart that separated us, it was the stories not shared that made the distance difficult.

In doing difficult things I never imagined, I began to imagine myself differently. I was living experiences I'd never known, creating stories punctuated with fewer question marks and more (lots more) underlines, bold and exclamation points. It's not that I was reckless. I wasn't. Or unafraid. I was. But playing it safe would put me in a story written by others, using a yardstick that didn't measure the unknown. Despite Aero Peru security team declaring our plane safe, some passengers returned to the gate, refusing to re-board. I could join them. I could book a flight home to Atlanta instead of Argentina. No. Gathering my bags, I returned to my seat on the plane bound for the unknown.

Upside Down Worlds

"Everybody wants to be a diamond but very few are willing to get cut."
— Eric Thomas

Despite hours of listening to language tapes, my Spanish was lousy and sometimes got me into trouble. It doesn't help that I can get lost driving around the block. In my defense, signs and markers in South America were often small, missing or mislabeled, making it easy for anyone to get lost. So I wasn't surprised to learn that I'd zigged when I should have zagged and found myself in the wrong place. I was, however, surprised to learn my mistake was life-threatening.

Instead of Bogota, the capital of Colombia, I had boarded a plane for Medellin, home of Colombia's cocaine cartels at the height of the drug wars. I knew instantly I was in the wrong place when there was no one to greet me at baggage claim. The teenage security guard/soldier, clad in too-big fatigues and a way-too-big rifle, also knew I was in the wrong place. His gun slightly raised and both of us on guard, we stared at each other, neither knowing what to do. Dammit. This was exactly the kind of danger my mom warned would happen, not that I'd ever admit it to her. I was in trouble, for real, and didn't have any idea what to do.

I found a pay phone, and after watching others, figured out how to place a call to the folks in Bogota, Colombia. They had been looking for me at the Bogota airport and went into 'holy crap' mode when they learned I flew to Medellin instead. I began to understand their concern once I realized that not only was I in the wrong city, I was in the wrong airport. I had flown into Medellin's *international* airport. The only flight from Medellin to Bogota, Colombia was out of Medellin's *domestic* airport several miles away. Taking a taxi to the domestic airport was not an option – taxis were notorious for kidnapping passengers. I might as well have been wearing a "Kidnap Me, please" sign.

By this time, the baggage area was almost empty, and the pubescent, nervous and heavily armed guard/kid was visibly agitated, motioning me to move on. I'd love to. Looking around, I approached what looked like a businessman. Using my best Spanish, I think I asked for help, but might have asked for something else entirely. Thank God he spoke English, and yes, he would take me to the domestic airport.

My relief was short-lived. We exited the building and he motioned for me to get into the huge black car waiting for him. Alarms were sounding in my head. I was terrified. Stranger Danger! Stranger Danger! Madonna Bernadette would *not* have approved of this. I hoped she had a candle burning for me back in Iowa, but said a quick prayer between clenched teeth just in case. I had to trust. There was nothing else to do. Looking from the businessman to the guard glaring at me with the gun, I felt time slow down as I slid into the cool, dark backseat beside the waiting man. I felt like a lamb entering the lion's den. As the car door slammed shut, I wondered if I'd just placed my head into the lion's mouth, its jaw slamming shut about me. Nope. The lion and I made small talk until, as promised, the lion's mouth opened and belched this little lamb safely to the curb of the correct airport. As when I'd hitchhiked in college, this was the second (and hopefully last) time an anonymous, kind man had delivered me from danger. I landed safely in Bogota a few hours later and a few years older. The reality of my situation set in when not a single person in the Bogota office teased me, underscoring just how concerned about lions they had been.

I was never sure which was scarier, traveling alone or traveling with my boss Juan Ernesto and his boss, Claudio X. González, CEO of Kimberly-Clark de Mexico. Claudio was a very powerful scion, revered and feared throughout Latin America and beyond. Traveling with Claudio involved armored cars whose doors were too heavy for me to open by myself, which was fine anyway because I wasn't allowed to exit until after the surrounding security guards had their guns drawn. Just in case. Just like on TV, only real. Really real.

There were always at least three vehicles, one in front of and one behind Claudio. Each had security guards inside and on (yes, hanging onto) the vehicle. The three never stopped, especially not in traffic, which sometimes required rerouting over lawns, sidewalks, etc., safely past potential bad guys. There must be some sort of armored car pecking order because I was always in the last vehicle, wondering if it was better or worse than being in the first. And if kidnapped, would I be worth much of a ransom or would I be a throwaway? I suspected (knew) the answer to both questions, but tried not to think about it. Juan Ernesto always said it was safer to travel in countries that were at war or revolution because the 'bad guys' were gainfully employed. I guess unemployed guerrillas have to make a living too, and thus turn to kidnapping, etc. to supplement their income. These are the things you learn and silently ponder, but never voice, when you're 31, the only woman, and a gringa traveling with powerful people in a dangerous country.

I had never, and have never since, experienced anyone command such respect, reverence and fear as Claudio. His mind was fast, clear and sharp, able to dissect issues, data and people with ease. Fear without respect or reverence is debilitating, making people cower and wither. Yet I saw men (there were no other women) raise to a level of performance beyond what they thought possible just so that they wouldn't disappoint Claudio. Staying in Claudio's good graces was a matter of professional and personal pride more than fear of recrimination, although fear was dispensed more than grace was received. And yet, upon learning I'd never seen the Southern Cross, Claudio kicked the pilots out of the cockpit of his personal jet as we flew from Buenos Aires to Mexico City one night, so that I could get a better view of the night sky while he pointed out the constellations to me. Then he changed clothes and went to bed (it was a big plane), commanding the rest of us to stay awake and finish the report for his review when he woke up. As if our sleeping was an option.

Throughout my life, I've seen men who were professionally fierce and unforgiving yet personally kind and generous. It's hard to reconcile but explains how leaders can be feared yet loved and people can be intimidated yet loyal. Claudio had a Grrr that stirred fear and, I noted, many of his managers led the same way or used the threat/fear of Claudio to drive action. But is being fierce and unforgiving necessary to command respect and achieve results? What did this mean to me for whom fierce and unforgiving commanded little and achieved nothing but being called a bitch?

Yet I am fierce. I am direct. I am unforgiving. I'll fiercely protect and support the work and my team, putting myself directly on the front lines to take the arrows while my team takes the hill. I am also unforgiving and merciless to those who don't deliver, who blame others instead of taking accountability. What is heard through action is louder than anything shouted, creating loyalty, not fear. The teams in South America responded to my style of leadership, respecting and following not out of fear, but in response to being championed and supported. I am told some are intimidated by my direct approach. Fine. And my folksy, midwestern style is too familiar for others. Fine. Put the two together and it works for me. Just like the folks in Carroll, you can trust me to tell you the ugly truth... as kindly as I can.

Adopting the style of managers I didn't want to work for might endear me to my manager, but didn't work for me or mine. I didn't recognize how much my teams reflected back my fierce loyalty until the Buenos Aires team came to work over the weekend to help prepare for a Monday meeting with Claudio. Three arrived dressed in suits and formal gowns. The three had left their friend's wedding and refused to return until all were fully prepared for Monday's meeting. Not because they were afraid of me, but because they didn't want to let the team down. All responded by working better and faster. We nailed the review and, more importantly, solidified the team's commitment to Claudio, who loved the story and appreciated everyone's commitment.

I was beginning to think I could do my job, maybe even well. I felt like Westley in *The Princess Bride,* who had finally figured out how to navigate the dangers of the Fire Swamp. I'd avoided getting blown up on planes, could manage enough Spanish to avoid sinking during conversations, and knew which guys were big rats to avoid in meetings. I was finally exiting the Fire Swamp, only to be thrown into the Pit of Despair by Prince Humperdinck. Juan Ernesto was my Prince Humperdinck. Juan Ernesto wanted me to go to Sao Paulo, Brazil to achieve the inconceivable: persuade Unilever, our competitor, to introduce Huggies diapers into Brazil using their sales and marketing teams. Oh, and convince Unilever to pay millions for the privilege. I was convinced the task was neither reasonable nor possible. It was inconceivable.

I had never been to Brazil. K-C sold almost no products there and had no offices. Also, I spoke no Portuguese. Nada. Nevertheless, I had gained Juan Ernesto's trust over the prior months. He knew I didn't back down from a challenge and wouldn't quit, which was not the same as being successful, I said to deaf ears. Juan Ernesto felt it was important to have a Director in Sao Paulo to show Unilever that K-C was serious. He asked (told) me to stay in Sao Paulo until we had Unilever's agreement. I learned then that my boss was more stubborn than me. I also learned then that people perform up or down to the level of expectations. In the coming weeks, he expressed his faith in me over and over, until I too began to conceive how the inconceivable could occur.

I first arrived in Sao Paulo with my boss and our finance manager. It didn't matter that I knew no Portuguese because we stayed at a very nice, very upscale intercontinental hotel where everyone spoke English. I felt like Cinderella arriving at the ball each time I stepped into its gleaming, marble lobby, the whoosh of perfectly cooled air welcoming me to a world where everything was new and nothing was broken, where hangers were cushioned, towels matched, robes were thick, soft and cozy and where complimentary slippers were carefully placed beside a bed with sheets so luxurious my skin felt intimidated. And the soap! There were bars everywhere – two by each sink (one for hands, one for face), one by the jacuzzi tub and more in the shower. Surely these bars couldn't possibly be related to the scrawny no suds scraps of gritty soap I was familiar with from the motels where Scott and I usually stayed. In no way were these elegant bars like the soap I'd used all my life that promised to KILL ODOR and KILL BACTERIA long after I washed. No, these were treasures, not killers. Each bar was wrapped in beautiful paper and scented so wonderfully that peeling back the paper was like unwrapping a garden, or the ocean, or the woods.

Before leaving the room each morning, I'd swoop up and stash every bar in my luggage so that when I returned later, the cleaning person had a fresh new set laid out and waiting for me, an overwhelming abundance of prosperity. I'd repeat this every day, using only one bar of soap so I could schlep the rest home. Once home, I'd place the bars in my dresser drawers and throughout the house. I gave some away as gifts, but mostly I hoarded the symbols of my newfound affluence. I can't tell you the posh hotel was worth the cost but can say for certain that I got my money's worth of soap out of each stay.

Sure, I loved staying in posh hotels with safe, manicured grounds. Duh. Yet I couldn't reconcile a luxury hotel room after viewing the favelas from the windows of my chauffeured car each day. So when told to stay in Sao Paulo until the Unilever board meeting, I decided not to stay in the international hotel. In hindsight, it was super stupid to stay in a crappy room in the heart of Sao Paulo by myself, unknown to any but my secretary. My room featured a brownish Naugahyde sofa and a tiny TV that got only one English-speaking channel – CNN – that repeated the same stories every 20 minutes, over and over, until I had each story memorized and could lip sync with the announcer. I didn't mind. It was comforting to hear English in my room amidst the frequent shouting and loud noises that I feared were gunfire outside my door.

I left the room several times each day to explore the neighborhood and get a bite to eat, always sure to be in my room by dusk, having learned from the stares I received that my dorky Wisconsin attire and utterly awful grasp of Portuguese tagged me. São Paulo, Brazil was home to over 12 million people while Carroll, Iowa was home to less than 12 thousand. Clearly, I wasn't in Kansas anymore. Unlike Dorothy from Wizard of Oz, I couldn't return home by clicking my heels together while chanting "there's no place like home, there's no place like home." Black slip-ons were no substitute for ruby slippers.

As far as I could tell, I was the only non-Portuguese-speaking woman walking around the city in a good JCPenney white blouse. I didn't go far. The memory of George's kidnapping was still fresh in my memory. Mostly, I felt overwhelmed by the sheer number of people, languages, smells and sights. No matter where I turned, nothing was familiar. Not even the trees. I could do without fancy soaps, limos and room service. I couldn't do without nature. The concrete jungle surrounding me began to close in, suffocating and scary, amplifying all that was different. Up and down, street after street, was more and more of the same. More offices, more stores, more cars, more people. A merry-go-round I couldn't get off. Then I found it, or perhaps it found me. Like a long-lost friend who looked different on the outside but was the same on the inside, I befriended a nearby rubber tree, upon whose roots I perched each day while drinking the strong Brazilian coffee that put Folgers to shame. Sitting amongst the ancient tree's roots, I reconnected with Spirit and found my center until it was time to hunker down once again in my room to work, serenaded by the symphony of familiar voices on CNN.

After a few weeks and many calls with Juan Ernesto and his leadership team, we created a compelling board presentation that showed how in partnering with K-C to launch Huggies diapers in Brazil, both K-C and Unilever would benefit because P&G would have to divert resources and attention from competing against Unilever's businesses to defend Pampers against the launch of Huggies. Simple. Brilliant. Or so we thought. I converted the PowerPoint from English to Portuguese, hoping the translation was accurate at best and non-offensive at worst.

When the K-C leadership team arrived, Juan Ernesto told me that I'd be presenting the following day to the Unilever Board of Directors. Huh? The Unilever Board was the who's who of Brazilian business, politics, and society. This was a very important meeting with very important people. I didn't even speak Portuguese. Surely, I hadn't heard Juan Ernesto correctly. Yes, he reiterated, I would present the proposal. He and Claudio would support me if needed. Meu Deus! Puta merda!

As I faced the room of all-male global executives in their custom-tailored suits, I was literally and figuratively miles away from the Jane of hiking boots and Tractor Supply flannel shirts. Even in my 'good' white blouse, I didn't feel good. Fear doesn't care what you wear. There is a big difference between *feeling* afraid and *being* good enough. I *felt* afraid but I was capable. After all, I had created the presentation and knew the material better than any. I *was* good enough. I knew it. I could be afraid *and* capable *and* good enough. I was all those things. Fortunately, the executive's English was better than my Portuguese and after considerable discussion, a mutual agreement was reached that benefited all. I said tchau to the Naugahyde sofa, CNN and my rubber tree, returning to Atlanta exhausted but victorious professionally and personally. Sucesso!

The team invited me on trips to Patagonia, Machu Picchu, Iguazu Falls, etc, but time together as a family in Atlanta was more precious than anything I could do or experience in South America. Most likely, Scott had spent little time in the company of adults, and I'd spent no time in the company of kids, so I appreciated the opportunity to listen while Scott and I went for walks around the neighborhood, Andy in tow. I had already told the stories I could share over the phone; it was the sight, smells and sounds of home I longed to share. I got to be wife and mom for a while, even if I stretched the conventional definition of both according to the welcome wagon women. Scott and I were still figuring out our roles during the weekends – were we traditional husband/wife when we were together? So much was new and different – our home, our city, our jobs/roles, being parents. All was being traversed for the first time, without training wheels. We wobbled, and despite our attempts to stay upright, there were crashes.

Our relationship was strained more by the things that weren't said than by the things that were. We hadn't been apart since college and didn't know how to bridge the widening gap between us. He didn't want to share, and I couldn't bear to hear how difficult the transition to Atlanta, to work-widower and to full-time dad was. I didn't want him to know how scared, lonely and unsure I felt. We thought our time together was too precious to spend in disagreement or conflict, each seeking to fortify ourselves with gulps of love before submerging below the surface of uncertainty again. Back then, vulnerability was something to be hidden, not shared. Too bad we didn't understand that only in sharing our pain could we apply the healing salve of understanding to lessen, if not eliminate, our mutual pain. But we didn't know. So instead, we avoided conversations and feelings that were messy, until issues inevitably erupted, emerging like Hungry Hungry Hippo, to be whacked before retreating, dazed and done-in, resolving nothing despite the whomping.

During this time, our Latin America businesses were thriving, driven by the exceptional success we'd achieved in Brazil. I was offered the opportunity to manage the Southern Cone countries, which comprised K-C's high-potential, highest-growth markets. It was a high visibility, big-time role for me. Scott and I would relocate to Brazil, where we'd live in a gated estate with drivers, nannies, gardeners and housekeepers to cater to our every need. Scott was assured of a job with the US Embassy and I was assured we'd be safe, happy and successful, living a magical life happily ever after. A fairy tale.

So far, Scott and I had said 'yes' to every opportunity and adventure that came our way. Saying 'yes' was a cornerstone of who we were and what we believed. But saying yes to Brazil meant saying no to things that were more important to us. We wanted to raise our family without security gates or servants. Sao Paulo was far, far removed from friends, family and the Midwest roots and values so important to who and what we were. The role might be great for my career, but would be terrible for our family and relationship, which meant far more than any title ever would. It would put us on a divergent path that was never a part of our dream together. Our marriage was already stressed. Continuing to travel as much as I was and living in a foreign country was not going to help. Sometimes, it is just as important to know what you won't do as what you will do. I was about to learn how saying 'no' sometimes creates space for a better 'yes' to come.

And so, for the first time, we said 'no' to the fairytale opportunity. We wanted to live where folks celebrated the opening of deer hunting season, not Carnival. Believing our 'no' was the kiss of death for my K-C career, I nearly quit at this point. Almost. My line of sight was incomplete, and I was surprised to find that as one door closed in South America, another blew open back in Neenah, WI.

From Stump to Rump

It's okay not to know.

— unknown author

While I was working in Latin America, Kimberly-Clark was in the process of purchasing Scott Paper for $9.4 billion. It wasn't just a big deal, it was a BIG DEAL, the largest merger in US history, making K-C a huge consumer products company, second only to Procter & Gamble. Scott, Andy and I returned to Neenah just as the merger was closing. Tom Falk, my mentor and advocate, had been keeping tabs on me while I was in Latin America and, despite my saying no to moving to Brazil, chose to make another big bet on me. I was made the VP of Scott Products. At 32, I became the youngest-ever VP at K-C.

I was on a roll! Who would have thought it possible to be so excited about toilet paper? Me! Think about it. TP is one of the few things people worldwide use several times a day, is something you never, ever, ever want to be without and the more excited you are, the more you use it. Aside from booze, it's one of the few products people hoard. See? Isn't that exciting?

My enthusiasm was dampened a wee bit when it became obvious the merger was not all it seemed to be. Al Dunlap, the CEO of Scott Paper for the year prior to the merger, was notorious for cutting costs to the core and was later investigated by the SEC for massive accounting fraud. I'm not saying K-C's $9.4B merger was a massive turd, but it was unpleasant to be around. With investors and the press sniffing around, my job was to make something positive and pleasant grow from the smelly mess I had been given. I began by triaging the Scott business from end to end… what we affectionately referred to as the 'stump to rump' experience.

If you want to know anything about how to make, market and sell toilet paper, paper towels or napkins, I'm your gal. No? Trust me, it's cool. Imagine a business with hundreds of thousands of acres of timber, massive pulp mills and tissue machines so big they're practically bolted to the center of the earth. These machines make toilet paper a football field wide at 55 miles an hour. On top of it all, I got to wear a hard hat, steel-toed shoes and a blouse with my name embroidered on it!! I was in heaven, except for the Chester, Pennsylvania part.

Chester, Pennsylvania was the home of Scott Paper and where our turnaround would begin (and end if unsuccessful). It became my home away from home for the next few months. There are only two sentences in Wikipedia on Chester. One states its population (33k), the other its location (outside Philadelphia). Two sentences. Nothing more. No more to say.

Except. Except the 33k people of Chester were proud, hard-working and multi-generational, like the people from my hometown of Carroll. Only tougher. Whereas K-C manufacturing plants were always freshly painted, meticulously maintained, and filled with proud employees in their wrinkle-resistant K-C logoed shirts, the Scott mills were neglected, grimy and filled with pissed-off employees not afraid to show it. The Scott employees had been lied to, belittled, and dismissed by the prior CEO and his brand of leadership. Most were second or third generation, proud of the products they had made and the community they'd created, yet in the past few years, they'd seen both degraded beyond recognition.

Unlike the wrinkle-resistant K-C logo shirts we wore, the Scott union leaders wore obscene t-shirts to our first meeting. Evidently, they had looked up their new VP of Scott Products (me), for the blonde woman on their t-shirts looked like me, although her boobs were much bigger, and her body was positioned to offer something I wasn't. If this was their idea of intimidating, humiliating, or bullying me, these guys needed to up their game. I was uncomfortable and unsure, but not scared. But I understood that they were. I understood that they saw me and us as the latest round of execs who would lie to them. They didn't know me, didn't trust me and had every reason to be hostile toward me/us. What they did know was if the mill closed, they'd lose one of the few jobs to be had in Chester, PA. What they didn't know, and wouldn't have believed, was how hard I'd work to ensure that didn't happen.

Without uttering a single word, their shirt expressed the deep chasm between us. Us versus Them. Got it. Message delivered. Despite the hostility and awkwardness, we began the meeting, sharing our plans to rebuild the business. They merely glared in a way that said, "we've heard this bullshit before and know you're lying." It was a standoff. Then Tim, K-C's gruff and seasoned head of manufacturing, did something. He stood up and asked the union guys to walk the floor with him. I tagged along.

As they walked, the union leaders introduced Tim to the men on the floor. Tim repeated each man's name, asked what he did and for how long. Tim asked what was needed, looking each man in the eye. That's when Tim learned about the roof. It leaked. A lot. Try to imagine the science and skill it takes to convert pulp and water into a very thin web of tissue 100 yards wide flowing at 55 mph. Very exacting. Everything must be exactly to specifications to keep the machine running. A single drop of water falling from the ceiling can create holes or rip the web end-to-end, causing a costly shutdown. The roof, Tim learned, leaked like a sieve.

We hadn't known the roof was creating frequent stoppages, poor quality and higher costs. Tim listened and was impressed with the cunning ways the Scott employees had minimized the impact. The problem wasn't the employees' ability, aptitude, or attitude, as originally assumed. Just the opposite. Sometimes you have to stop talking about what you want and listen to what others need to achieve what both desire. Tim was wise enough to look past the glares and the stupid shirts to find and focus on what was common to all. The enemy was on the roof, not in the conference room. The facility was rundown and in disrepair, not its people. Why are we so quick to associate surroundings with success, or lack thereof? Of all people, shouldn't I have known that?

Over the following months, I flew often to Chester and the rest of the Scott mills, listening and learning. Trust and teamwork take time; meeting face to face helped us see eye to eye. During my visits I learned the complexity of the problem. Kimberly-Clark's purchase of Scott Paper meant we were completely vertically integrated, from managing and owning thousands of acres of timber for logging, to barges to transport logs to pulp mills, to tissue mills, to distribution centers to get paper products to retail. It was a massive enterprise that had been cost saved nearly to death. The reason ScotTissue had holes you could stick your thumb through was that the quality of the pulp had declined because our loggers had been directed to harvest low-cost, inferior trees. Crap in, crap out. No pun intended. So many corners had been cut that of course the tissue looked like Swiss cheese.

In the first months after the merger, there weren't enough fingers to plug all the holes in the dike, but Tim and the team triaged the worst holes and began to get the mills squared away. Simple things like repairing the roof fixed far more than the leaks. There was much more to do, but as we began to work with instead of against one another, it was clear the mills were on track to making a product all were proud to sell. People began walking with shoulders back and chin up. The 'stump' part of the business was stabilizing. But we still had to get people to trust, try and buy Scott Tissue again. It was time to double down on the 'rump.'

Founded in 1872, Kimberly-Clark's heritage was premium brands of high quality, high-performing products marketed with integrity and excellence. Scott value products didn't fit that mold one bit. Scott brands were practical, hardworking and got the job done without fuss at a fair price. Scott was the reluctant stepchild who didn't really fit in a beautiful family of premium brands like Kleenex, Cottonelle and Huggies. I understood Scott products; I *was* the Scott brand. Conversely, my new boss Steve was an Oxford graduate who wore Italian loafers and form-fitting suits, had perfect white teeth, no body fat and never once had to worry about missing a mortgage payment. Like Cottonelle, Steve was a premium product.

Steve appreciated premium quality and rejected the concept of Scott 'value' brands having value. He dismissed all data showing Scott brand loyalty was multiples greater than Cottonelle and so rejected each of my revitalization proposals to invest in Scott Products. It was all about the numbers with Steve, and the Scott business was hemorrhaging money, losing millions. Steve needed results, not relationships. I shared his sense of urgency to get the Scott business healthy again but needed an infusion of money to get it off life support before we could get Scott back on its feet. Steve didn't want to invest in an ailing business. It was a classic chicken and egg conundrum. Steve saw the sickly business it was, which reinforced his low image of 'value brands.' I saw the strong, proud business Scott once was and could be again. My team and I put together plan after plan, but Steve remained unconvinced, unenthusiastic, and unsupportive, choosing to instead invest in premium brands. It wasn't personal, he said. It was business.

But it was personal to me. I saw in Steve the characteristics I questioned in myself – confidence, smarts, decisiveness, ability, premium quality. Compared to Steve, I felt more and more unsure and inferior – a second-tier leader leading a second-tier business. I felt the weight of the business heavy in my heart and on my shoulders as I played defense during discussions on mill closures, on capital investments and on marketing spending. I pictured the folks in the mills and on the marketing teams who had placed their trust in me. If Scott brands didn't show dramatic improvement soon, mills would be closed, jobs would be lost, hundreds of families would be hurt. It seemed I was responsible for every job, every family. I felt like the awkward stepkid with zits and braces trying to be seen while being pushed to the back row of K-Cs family portrait. Yes, it was business. It was also personal.

I worked hard to make everything work but the harder I worked, the less worked. I was exhausted yet unable to sleep, my mind a gyroscope attempting to figure out the 1000-piece Scott jigsaw puzzle that refused to make its shape known to me no matter how I turned the pieces. Yes, it was personal as I lay suffocating in my bed each night unable to breath, crushed by the weight of responsibility I felt but didn't want to show.

How do you earn the confidence of your team when you don't believe in yourself? It's said that no one is going to see in us what we don't see in ourselves. The thing is, confidence isn't seen, it's felt, and respect isn't given, it's earned. I was a VP who did not feel the confidence, respect, and support of my boss. I wasn't sure I ever could or would. To me, it seemed Steve was a non-believer in the Scott business and in Jane. Both challenged his image of success. Over the years, there had been lots of times when others didn't believe in me yet I flew my 'fuck you' flag and went about the business of doing what couldn't be done. This was different. The stakes were much higher. Others' jobs were on the line, and they relied upon *me* to fix the mess. The old voices began to nag, saying I didn't deserve the VP job, I wasn't ready or good enough to fix this problem, I didn't belong and wasn't one of *them* and *they* knew it. I felt like an outsider, an imposter.

My fellow VPs and business leaders were all accomplished, experienced men. Every single one. I longed for another woman to confide in and learn from. What I would have given to talk with another woman who was trying to figure out how to manage home, husband, kids, work, bosses, teams, leadership. The women I worked with then didn't allow space for others to see beyond their armor. There was neither time nor energy for such things and executive relationships were generally kept at a cordial but superficial level. Maybe it was just me who was too afraid to confide in others. I was surrounded by people every day yet was desperately lonely.

At that time, K-C had one female President. Kathi was viewed by my boss as more cheerleader than business leader because her style tipped heavily on the rah-rah scale. Her presentations sometimes included more animated characters and cheers than numbers. But she *got* the numbers. She *achieved* the results. Quarter after quarter, year after year, she and her business were successful. Steve's style was thoughtful and strategic, reflecting a more formal Oxford education whereas Kathi's was relational, more typical of Happy Valley where she was born and raised. Both were successful in their own way.

But it didn't seem to me that Kathi or her way was sometimes respected; thus, I was reluctant to reach out to her for guidance. I didn't want my peers dismissing and rolling their eyes at me the way they did her. The other two female VPs were in HR and R&D. Our roles as VPs were very different and I didn't really connect with them.

Even when Steve tried to bridge the gap between us, it seems we missed. We came from different worlds and struggled to find common ground.

For my 10th wedding anniversary, Scott had bought me a new wedding band with a flawless diamond to replace the diamond chip and gold band that had been giving me rashes and discoloring my finger for years. The new ring was beautiful. Perfect. Steve complimented it, then frowned, asking why I got a yellow gold band instead of platinum. I told him I didn't want white gold. After chuckling, he explained that platinum wasn't white gold, it was better, better than yellow gold. Oh. How was I supposed to know that? I went from feeling proud to feeling foolish. Even if I did, Steve wouldn't have seen or understood the barb or the ways he inadvertently kindled doubt in me.

Steve's barbs found and left their mark. Little pricks, small cuts, nothing that couldn't be shaken off but which eroded my confidence and wore me down so slowly, bit by bit, I didn't know I was bleeding dry. Self-doubt led to isolation led to reluctance to ask for help, which further fueled my isolation and so on and so on…

After going a few rounds with Steve and the leadership team, I would head to the women's restroom for privacy. My office had glass walls that made me a fish in a tank for all to watch, so I hid in the bathroom to regroup, unwilling to let anyone see me as anything but strong. I was unsure what to do, who to talk to, where to turn. Was I the only woman sitting in a bathroom stall shoving feelings of fear, uncertainty and doubt aside, trying desperately to keep the mask in place, averting my gaze so no one could see the desperation in my eyes? Maybe if I'd known a few or even one other woman in whom to confide, I wouldn't have felt so alone. But I didn't know. So I sat, a queen on her throne in a lonely stall, the roll of Cottonelle tissue at my side, mocking me.

FUD
(Fear, Uncertainty and Despair)

"What if I fall? Oh, but my darling, what if you fly?"
— Erin Hanson

*"I put my hand in yours and together
we can do what we could never do alone."*
— Overeaters Anonymous

Hiding in bathroom stalls wasn't new for me. I'd been doing it since I was a teenager working at McDonalds, then in my dorm and then in public and private bathrooms ever since. Only now, the bathroom was outside my glass-walled executive office. Yet the view was the same.

When feelings of fear, uncertainty and despair (FUD) overwhelmed me and "not good enough" voices consumed me, I sought to swallow my emotions by shoving anything down my throat in an attempt to silence the voices, numb the pain and seek an escape. Any food would do, but ice cream was easiest to purge and thus consumed by the gallon. But the relief was temporary, if at all, and minutes later I'd kneel over the toilet, sticking fingers down my throat to bring up the ice cream just eaten, still cold. As was my fear. No matter how hard I tried, FUD wouldn't be swallowed or squelched. Fear, uncertainty, and despair (FUD) was too clever to come up with the contents of my stomach; FUD would not be purged in such a way. Relief could gain no foothold on the slippery slope of my shame and regret, accelerating the cycle of insanity and anguish that became my secret for decades.

Each morning, I looked in the mirror and saw reflected there the confident, capable, vibrant Jane who could achieve anything… only to see a different Jane reflected from a toilet bowl hours later, ashamed and discouraged after having just purged. The two Janes were not friends. The two Janes had fought on and off over the past 20 years, but the confident, capable, vibrant Jane usually won. While trying to save the Scott business, live up to the VP title and Steve's expectations, the confident, vibrant Jane was reflected less and less often in the mirror and discouraged Jane showed up more and more often from the bottom of a toilet bowl. I didn't know where to look for vibrant Jane or where to find help but knew neither would be found lurking in a bathroom stall.

A friend who attended Alcoholics Anonymous suggested I might benefit from a 12-step program, Overeaters Anonymous. But *I* wasn't like him or them. Besides, I'm not much of a joiner and ice cream was not booze, after all. But despite every promise I made and broke to myself, I was unable to stop using and purging food to ease my pain. Every part of me had wanted to deny my disease, to remain hidden behind locked bathroom doors. How could I tell others what I was doing when I wasn't even telling myself the truth? How could I ask for help when I refused to admit I was in trouble? I wasn't sure, but I knew I couldn't keep hiding the truth.

On a Tuesday night I exited the bathroom stall and knew I needed help. I was desperate. As soon as I walked into my first OA meeting, I knew right away that I didn't belong there. I wasn't *that* desperate. I wasn't like the others. It would be rude to say they were losers, but let's just admit they weren't accomplished, capable and strong like me. *Their* lives were a mess. Many didn't have decent jobs, were whiny, lived day to day and shared things I couldn't (didn't want to) relate to. Cripes.

I'd made a mistake coming here. But they said to keep coming back, promising it works if you work it. So I did. And the losers saved my life.

At Overeaters Anonymous I finally acknowledged my eating disorder and reluctantly put a name to my insanity – bulimia. For the first time in years, the mask slid away and the façade crumbled. I was exposed. I examined my life in the light of day and the love of my OA friends. With them, I need not solve any problems but my own, take care of or be anyone but me. I only needed to come to the meetings. The meetings came and went. I said the words but couldn't get beyond the first step, that I was powerless, and my life had become unmanageable. Okay, so yes, my life had become unmanageable. But I WAS NOT POWERLESS! I was a success! I was a VP! A wife! A mother! I just needed to try harder for crying out loud!! And that's exactly what I found myself doing, crying out loud. The dam was breaking, and I couldn't keep it together or stop the flood of tears any longer. I knew I couldn't do it by myself but didn't trust how to ask for or accept help. The tenacity and self-reliance that had enabled me to survive and thrive for the past 32 years was killing me.

Fortunately, the second step is believing that a power greater than myself could restore me to sanity. That's where the losers came in and saved my life. For now, they were a power greater than myself. Together, we worked the 12 steps to the best of our ability, and over time, I learned how to be enough. The OA losers became my lifeline of lifelong friends whose experience, strength and hope enabled me to examine, repair and rebuild the brokenness that was me. I shared, rather than swallowed, my feelings. I exposed myself and all I feared – being overwhelmed, inadequate, unsure, dumb, a fake, a jerk, unloving, unlovable, unworthy. When I spoke my fears aloud, no one ran screaming from the room in horror. Which was a little disappointing, to be honest.

FUD (Fear, Uncertainty and Despair)

In fact, no one judged me because they had been there, done that. I wasn't alone or unique. I began to see that my alter-me wasn't a nemesis to purge, it was just me. One Jane. It was time to stop judging myself as 'good' or 'bad.' Dammit, I was going to miss Superhero Jane who had Archnemesis Jane to blame for everything. Doubledammit, I learned my true strength wasn't achieved by what I excelled in. It was my weaknesses that created the space for grace, the space where others contributed their strength and support, so that together we could do what we could never do alone. Like epoxy glue, I was nothing separate, but when combined with others, had super-duper strength. Who would have thought that weakness provided the first, crucial ingredient to my secret sauce of life? My loser friends at OA, that's who.

I worked the program and it worked for me. For years, my 'us' vs 'them' thinking made me judge everything and everyone as 'better than' or 'worse than' me. Falling short in my analysis, I secretly felt that I belonged nowhere, wasn't good enough for anyone or deserving of anything. I was highly educated and employed, but my upbringing and values always made me feel like an outsider with the "thems" yet clearly not one of "us." How ironic and humbling that when I most needed help, the woman who stepped up to be my sponsor and lifeline was a union mill worker?

She was no different. Her problems were no more or less worthy. She challenged my us versus them perspective that assumes worth is based on a bullshit scale of title, status or bank account – a scale that kept me separate, fear-based and hiding. Exposing my cracks didn't mean I was broken; the cracks allowed light and others in.

In the program I learned I was only as sick as my secrets. I shined a light on behaviors that hurt me and others and gradually let go of the secrets and thinking that were keeping me sick. I stopped judging myself as good or bad, strong or weak. I am all those things, perfectly imperfect, no better or worse than anyone else. There is no them and us; there is only us, for we are all the same. Surrender wasn't losing; letting go of a 'them' mentality meant gaining an 'us' reality. I was not alone.

Fear, uncertainty and despair isn't about age, title or gender; it's about being human. My seeds of fear, uncertainty and despair germinated in childhood and secured a stronghold during adolescence, waiting in anticipation of puberty to bud and blossom into adulthood where their poisonous flowers dispersed evermore seeds that flourished in the fertile soil of insecurity. Even the most caring, nurturing gardener can't prevent FUD. It can't be treated by chemicals or yanked up by the roots and chucked into the mental trash bin. My FUD needed to be acknowledged and accepted, diligently managed, and pruned so it didn't strangle or keep me from moving forward. Or keep me in bathroom stalls.

Over time, meditation, medication, movement and my OA program became my pruning shears of choice. When FUD threatened to overwhelm me, I reached out to friends whose names were not Ben & Jerry.

As I began to take my life one day at a time, redirecting the time, energy and angst wasted on my soul-sucking bulimia to life-giving recovery, I rediscovered the vibrant Jane in the mirror and was able to step out of the bathroom literally and figuratively. Instead of putting my fingers down my throat, I put a coin in my pocket that read, "I put my hand in yours and together we can do what we could never do alone."

I left the bathroom and returned to my glass-walled office where people could see me and I them. Let them look. Let them in. I stopped behaving like it was up to me to save the world. I began inviting my marketing and sales leaders to join and participate in meetings around the conference table. I asked my finance and operations folks to present and represent. I stopped pretending to have answers when I didn't. "I am good enough. It's okay not to know," I told myself over and over again. Like the freezer beast of my youth, once I faced my fear and

FUD (Fear, Uncertainty and Despair)

made room for others, the conference table lost its power over me. It became just a table and not a battleground. I stopped talking and began asking Steve questions, creating plans that addressed his concerns. As I fought less, I feared less and led more. The more I invited the help of others, the more credibility and support I received and the more respect I gave and earned.

Over the next few years, we did what many thought couldn't be done. We resuscitated Scott Paper, returning it to growth and profitability. Most would never know how close we came to failure, how often we despaired of shutting down mills and laying off the people who had come to trust us. Instead, Scott the value brand became a very valuable addition to the K-C family.

Only after letting go and accepting help from the many people around me did I too avoid shutdown and begin the hard work of accepting and appreciating the Jane in the mirror.

I emerged from hiding to find I wasn't unworthy or incompetent. I was worthy. I was capable. I was not the awkward kid with zits and braces pushed to the back of the family portrait, even though I sometimes felt that way. I deserved to be the VP of Scott Products, for what was once a whopper of a turd had emerged a jewel in the K-C family crown of strong brands. Slowly but surely, I too emerged stronger and healthier of mind, body and spirit. I began to realize my achievement was not based on fixing either the stump or the rump, but on mending my own heart and learning to honor the Jane in the mirror who was the most precious jewel of all.

Jack

"It was clear by the smile that radiated from within him that God had given us a special gift."

— Jane Boulware

Scott and I decided to conceive a second child soon after Andy was born. God just laughed, not in any hurry to lend us Jack's kind soul. Maybe I wasn't ready. It's hard to bring a new light into the world when your own light is flickering and fading, as mine was at the time. I may have failed miserably at babysitting others' kids but loved spending time with my own. I am proud to say I never once acted on the urge to run screaming from the house as I had while babysitting the Koeking kids years ago. But toggling work, wife and motherhood was a grind. The more I tried to be good at everything, the more convinced I was of failing. Hell, I wasn't even sure what 'good' was but knew I was bad at it.

The only thing I wanted more than being successful at work was to be a good wife and mom. Since things weren't going so well on the work front, I doubled down on the home front. Upon returning to Wisconsin, Scott went back to work as the manager of a high-end audio store, which meant working lots of evenings and weekends. He loved his job and was very successful. He was the go-to guy for audiophiles for miles around and was even invited to California to preview and assess elite audio equipment before it was introduced. He loved it and was thriving, but Scott's retail hours, especially during the holidays, meant I was essentially a single parent many evenings and weekends. For the first time, I truly understood and appreciated what Scott had done for us, caring for Andy while I traveled. How had Scott made parenting and managing our home look so easy?

I tried to be a good mom. I fed Andy wholesome, nutritious food. I did not buy him toy guns. Instead, he ate gum stuck to the sidewalk and chewed toast into gun shapes to shoot me while gleefully shouting "BANG! You're dead, Mommy!" Andy lived with gusto. He would play quietly next to me one minute, then push toy trucks into the street the next, proclaiming he was "starving of thirst" from his hard work.

To add insult to injury, Andy refused to toilet train. Despite working on Pull-Ups for years, I couldn't get my own kid to pee in the friggin potty. I tried everything. I bought Barney and Bob the Builder underwear. I encouraged, cajoled and bribed. Nothing inspired so much as a tiny tinkle from him until one day Andy saw a huge man using a huge jackhammer. The large man wore small tighty whitey underwear that revealed a big butt crack. I don't know if it was the butt crack or the jackhammer, but Andy was inspired; he wanted to be just like the man. Out went Barney and Bob the Builder. In went tighty whiteys, which remained tidy and white from that day forward. Find someone's butt crack and you will crack the code of inspiring others.

Our family felt incomplete but as I approached 35, after five years of trying, Scott and I figured Andy would be an only child. That's when we became pregnant, and our sunshine boy was born. It was clear by the smile that radiated from within him that God had given us a special gift. There was a soft click the moment Jack was born, pieces falling in place, the gears of our family finally fitting seamlessly, filling the gap we could feel but not see until Jack was in our arms and in our home. Jack made our family whole, complete.

Whereas Andy was a small, adventurous, noisy ball of perpetual motion, Jack was bigger, more thoughtful, easygoing, kind, calm and content amongst the chaos of our clan, his smile often triggered from within, making us wonder what he knew that we didn't. Jack was the child who quietly taught himself to read when no one was looking, already reading chapter books in first grade because that is what his brother was doing in fifth. Jack did not seek permission or recognition. Learning was his passion and our gift, teaching us to open our minds to so much of which we knew nothing. Jack stole our hearts and joined the heartbeat of our household without skipping a beat – strong, solid, sure.

Maternity leave was different the second time around. I enjoyed my pregnancy and every moment home with Jack, aware this precious time would not come again. I already knew which end to feed and which to diaper, which allowed time to slow down and me to be able to savor quiet moments with Jack and to cherish being a mom of two joy boys. I rued returning to work. With Andy, I didn't know what I was missing, but now that I did, it made the missing harder. It did not change the fact that I needed to return to work for many reasons. It was just harder the second time. Harder to let go of what could never be and return to what was.

After Jack was born and I began attending OA meetings, I came to the realization that I couldn't be the best mom, wife, daughter, VP, and friend. I could only be me, which on some days was pretty fantastic and on some days was pretty lame. I was never going to be the best at everything, but I had lots of people to learn from and on whom I relied to supplement what I could not do/be.

Enter the McHughs. The McHugh family was a godsend. Terry, the hunter, and neighbor I'd encountered from my balcony on our first day in Neenah, and Shannon, his fun, wonderful wife, would become surrogate parents to my children. Shannon was pregnant with her third child, Kyle, while I was pregnant with Andy. Shannon was an amazing mother, the kind of mom into whose arms kids naturally sought shelter and love. Her hands could simultaneously cook, wash and feed children while toggling effortlessly between sharing witty banter with me and threatening the kids to stop doing what only she could see from eyes in the back of her head.

Shannon took pity on me after Andy was born, teaching me the tricks of the trade as if it were no big deal, never acknowledging how clumsy I was at all she did so gracefully. How we became good friends is a wonder. Must have been the margaritas. After returning from Atlanta, we bought a house close enough to the McHughs to walk together to Dairy Queen, but far enough away to never again see Bambi hanging from Terry's tree. Scott was keen to stop being a full-time dad and start managing the high-end audio business he enjoyed so much. Shannon was keen to give up her job and be a full-time mom. So when we returned from South America, it was into Shannon's home that Andy was welcomed each day while Scott resumed managing Sound World and I navigated the stump to rump of Scott Paper. The McHughs made Andy their fourth child. And when Jack was born, they made our second son their fifth.

Time with the boys was cherished, filled with rituals and traditions, many still practiced today. Bedtimes were choreographed, finishing with a prayer that evolved and grew over time, as evidenced by the number of 'amens' and 'ands' as follows:

(Take big breath here for part one)

"Angel of God, my guardian dear,
to whom God's love entrust me here,
ever this night be at my side,
to light, to guard, to rule and guide
Amen…

(Take BIGGER breath here for part two)

God bless Andy and Jack, Mom and Dad,
Grandpa and Grandma,
Kyle and Shannon, Nick and Leah and Terry,
Nana and Poppo,
Patti and Keith,
Mack (neighbor's dog) and Titus (our dog) and Tucker (dead dog) too
and…

(Gulp final breath here for the homestretch)

Grandma Phyllis and Grandpa Herb in heaven
and Uncle Tracy in heaven,
and all the people in the world
that need your help tonight
and…

Please don't let us have any bad dreams…
…and please let us have a good night's sleep.

AMEN!
(clap once while saying amen… not sure why)

(Exhale)

Everyone who has been with our family at bedtime has heard us say this prayer. Heard the Amen clap. Done the Amen clap. Even when I was out of town on business, even from other countries I called home each night for bedtime prayers. I've excused myself from business dinners, meetings, and customer socials to pray/sing into the phone with my kids before they nodded off to sleep. Let me tell you, there is no good way to sing or recite a bedtime prayer into the phone during a snowstorm from the curb outside a swank NYC restaurant, a paper mill cafeteria, a television studio or in front of a peer or customer. I neither cared nor made apologies. Of course, it wasn't about the prayer. I called home so my kids knew I was thinking of them, and they were most important, no matter what I was doing or where I was. That was my thing. To hell with what others think; all that matters is what family knows.

Between my travel and Scott's retail hours, we relied heavily on the McHugh family and the boys' godparents, Patti and Keith, to be there when we weren't. Friends became the family we chose, each offering their unique gifts to the collective soup, ladling generous portions of love, support, and laughter… with occasional boil-overs and burned feelings. Our collective soup filled and nourished us all. The boys were happy. But Scott and I spent more hours apart than together, both successful in jobs we didn't want to quit. Something had to give. From the outside, all looked well but, on the inside, I was out of whack, swinging between roles on a rope both frayed and worn. My hours were too long, the responsibility too great. I resented and wanted to be among the men whose wives picked up their dry cleaning, made dinner, cared for the kids and kept their lives tidy. It's not that Scott wasn't helping. He was. But his evening and weekend hours meant I used most evenings and weekends catching up on the things done by 'wives' during the week. I wanted a wife too. But I *was* a wife *also*. It's the *also* that gets ya. I understand why so many women leave the workplace at this point in their family and career. I nearly did. I seldom took time for me, and if I did I felt guilty about what I wasn't doing, such that doing nothing became too stressful to do. Yes, something had to give before I gave out. I decided my job at K-C was the something that had to give. I would quit K-C. At least for a while.

Scott and I had talked about the pressure, but so far, I had been unwilling to fully admit to myself or him how precariously the plates were spinning on my wobbly sticks. I wanted to do it all and tried. But on yet another day when I had to call Shannon to say I would be a half hour late, then another half hour, and another, I arrived harried and strained, trying not to let the boys see me cry on the way home. That night I talked to Scott about quitting my job. I'd given it serious consideration and we had a serious discussion. He asked me to wait and to give us both time to think and talk some more. We didn't have an extravagant lifestyle but living on his income would require adjustments for sure. That didn't scare me nearly as much as not knowing how or if I would/could be a good full-time mom. All I knew for sure was the life I was living wasn't sustainable for me, my marriage, or my family.

A few days later, Scott said he would leave the job he loved to become a full-time dad for those he loved more. Scott walked away from a fulfilling career where he was well recognized and respected to take a job that was neither recognized nor generally respected at the time. By anyone but me. Scott was an amazing dad. He was an even better full-time father than full-time audio manager, able to do what I could not. His decision was the most loving gift ever given to me and the boys. We agreed to re-examine the arrangement every few years, deciding whether to renew, renegotiate or switch our roles. As the family flourished, we came to appreciate that each of our roles had advantages, stresses, and sacrifices. Our chosen roles had enabled us to be "family first," putting our family at the center, just where our yardstick for success told us it should be and stay.

Perspective

"One of the best gifts you can give to someone is a wider perspective. It's also one of the best gifts you can receive."

— C. JoyBell C

No matter how rich or poor, everyone in Wisconsin loves the Green Bay Packers. The only NFL team not owned by a kazillionaire, the Packers have been publicly owned by the good citizens of Green Bay (pop 100,000) since 1923. The Pack is to Wisconsin what the Pope is to Catholics. Both are revered and invoke prayers on Sundays. "Go! Pack! Go!" are often the first words uttered by babies; attending a Packer game in Lambeau Field is a thrill for any football fan and is the dream of every boy and girl in Wisconsin. Or so I thought.

Kimberly-Clark had a luxury suite of box seats in Lambeau Field, mostly used to host customers and reward employees for exemplary work. As a K-C executive, I occasionally had access to the suite, creating anticipation amongst my teams and vendors, all of whom jockeyed to be invited. During this time, I was an active board member at the local Boys & Girls Club and knew the kids we served might never have a chance to attend a live game, much less in an executive suite. It was an unusual request, but I was given permission to use the luxury box suite to host almost two dozen Club kids.

It was a beautiful fall Sunday when Scott and I filled two large rental vans with the excited boys and girls who were heading to Lambeau with us. A little apprehensive, I couldn't help but wonder if this was another of my ideas that was better in my head than in reality. Were we crazy to take kids we barely knew from the Boys and Girls Club to a stadium of 70,000 people? But there was no turning back as, together with a Boys & Girls Club employee, we set off for Lambeau Field, the vans propelled by the kids' anticipation and happy chatter. The miles flew by as quickly and easily as the laughter flowed, the kids' enthusiasm overpowering any insecurity and my face reflecting the same eager anticipation as the kids from the Club.

We clasped hands and snaked our way through the crowd, feet barely touching the ground. I sensed something had shifted. I could see it by the way the kids walked, the way they held their heads. They weren't just excited, they were proud. For each had been selected, chosen, to be there. Chins held high, their silent shouts roared, "Look at me! I'm special!" These were not kids often chosen, especially to do something other kids didn't get to do. But today they were VIPs as never before, passing through a private door to a place few would enter. It wasn't the *event* that was special, it was *they* who were special, and for once, they wanted to be seen and recognized.

The kids didn't know that we had a big surprise waiting for them – Brett Favre and others had signed and donated Packer shirts, hats, etc. to make their visit memorable. Entering the luxury box was magical, offering a bird's eye view of Lambeau Field in all its glory. It's impressive even if you're not a Packer fan, even if there wasn't autographed Packer gear strewn about. As they entered the luxury suite, the kids' excited chatter stopped. It became quiet as the kids took it all in.

"Is that for us?" someone whispered.

"Huh? What? Yes, help yourself," I said as I realized I was being asked about the buffet of food spread out before us.

"Which part?"

"All of it."

"Are you sure?"

"Yes."

It wasn't Lambeau Field, the luxurious suite, the box seats, or even the game that held the kids' attention that day. It was the smorgasbord laid out before us, a cornucopia of hamburgers, hot dogs, brats, nuts, cookies, brownies, chips, etc., around which the kids hovered until the game was over and it was time to leave. The kids had eaten until they could eat no more, but still the food buffet was full, having been replenished throughout the game.

"Who's going to eat all of this when we leave?" a boy asked me, others listening intently to my reply.

"What? Oh. I don't know. No one."

"Can I take some home for my little sister? It's not her day to eat and she'll be hungry," responded the boy shyly.

I was silenced as his words ripped a hole in my heart. Looking through his eyes around the room at the food, I felt ashamed, realizing I'd completely lost perspective. But shame doesn't fill bellies. We mobilized quickly, emptying buns from bags. In just minutes, we filled bags with the remaining nuts, hamburgers, chicken and anything else that could be reasonably transported home. Upon leaving, I gave the room one final look and smiled, knowing no other suite could have been filled with more gracious guests nor emptied with more gratitude than our suite that day.

I can only imagine what the other VIPs thought as we filed out of our suite, Old Home bun bags clutched tight in small hands, snaking our way through the crowd and out the private luxury box exit to the two vans. The drive home was comparatively quiet, kids full, happy and tired. A few hours later, after all the kids were gone, I found the young boy's new Packer hat in the van. Perhaps he left it by accident; perhaps on purpose, fists too filled with bags of food to carry both.

Either way, I knew his memory of the day would not be of the football game or the field. His would be the pride of being chosen, of being special for the day, and of bringing bags full of food home to his sister. I expected to feel like a hero for having given these kids the gift of attending a Packers game at Lambeau Field. Instead, I had been given the gift of perspective from a shy, unassuming boy who made sure his little sister would eat that day, even though it wasn't her turn.

The Only Constant Is Change

*"Life is a series of natural and spontaneous changes.
Don't resist them; that only creates sorrow. Let reality be reality.
Let things flow naturally forward in whatever way they like."*

— Lao Tzu

In early 2000, I moved from Scott Products to head the marketing, media, advertising, promotion, design and marketing research departments for K-C's consumer and commercial businesses. Tom Falk, my sponsor and COO at the time, set in motion an initiative to examine and challenge K-C to be more efficient and competitive. I led the charge of marketing efficiency and effectiveness. It was a big move. I hadn't a clue where to start and made mistakes along the way.

Mistake #1 was hiring consultants in K-C's no-consultant culture. Mistake #2 was assuming consultants knew more than K-C did about marketing. Mistake #3 was allowing the project to become so complex that my presentations had to be scripted by others to explain what we were doing. When words feel foreign on your lips, it's best to remain quiet until the voice you hear comes from your head and not that of another. I should have recognized and stopped the insanity. But I didn't. I realized too late that complex processes don't create progress, they just create complexity.

John Wannamaker said *"Half the money I spend on advertising is wasted; the trouble is, I don't know which half."* Seeking to identify the half Wannamaker insisted was wasted, I began working with big tech companies to create software that analyzed market data to spit out marketing insights and return on investment, the holy grail of marketing. Many changes were made that improved results, created millions in savings and reduced time-to-market. On paper, I had done a brilliant job. The consultants were beaming.

But I wondered if in the process of hiring outside consultants to tear apart and reconstruct our processes to drive efficiency, we unwittingly destroyed the secret sauce that had made K-C so successful through the years. Identifying the 'best' marketing practices and championing the 'best' campaigns pitted internal marketing teams against each other rather than the external competition. Had we become our own competitors? That was not the legacy Dudley, Patti and others had entrusted to me.

In time, the old guard was viewed as old school. Their guidance was minimized and considered misguided as we ushered in a new generation of marketers who were born and raised in the here and now. It's hard to honor a brand hallmark when your goal is to make your mark and move on. Marketing by the numbers made it too easy to fund short-term wins at the expense of long-term strategic investments. Like all great relationships, tactics may change day to day, but brand equity accrues year by year, experience by experience, honored and reinforced over time.

Magic happens in the space between what was and what can be. Dudley and Patti mentored and taught me, making way for me and others climbing the ladder behind them. It's always been so. Yet in our fast-forward lives, there is more need, but less time, than any generation before to look back on the experience and support of those who blazed the trail before us. And so early retirements were given and soon the old guard was gone as K-C's marketing was overhauled to make room for new people and processes.

At the same time, I made the cover of marketing magazines and spoke on stages with spotlights, heralding K-C's new marketing approach nationwide. Tom, successful in his quest to drive efficiency and effectiveness, was promoted from COO to CEO. I became a member of a new executive team. At 40 years old, after 17 years with K-C, I was at the top of a ladder I'd neither dreamed existed and nor set out to climb.

When we married, Scott and I promised to take on new challenges and never let ourselves get complacent or comfortable. We swore we wouldn't become fat, dumb and happy or be the kind of people who resist change and declare why something won't work before attempting it. In the past 20 years, we'd experienced plenty of change and challenges with one marriage, two kids, three degrees, four states, eight homes and umpteen jobs under our belt. So when we hit 40 and found ourselves kinda fat and mostly happy…we wondered if we were dumb to keep pushing ourselves outside our comfort zones. Is it so bad to like the comfort of being comfortable? We were hunkered down in Wisconsin with two great kids, two lovely homes and two powerful snow blowers. Yup, we were living the dream and smack in our comfort zone.

But a life of ease is uneasy for one whose engine cannot idle. It seems I am better at changing and creating what isn't yet than managing what has been. There were no major K-C business/departments that needed to be created, overhauled or changed. Having been at the helm of so much change through the years, it's ironic I found myself chafing and out of step with the culture and crew of Tom's new executive team. I did not feel or have a home in the company I'd considered home for 17 years.

I was considering the course forward when, as had happened so often before, there came an unexpected phone call that would redefine our life. I remember the call clearly because Scott and I had sprung the boys from school and were playing hooky on the first beautiful day in spring 2004. The conversation was brief. "Uh huh, uh huh. Not interested. Thanks. Goodbye," Call forgotten.

From April to July the Microsoft recruiter kept calling. For months, I listened politely but expressed little interest in uprooting my family to change jobs, industries, cultures, states, and lifestyles. Why swap Wisconsin for Washington, Packers for Seahawks, brats for salmon?!? Cripes almighty, that's just fishing for trouble.

And yet, I couldn't help thinking about it. The next time they called, I stayed on the phone, listening, before saying, "no thanks, not interested." The pinball was pinging in my brain. Then Microsoft upped the ante and sent an Xbox to Andy and Jack. Bribing our boys achieved what no telephone call could. The boys were thrilled but Scott was not. "Enough is enough! Either tell Microsoft to stop calling or go meet with them." Scott was done with the "what if" conversations and wanted us to move forward, one way or another. Like the job in South America, Scott would not let me dismiss the opportunity lightly. He encouraged me to learn more.

Within a few days, I found myself on a flight to London to meet the woman who would become my new boss. The meeting went well enough that I flew from London to Seattle to interview with the MSN team. I was back in Neenah only briefly before finding myself back on a flight returning to Seattle. This time, Scott was sitting in the first-class seat beside me.

Scott had been researching housing, schools etc. while I'd been taking a crash course on Microsoft. We had learned a lot over the past few weeks, but still hadn't a clue. Like my interview with Kimberly-Clark years prior, Microsoft had assigned a driver and realtor to show Scott the area while I spent the day doing a final round of interviews, the last of which was with Steve Ballmer, CEO of Microsoft. That night, Scott and I celebrated our 20th wedding anniversary. We dined at a restaurant overlooking a huge and powerful waterfall, never realizing that our lives were about to take a similar plunge.

The interview with SteveB was fiery. Within minutes, Steve had jumped up from his chair and began diagraming his thoughts on the whiteboard in his office. His energy was contagious, but I disagreed with much of his thinking regarding branding and was soon on my feet drawing a diagram that looked much different. This went on for almost an hour, each challenging the other. I didn't expect to win but wasn't about to back down.

So it was a big surprise when the next day Scott and I were invited to extend our stay to do some house hunting and check out schools for the boys. Just days before, it seemed wildly inconceivable to spend a million dollars on a house. Such people were idiots, we joked... until we realized a comparable house in Bellevue, close to work and schools, was 10X the price of our Neenah house. Within weeks, we became the idiots people joke about. And unlike the midwest, where Catholic schools were a dime a dozen and practically free, we learned about waiting lists, applications, letters of recommendation and connections. It wasn't long before we were swept away, bobbing and gasping in the rapid current.

We bought a new home in Washington down the road from Bill Gates and sold our home in Wisconsin down the road from Dairy Queen. Within weeks of receiving an Xbox in the mail in Neenah, WI, Andy and Jack started school in Bellevue, WA while I started my new job as a Corporate Vice President of Microsoft's online business. I was one of the top 150 executives (one of less than a dozen women) in a company of over 60,000 employees. Everything happened so quickly that there was little time to reflect. We leaped, leaving behind a secure and stable life and lifestyle and hurtling into the great unknown.

Part III

Worth Beyond Wealth

Lifting Up

"Encouragement is free and beyond measure."
— William DeFoore

Andy was in fifth grade and Jack in first when we left Neenah, WI and moved to Bellevue, WA. The boys slipstreamed into their new life, unaware that their milk and cookies were now organic and gluten free. Scott jumped into superhero mode and dove into his new job managing the move to a new house and school. Andy made friends quickly and became the kid others wanted to be around. Especially his little brother, Jack. Jack adored Andy. He wanted only to be by his big brother's side, to be like him for Andy could do no wrong in Jack's eyes.

Unfortunately, Jack could do no right in Andy's eyes. By the time Jack was in second grade and Andy in sixth, Andy thought and treated Jack as a pesky little brother and did not appreciate his sidekick. Tears were shed and hearts were breaking when Scott and I pulled Andy aside and told him something I've tried every day since to embrace.

We asked Andy if he knew he was Jack's hero. Did Andy understand that he stood high upon a pedestal in Jack's eyes? It didn't matter that Andy didn't ask to be Jack's hero. You can be your own hero, but only others can make a hero of you. Jack had made Andy his hero and that's all that mattered. We explained that in Andy's entire life, no one would ever place him on a pedestal like Jack had done – not his friends, not his wife, not his coworkers. If ever Andy came off the pedestal, he might never get back up. Each time Andy tore Jack down, Andy came down a step. When Andy lifted Jack with kind words and actions, both rose. Andy could lift Jack up until he too stood on a pedestal. Or not. Andy could earn and remain Jack's hero or tear Jack down and go to zero. Lift up or tear down. Hero or zero. Andy's choice, Andy's consequences.

Nothing good has ever been built by those who tear down; something good is always achieved by lifting up and exposing the greatness in others. It's been many years since that conversation and despite different interests and talents, both of our sons have helped the other become a man to look up to.

We have a rule in our family. Big takes care of little. Being big means more than size and age. Being big means using your talents and capabilities to look out for people in need of support and help. Being little means honoring and listening to the unique talents and capabilities that make others big. Sometimes being big means standing up for little even when it's hard or against the rules.

Within months of moving and starting school in Bellevue, Scott and I were called into the principal's office. Andy, a fifth grader, had gotten into a fight with an eighth grader. What?!? Andy had never, ever been in trouble. In tears, Andy kept repeating, "Big takes care of little!" as he explained how an eighth grader had been bullying some of the young kids. Andy was 'big' to the young kids and had stepped in to defend a little guy. Andy knew he'd be in trouble. He knew he was breaking the rules. He feared the consequences. But 'Big takes care of little.' That was the rule Andy had heard so many times at home. Scott and I supported the school's decision to suspend Andy for a few days – that was the consequence of breaking the school's rules. Scott and I also supported Andy's decision to defend the little boy, allowing Andy to watch TV while suspended – that was the consequence of honoring our rule. Big takes care of little.

If only we sought to be heroes for one another, to defend against bullies who push and tear down vs build up. I always believed once I got the next promotion, when I reached a certain age, I'd be confident and more worthy to help others. But being a hero has nothing to do with title, age or income and everything to do with having the courage to get out of my rut to lift someone out of theirs. It's simple; it's just not easy. It's hard because we make it so, because even though we want to do what's right, we fear being associated with the weak, the losers, and look away lest we become the bullied.

Ugly ducklings turn into swans. Caterpillars into butterflies. Frogs become princes. Flowers bloom. That is the way it works. There are no examples in nature or children's books of the beautiful and strong transforming into duds. Mother Nature prefers to see her creations gain strength and beauty as they mature. And so it is with humans – we worship the winners, averting our gaze and stepping away from those who have fallen back or down. So I learned.

My first years at Microsoft is the story of a butterfly getting smooshed back into the cocoon, emerging a plump squishy gray moth. Big didn't help little, the caterpillar didn't turn into a butterfly, it got squished while everyone averted their gaze.

Microsoft

"If you're offered a seat on a rocket ship, don't ask what seat! Just get on."
— Sheryl Sandberg

When I joined Microsoft in 2004, I was full of spit and vinegar. I felt bulletproof. I had the pedigree: active member of Forbes's CMO Council, on the ACNielsen Marketing Innovation Advisory Board and SAP's Global Advisory Council, a member of the CMO Group and Forrester's Leadership Board, was recognized as a Master in Marketing by the Association of National Advertisers, blah, blah, blah. I had checked the boxes on a long line of career successes – launch Pull-Ups and GoodNites, now billion-dollar brands (check), work internationally (check), lead a $9B Scott Paper merger/resuscitation (check) and a corporate restructure (check). I "would clearly be an asset in the MSN role" according to the in-depth review and analysis done for Microsoft by the Hay Group during my interviewing process. Their report stated "Jane's ability to challenge established systems and identify potential enhancements and to match individual skills with key roles would make her an effective leader in driving the brand vision and marketing strategy. Jane's ability to analyze, simplify, create, 'sell' and implement concepts would serve Jane well in the MSN marketing role." Yes, I had the pedigree, the experience and the desire to succeed as one of the most senior officers at Microsoft. No, it would not be enough.

My joining Microsoft was kind of a big deal, with articles in *Brand Week*, *Media*, etc. I even made the cover of some business publications. Still, neither Mom nor Dad owned a computer or a cell phone and neither were impressed when I told them I was going to be a Corporate Vice President at Microsoft. "Do you get a uniform, a pension and days off?" Mom wanted to know. "Because the Post Office even gives President's Day off. President's Day!" And I liked to walk, she pointed out. She was sure that being a mailman was the perfect job for me – reliable employment, great benefits and I wouldn't have to travel anywhere outside the neighborhood. Mom couldn't hide her disappointment and slight disapproval despite my assurances that Microsoft was a good company with great benefits. I had always been stubborn, she said.

I was proud to join Microsoft, a company of winners, people who believed and went about the business of changing the world. They were more global, more informed, smarter with better pedigrees, quicker and more convicted than any group of people I'd ever spent time with. They literally expected to change the world for the better, believed they could... and arguably, they did. When Steve Ballmer roared, "I LOVE THIS COMPANY!" each year at MGX, our global Sales and Marketing gathering, I cheered along with 25,000 others, having just witnessed demos of the amazing technology we were about to unleash to save lives and make the world a better place. It was heady stuff, more like an evangelical rally than a technology conference. All I knew was that I BELIEVED! By the time I left my first MGX conference, I had drunk the Kool Aid and was all in, for I too wanted to change the world!!

Employees (called Softies or Bluebadges) were proud to work at Microsoft and wore Microsoft blue security badges with pride, knowing it sparked envy in less fortunate people employed anywhere else. The Bluebadges were worn prominently, a beacon of prestige displayed chest-high from lanyards or clipped conspicuously to the hip of designer jeans and cargo shorts alike. Commonly worn seven days a week, several Bluebadges could be spotted at church each Sunday just in case God lost track of who was and was not among Microsoft's 'chosen people.' Membership had its privileges and to be a member of the Microsoft community was a privilege. We showcased that privilege through the proliferation of Microsoft logos adorning our shirts, jackets, vests, hats, sunglasses, pens, lanyards, notepads, umbrellas, and skin (often tattooed in places I'd rather not have glimpsed).

Unlike K-C, Microsoft was all about hierarchy and title. It was critical to understand the pecking order so as to be clear on who was the pecker and who the peckee. Executives were treated as all-knowing and were seldom challenged. Execs were always the peckers. Managers were a privileged class (although less privileged than Execs), followed by the vast majority of full-time employees who were generally some variant of peckees. Developers were a special class — brilliant, nerdy prima donnas, generally feral and better left alone. I was not technically savvy, thus unable to talk directly with developers, despite my lofty title. I could recognize developers from a distance by their cargo shorts, flip flops, saggy t-shirts and Bluebadges, although daytime sightings were rare; it was best to avoid them outside their natural habitat. Regardless of pecker or peckee, Bluebadges were gods compared to all else, who were mere mortals.

Next on the Microsoft hierarchy were vendors. For every full-time Microsoft Bluebadge employee, there was at least one (usually more) Microsoft vendor on payroll who actually did much of the work assigned to the Bluebadge. Vendors wore orange badges, and despite doing the work of the Bluebadge, were typically dismissed, overlooked, and unappreciated for their badge was orange and not blue and thus, were those who the peckees pecked.

Microsoft

Finally, there were Microsoft Partners, the people who made Microsoft's software work for customers. Think of Microsoft Partners (mostly men) as Lego builders who receive from Microsoft a large box with a cool Star Wars Millennium Falcon picture on the cover. The box contains thousands of Lego pieces (some pieces are missing but may come in a later build) and instructions (mostly missing but may come in a later build). Microsoft Partners are very skilled. They finally build the Millennium Falcon despite missing pieces and poor instructions, at which point both customers and Microsoft ask what took them so long.

Everyone else in the world was referred to as 'the unwashed masses' whose opinions and needs were widely disregarded as irrelevant, since they were not Bluebadges and thus not changing the world.

I was excited to be hired by a strong woman with great industry experience from whom I could learn and receive air cover while finding my footing. Being able to finally work for and learn from an executive woman was a big draw in accepting the job. It took very little time to realize that the good folks at Microsoft were being led by a herd of Kents. Within weeks of starting as a Corporate Vice President pecker, I realized my division was so hostile that my new boss, the person who hired me, was suing Microsoft for harassment, hostile work environment and discrimination. Whaaat? The pecker was being pecked? She pulled me aside one evening and shared her experiences, which paralleled what I too was encountering, and provided a foreboding of what my life would become. She encouraged me to join her in the lawsuit. WTF?!? Are you kidding me? My family and I had just uprooted and moved cross country. I had signed on to achieve success in the marketplace, not the courtroom. My motherboard overloaded and began misfiring as I tried to process this information.

I had been in difficult situations before and had spent my entire life finding a way to 'make it work.' Usually that meant working harder to figure it out. At the end of each day, I shared my experiences with Scott, but he sometimes found my experiences a little hard to believe and often said, "it can't be that bad" or worse, "if it's that bad you need to quit." I interpreted this as "fix it, quit or quit complaining." I didn't know how to fix it (hence the complaining) and quit was not in my vocabulary. Meanwhile, Scott was experiencing adjustments of his own. He continued to drive a Ford Explorer and wear $30 Eddie Bauer khakis amid a sea of Range Rovers and parents wearing jeans that cost more than the mortgage payments on our first house. We had moved from Happy Valley into the Belly of the Beast, as we later learned our neighborhood was called due to the number of millionaires, billionaires and Microsoft executives who lived there.

Still, together we could make this work with time and effort. Or so we told ourselves. Naïve and in denial, we weren't ready to remove the blinders created during 17 years at K-C where the corporate culture was competitive but respectful and where the ruthless weren't tolerated or successful for long. I should have heeded the warning signs and ripped the blinders from my eyes, faced the harsh glare of my new reality and boldly navigated a path through the viper pit that was Microsoft at that time. But this was no fairy tale. The snakes were real. And poisonous.

The Battlefield

"The world ain't all sunshine and rainbows.
It's a very mean and nasty place and I don't care how tough you are it will beat you to your knees and keep you there permanently if you let it."

— Sylvester Stallone

In 2004, when I joined the Online business, Google and Apple were gaining traction by making technology accessible and easy for 'the unwashed masses' to use. The more tech savvy the masses became, the less tolerant users became of Microsoft's complexity and incompatibility. Many were buying into Apple's marketing that said PCs should be 'personal.' People didn't like groveling at the feet of the nerds they'd teased in high school and were tired of using computers that made them feel dumb and incapable. And so began the revolt that challenged the power and control wielded by computer nerds.

Microsoft was a technology-driven company that had become successful designing stuff for computers, not people. The culture thrived on complexity, developing features and functions that coders thought were cool and fun to *create*, but weren't necessarily functional or fun to *use*. "Build it and they will come" had been the approach since inception and 'they' did. How dare Apple disrupt this by making computers friendly, intuitive and easy to use?

Microsoft (the brand) was and is one of the world's most recognized, valuable, trusted brands yet Microsoft's (the company) product and branding strategy reflected the culture of the time – complex and competitive – it worked separately but not well together. Across the Microsoft businesses, there was no single brand owner, little shared accountability, deliverables or strategy, and layers and layers of people and product efforts, each doing their best to create the best independently. Teams aggressively staked out their product and created separate brand hills to climb, each competing for resources, defending their hill to the death. Meanwhile, Google and Apple aligned their brands and products around a consistent value proposition that became the one mountain all ascended.

But Microsoft couldn't lead the world by chasing the taillights of Apple and Google. Realizing they were losing ground and getting left behind, Microsoft doubled down on products and people, determined to take all hills and thus reclaim its rightful place in the world. When I joined, there were product and consumer efforts underway across Search, Security, Music, Email, Messaging, Homepage, News, Entertainment, Start, TV, Video, Health, Money, etc. Each had its own product and brand strategy. For email alone, there were four consumer brands – MSN, Hotmail, Outlook, Live – none of which worked as well as the competition, each of which were competing internally against the other for resources and externally for awareness and usage. I learned this from the five different brand trackers that told me thus. Each project was cloaked in secrecy and so given code names – Skylight, Moonshot, Longhorn, Alchemy, Monarch, Wave 10, Flashlight, etc. Making sense of the disparate brands and product launches was harder than solving a Rubik's cube blindfolded. This was deemed brand marketing's problem to address. My problem. To do so I would need to lasso in the wild, wild west that was Microsoft.

Known for eating its young, Microsoft's culture resisted those who threatened what had been so successful for so long. There was a way things were done – the Microsoft Way – and making things easy to use and integrated was not top priority, as evidenced by the eye rolling I received for having suggested such a thing. No, Microsoft was in a race to be first with technology, not the best, and would fix any bugs in subsequent updates. Innovate then iterate. Launch and learn. Problem is, coders like to work on the shiny, new projects, not debug the products already released. That's why there is a Microsoft graveyard full of great, innovative products and features that Microsoft was first to launch but were executed poorly or left to wither and die of neglect after resources moved on to the next sparkly product/project.

In my very first review with Billg and Steveb, I was told emphatically to stop using the word "consumer." It was explained that people didn't "consume" our products, they "used" them and that's why traditional rules of consumer marketing and product development didn't apply to Microsoft. What?!? Wasn't I hired for my consumer marketing experience and success? Besides, they said, we didn't need to do user research like consumer companies because our users didn't know what they needed until Microsoft gave it to them. Oh. That explained a lot.

Meanwhile, my Online business was getting hammered by Google and Apple, who apparently *did* think it was important to build products that consumers wanted and liked to use. The "like it or leave it" approach that had worked in the past was now creating a mass exodus as the great unwashed masses *didn't* like it and chose to leave, choosing Apple and Google instead of Microsoft. Market shares plummeted. No amount of spending could stop the hemorrhaging, as we executed a strategy de jour that added more confusion than clarity. Ours was an unruly business that even Steveb, the CEO, couldn't wrangle. Bodies were getting shot everywhere and I soon learned that I was not bulletproof after all.

As a successful consumer marketer with a proven track record of creating successful brand strategies and effective consumer marketing campaigns, I was ready to transform the Hotmail/MSN/Live/Skylight/Outlook/Messenger brand muck into a clear, integrated consumer brand portfolio. Something consumers could understand and want to use. I was determined to translate Microsoft's geeky tech talk into language the average Joe and Jane could understand. Only I didn't realize that there was no credibility granted, no recognition given, for achievements outside the walls of Microsoft. It didn't matter how successful I'd been before joining Microsoft. It didn't matter how many successful business and marketing campaigns I'd led, nor how many boards or recognitions I'd received. None of it mattered. If it didn't happen in tech, at Microsoft, it was dismissed as irrelevant. Ergo, I was dismissed as irrelevant.

An integrated approach threatened the Kents of the kingdom, who didn't appreciate anyone trying to bring the independent armies under one banner. Although both my talent and tenacity were underestimated, I was intent on doing the work for which I was hired, wild west or not. Shortly after I joined the team, a fellow CVP informed me that my position wasn't needed, he was against my hire and against me for there were others more qualified for my position. And by "others" he meant a woman with whom he was intimate. Meanwhile, the admin I'd been assigned was being fired for misusing corporate expenses, my office was relocated to a remote corner of the complex, and my meeting and conference rooms were reassigned. There were awkward pauses as I arrived late to critical meetings, having not received updated locations and times because, like me, my new admin was being rejected by peers. My name was often excluded or dropped from key leadership email strings where budget decisions were made during the day and 'revisited' in the evening. I began to hover near my computer each night, afraid to stray too far lest I miss an email thread that unraveled what had been achieved in the light of day. I had dodged bullets before, but it's hard to dodge bullets that you can't see coming.

This probably sounds stupid and childish, like little kids playing a game of keep away. It was, only the balls represented billion-dollar businesses, my career, my credibility and my sanity. I was a foreign organ being rejected by the host, going into complete organ failure. I was easy pickings for those who saw any success I might achieve as coming at their expense. There were few allies to be found. As I went up and introduced myself to peers at Steve Ballmer's annual BBQ for his executive team, some were friendly while some, upon learning my role, rolled their eyes and turned away, ignoring my outstretched hand, leaving me standing with no hand to shake. One guy said what many were thinking. "You probably won't make it, but if you're still here, come find me next year." I focused on those who were friendly.

I was one of 10 wide-eyed executive newbies hired from outside Microsoft in 2004. All were experiencing similar culture shock. Almost half left after the first year. The five remaining banded together for support. Some had landed in places that were less hostile, but each was struggling to get traction, much less excel. Scott and I hosted a dinner party, which became a regular occurrence, where we swapped stories and laughed anxiously at the insanity, pledged support and talked of how we'd leave Microsoft once the stock hit $40/share. It remained in the low $30s, yet within a few years, nearly all left Microsoft until I was the last standing. Well, more leaning than standing, truth be told.

The culture in my division was more about talking than listening. Uninterested in what I had to say about marketing, I was given 'helpful' advice on what to wear (black, not white), what to say ("user" not "consumer") and what not to do (don't say what you think). In other words, fit in, shut up and don't rock the boat. Uh, no. So I tried harder, thinking that good ideas and strategy eventually win and that business leaders ultimately pursue what's right for the business over what's right for themselves. In the meantime, I hired a professional shopper at Nordstroms who picked out $300 jeans and designer jackets I would never have selected, none of which fit me physically or mentally, but would make me look as if I belonged. My closet was filled with padded hangers upon which hung trendy clothes, price tags still attached, when what I found I really needed were padded bras that hid my nipples so guys would stop staring at my chest. Each day, I could feel those designer clothes snubbing the clothes that I continued to reach for as I promised myself that *tomorrow* I'd begin wearing the cool new clothes that would make me more like them and less like me. Even the clothing labels made me feel inadequate – Free the People! One for All Mankind! True Religion! Sigh. You know it's bad when you feel like a loser in a pair of Lucky jeans.

I really did try to fit in. I started using PowerPoint and stopped telling stories. I used cool buzzwords and tech talk instead of using the language of our customers. I got bullied into strategies I knew would fail because they didn't reflect what our users wanted. I knew, but didn't want to acknowledge, that there was nothing I could wear, do, or say to succeed or fit in. The more I tried, the faster and more completely I failed. The internal focus and in-fighting made it possible for both Google and Apple to do what we could have and should have done, but were unable to get out of our way to do.

I went from Chief Marketer to Chief Fuckerupper. Over the following months, the success I'd experienced throughout my life and career faded into the background as if done by another or not done at all. I'd spent my life challenging, overcoming, competing and creating, but my life skills didn't prepare me for death-by-a-thousand-cuts warfare from within. The "you're not good enough" whisper in my head began roaring "YOU'RE NOT GOOD ENOUGH! YOU'RE A FAKE! YOU DON'T BELONG HERE! YOU'RE SCREWED!!"

I was losing track of what was the real me and what was the persona I projected to appear that all was well, deceiving even myself. I was a beautiful butterfly that wasn't ready to admit to being squashed, shoved and smooshed into an ugly cocoon, so instead, I folded my wings tightly around me and tucked my head tight to my chest. I didn't let anyone in, didn't share how dark and murky it was within my cocoon, how lost I felt, how unsure of the way out. Tethered to my PC, lest I fall further behind, I worked late into most nights, responding to the flood of emails and texts, proving my commitment and worth by being "always on." If only my worth was measured by the number of emails and strokes on my keyboard.

Scott and I had agreed that if Microsoft didn't work out, we'd return to the Midwest. But while I dodged bullets at the office, it seemed Scott was hitting the bull's eye getting himself and the boys settled in school and after-school activities. Scott knew all the boys' teachers and coaches and was an active volunteer, a favorite amongst the school kids and teachers alike. Scott was no longer the only full-time dad in town and became friends with men whose lives mirrored our own. It was a big adjustment, but the boys were happy and Scott was doing his part. I needed to do mine. After all, it couldn't be that bad given what I'd already been through. Right? Right? Squish.

I spent that year driving by entrances. I drove by the entrance to my office building until I was sufficiently fortified to tackle what waited for me behind the doors. I drove by the entrance to our home on evenings I hadn't fully regrouped, my spirit shattered and not recognizable to those within. I was lost and lonely having made no 4 o'clock friends in which to confide and unable to share with my 4 o'clock friends in Wisconsin for fear they could not relate.

I was assigned a mentor, Chris. In our first meeting, Chris gave me the lay of the land using so many acronyms that I recognized only the verbs in his sentences. Prior to our next meeting, I had done my homework and felt fluent in Microsoft jargon, only to find out I was still at a remedial level. In hindsight, I wish I had relied more on Chris, a genuinely good guy who had earned a great reputation and was willing to help me. Chris was a homegrown Softie; tech acronyms rolled off his tongue as naturally as prayers passed Madonna Bernadette's lips. Everyone liked and respected Chris. I wanted Chris to like and respect me, so was unwilling to let him see my insecurity or know the challenges I was facing. I was a hot mess, but if he sensed the heat, he didn't say so.

Had he been given a chance, maybe Chris could have been my Big and given me perspective or air cover. He could have provided tips on how to survive, if not thrive, in the Microsoft culture. He could have told me the importance of having lifelines, of going to dinners with peers to create alliances, of knowing that most decisions weren't made in face-to-face meetings, but played out in emails or texts outside of conference rooms. That decisions and people were Teflon – neither stuck for long. But I was overwhelmed, thought asking for help was admitting failure and was too ashamed and afraid to be honest, so I stubbornly fixed a smile on my face and tried harder. Like I always had. Only this time it wasn't working. My eyes, dull and dark, betrayed my smile, which would no longer stay fixed to my face.

After the woman who hired me left the company, I was shuffled from boss to boss. In total, I reported to four different people within my first year. Re-orgs were common at Microsoft, but even so, that was a lot of shuffling. My third boss, Dave, called me into his office late one evening to better understand the branding strategy I'd developed. Dave was a technical guy through and through, a fish out of water when it came to marketing. He slowly, reluctantly, pulled my marketing PowerPoint deck from the pile of product plans on his desk, a look of grim determination and pain on his face, as if steeling himself for something horrible. As he flipped through the deck, I could see that he had circled and scribbled very specific questions in the margins, with arrows highlighting several things written in the small font no one was supposed to have read. It was clear Dave wanted to understand my proposal and wanted to create rapport to better understand me. I knew this discussion was a pivotal moment. He was tossing me a lifeline. I desperately wanted to catch it.

Dave, like all seasoned Microsoft executives, had been trained and steeped in the art of Precision Questioning, a critical thinking technique for problem solving that uses a highly structured, one-question/one-answer discussion format to help solve complex problems, conduct deep analysis and facilitate difficult decisions. The Online branding problem was complex, requiring deep analysis and difficult decisions. Perfect. Unfortunately, I knew nothing of Precision Questioning and Dave knew nothing of marketing/branding.

Dave dove straight in and began drilling down, asking a series of specific, precise questions he had prepared, for which he wanted specific, succinct answers. "On page 5, column 3, row 4 you state that Brand A, feature X should be compatible with Brand B, feature Y." I nodded and said yes, making brand and product features compatible was important. "Yes, but exactly how much market share will be gained by that change?" As I began to answer, Dave's face became red and I felt a whoosh as the lifeline he'd hurled very precisely at me went whizzing past, just beyond my grasp.

I later heard Precision Questioning at Microsoft explained this way:

> The way precision questioning works is that executive X is going to ask you a question, and then after you answer it, you'll be asked a follow-up question, and so on until you finally say "I don't know." You want to last as many rounds as possible before finally reaching the point where you're asked a question you cannot answer.

Marketing isn't precise nor were my answers. I got knocked out in round one with the first question. I was unsuccessful in translating traditional brand-building knowledge and experience into a strategy that landed in a meaningful way. The tried-and-true strategies that had built traditional billion-dollar businesses of high brand loyalty were dismissed as old school and uncool, like me. We threw away millions on cool, fun, but ineffective tactics. There is no such thing as a quick fix or silver bullet, though we spent lustily on things that *looked* good even though they didn't *do* any good. Being cool was the important thing to the Kents of the day.

I was dismissed, a fate worse than failure. Failure can be learned from and overcome. Dismissal is a conviction against which no one can fight or overcome because dismissal says *I,* not my actions, am the failure. Dismissal said *I* was unworthy. I was KO'd shortly after entering the ring. Within one year, I was unable to persuade anyone of anything because I'd lost my confidence and was unable to get beyond my self doubt. Within one year, I found myself kneeling over a toilet trying to purge the fear, uncertainty, and despair that had again found a foothold and threatened to overwhelm me. For the first time in my life, I didn't know how or if I could be successful in my job. I had lost the distinction between failing in a job and failing as a person. They had become the same.

I confided in HR, who was sympathetic. They saw but couldn't heal the dysfunction that had taken root in our organization. My HR Director gave me a plaque that said, "And the day came when the pain of staying in a tight bud was greater than the risk it takes to bloom," knowing that no matter how great the pain, I would not bloom there. Within a year, I left the role for which I was recruited, qualified and hired, hoping I could bloom in another division.

Few times in my life have I been unable to find a way to make something work. This was one. Perhaps the Kents had bested me, but in the end we all lost the battle. In a few years, six of eight CVPs in my division left the company after failing to achieve objectives as did nine of the ten CVPs hired the year I joined Microsoft. The internal focus and in-fighting made it possible for both Google and Apple to do what we could have and should have done but were unable to get out of our way to do. Microsoft had superior technology and brilliant people but at that time, the Kent culture made it virtually impossible to win without getting shot. So people either remained heads-down in their bunker or fled the battlefield. I fled the battlefield. Before I was removed on a stretcher.

Out of the Frying Pan

"If you're going through hell, keep going."

— Winston Churchill

Perhaps because someone feared a lawsuit, I was shuffled to a new role working for Microsoft's CMO who was among Microsoft's first employees. And a woman. Like me, she was one of only a dozen women among the executive ranks. I would be her right hand in managing the Central Marketing Organization.

My new office was in Building 34, Microsoft's equivalent of the oval office, the epicenter amongst the really big guns – the CEO, COO, CMO and CFO of Microsoft. The area had a sense of energy and urgency and I knew right away that I was breathing rare air. People entered this domain with a mixture of excitement and fear. Not so much because these guys were billionaires, although they were, but because they were forging the visions and making decisions that influenced billions of people and companies around the world. So you can imagine how it took a while to get used to seeing the CEO padding around the halls in his socks, sticking his feet up on the desk complaining of sore feet.

Steve Ballmer (aka Steveb), Microsoft's CEO at the time, was a force of nature. His energy, intellect and intent were unrivaled. In that way, he reminded me of Claudio. His judgment and leadership style, however.... well, he didn't exactly foster the kind of environment needed to capitalize on major industry trends of the day. Professionally, most were intimidated by Steve. Personally, I thought Steveb was a genuine, honest, well-intentioned guy who neither asked for nor received special treatment. Several times Steveb was in line with Scott to pick up football gear for his son, refusing offers to trade places, content to stand in line just like the other dads. Pretty cool considering Steveb was one of the wealthiest guys in the world. In a community where Mercedes and Porsches were the norm, he drove a Ford because that's where his dad had worked. Steveb parked in the same parking garage as everyone else, although every now and then I saw security guards discreetly keeping watch and figured it wasn't me they were looking out for.

Steveb was a mere mortal until it came to business, then Whammo! He relished going *deep* into the details of the business and sloshing around in the numbers until he made the connections, or found the disconnects, in what was being presented. Steveb loved numbers. The more the better. Presentation decks were packed so densely with numbers in fonts so small that magnifying glasses were distributed along with handouts. Seriously. I kept a collection of magnifiers in my desk drawer. A successful meeting with Steveb was one where no data errors were found, not necessarily where the right conversations were had.

None of this fazed my boss Mich, who had been working beside Billg and Steveb since the early days. She would see the struggle, hear the stress swirling and do her little chuckle, chastising me for worrying too much because "it's all just a game." Perhaps to her, but like the days on the Scott business, I didn't like being a pawn in others' games nor did I like playing with people's jobs. Mich and I worked shoulder to shoulder. I learned a lot watching her deftly orchestrate Microsoft politics, using her experience, relationships, intelligence, and British accent to direct pieces on the board in the game she was playing. Over time, I let my guard down as we talked about work, kids, marriage and all the things that make people personable, enjoying the camaraderie, forgetting she was what I was not. Mich was the chess master.

Steveb liked numbers and when it came to marketing, he didn't have them. I was asked to lead a project to identify where, who and how many marketers and billions of dollars were being spent on marketing each year. Aha! I had done something similar at Kimberly-Clark and knew I could do this. A small but mighty group of Bluebadges, together with a few folks from McKinsey & Company, led an initiative we called ROMI (Return on Marketing Investment) to shed light on the deep abyss that was marketing at Microsoft. It was like trying to boil the ocean. There were people and budgets and campaigns and dollars being spent everywhere by everyone.

Despite being a fellow CVP, the heads of marketing were initially reluctant to meet or share their data with me. But like a Girl Scout selling cookies, I wore them down and was tenacious in getting most to support the project despite their initial reticence. Over the year, we developed recommendations that would save hundreds of millions of dollars. Had I been a Scout, I'd have earned a badge for sure. Week by week, month by month, I felt my balloon of self-confidence re-inflating. Perhaps it was the rare air.

I was excited to present the findings and recommendation to Steveb. For weeks, we scrubbed the data and pre-sold the recommendation to ensure all were on board. I practiced the presentation with Mich, anticipating every possible question and objection. I was ready. The meeting was my redemption, when I'd present ROMI findings and prove to Steveb and others that I did know my stuff. I had done a good job and they'd realize my worth. Yes, I'd have a bright future at Microsoft.

I entered the meeting feeling confident, ready and bulletproof...so I didn't see the bullet coming. Just as I was taking a deep, confident breath to begin, Mich reached her hand in front of me and said, "I've got this." It was her chess game, and she was the queen. She presented the work, barely mentioning me or the team. It was a betrayal of the worst kind because I had come to think of Mich as more than my boss – I thought of her as a friend and advocate. She knew this meeting meant a lot to me yet buzz-sawed me anyway. I sat there while the rare air leaked slowly, painfully, mercilessly from my body.... NOOOOOooo... leaving me completely deflated.

I seldom cry, but that night I went home and had a snotty howler, surrendering to the disappointment, betrayal, anger and pain of the past few years. I wasn't crying because I was weak, but because I had been struggling to be strong for too long. I'd put on a brave face at the office, but now lay broken, not wanting or able to get up as I lay crying in a fetal position in my closet. Gone was the Jane who rode Buster fearlessly, who sold used carpet, who built GoodNites, who was wife and mother. I had betrayed that Jane when I became so desperate to fit in and 'succeed' that I'd begun using another's yardstick to measure my success, a stick that didn't measure what was important to me and for which I didn't measure up. There would be no regrouping; this bullet hit me square in the heart. I didn't want or know if I could get up. So I didn't. I just laid there and cried for a good long time. Until Scott joined me, gently handing back the yardstick I'd misplaced but not lost.

Broken But Not Busted (again)

> *"I can't let you walk out of here without crutches.*
> *Your leg is broken; the only thing keeping your knee from your ankle*
> *is a metal rod that was never meant to be weight-bearing.*
> *You're damn lucky that rod never broke."*
>
> — Dr. H

After getting buzz sawed by Mich, Scott and I had some big decisions to make that involved leaving Microsoft and probably relocating. We took the boys skiing in Canada for a few days to get some fresh air and perspective. Maybe a 43-year-old flatlander from Iowa should have questioned going down a snowy mountain on two skinny sticks. Especially one who had already broken her leg at 11 while ice skating with Robbie Feltman. Sure enough, it wasn't long before half of me zigged while the other half zagged, and I found myself standing upright with skis facing opposite directions. Unfortunately, my feet were still in my skis. I didn't need to be told that my leg was broken; I'd seen and felt this before and knew it was bad. SON OF A … I wanted to scream, but Jack was with me, so instead I found my way to the ground and waited with my 8-year-old son for help to arrive.

X-rays confirmed I had spiral fractures in my tibia, fibula, and ankle. Again. Doctors told Scott my leg was broken too badly to address locally. After agreeing it was best to return to the US, I was pumped full of enough drugs to keep me in la-la land while Scott sprang into action, returning all ski equipment, checked us out of the hotel, and sped the family through border patrol and back to the USA, all with me drugged in the back seat and the boys wondering why I was drooling.

The Bellevue hospital had been informed I was coming and lucky for me, an orthopedic surgeon on call was waiting to take me into surgery. Unlucky for me, the on-call surgeon was not skilled enough to handle my break. He put a metal rod (doctors call it a nail) from knee to ankle and used nearly a dozen screws to put Humpty Dumpty back together. Or so he tried. He didn't actually put all the bones together before screwing everything in place. Unlucky for me, that was a pretty big miss because, like Humpty Dumpty, I couldn't and wouldn't heal over the next year.

Walking is as critical to my sanity and survival as food, water and beer. It provides the mental and spiritual lubricant that keeps me sane and moving forward. I walk everywhere and all the time – before dawn, late into the night and anytime in between. According to my Fitbit and my car's odometer, I walk more miles than I drive each year. Like most people, my day is spent focusing only a few feet in front of my face – in conversations, in meetings, in front of a computer screen. But perspective dies and life can't be truly lived in the space between your eyes and a phone or computer screen. When walking, I lift my gaze up and out and my thoughts follow, up and beyond to the beauty surrounding me. Looking up and out reminds me that I'm part of something bigger than myself, something much bigger than the inches separating me and my device.

As often as possible, I'd walk with Scott and the boys and listen to stories of the day. During solo walks, I saw and heard nothing specific, each step liberating the thoughts pinging about in my head, creating space for grace and gratitude. I exhaled during late night walks through the neighborhood, as lights softened and stillness settled in. Early morning walks were the best, filled with hope and the anticipation of a new day as the morning sky filled with pink and promise. It was during walks that God and I had a chance to chat. I liked that. I needed that.

After getting cut down at work and on the ski slope, God and I stopped chatting. Or maybe I just stopped listening. In hindsight, it seems God was speaking pretty clearly. "Slow down, Jane. Redirect. You're on the wrong run." But like Wile E. Coyote trying to catch the Road Runner, I would not stop no matter how many anvils fell from the sky upon me. Days after surgery, I dialed into work from my bed at home to resume leadership of the ROMI meetings. Hopped up on pain meds, my comments were not as strategic or insightful as they seemed to me. The next day, a stack of books – *Little Women, The Secret Garden, Jane Eyre* – were dropped off at the house along with a message that Mich would take over ROMI while I recovered. Given my recent gutting in the Steveb meeting, I took this as another sign of dismissal, not support, and became more determine to return quickly. Yup, Wile E. Coyote.

Scott and the boys put me in a wheelchair and rolled me through the neighborhood to keep my spirits up; yet I was so grouchy I wouldn't have blamed them for ditching me in a side street. How many times had I run up the staircase, never appreciating my strength and health? There were 17 steps, 10 feet and humility separating my wheelchair and me from the base of the stairs to the top, but undeterred, I scooted on my butt, carefully dragging my leg in a race with Jack (he beat me). Pain pills made me too loopy to read but not loopy enough to enjoy daytime TV. The weeks went slowly by. Finally, I was allowed crutches. The crutches felt familiar in my hands, having spent so much time on them as a kid, but the pills made me unsteady so Scott tied a belt around my waist while holding me from behind as I insisted on navigating the steps on my own. If not for Scott, I'd have gone ass over teakettle down the steps more than once. He had a third sense and knew when I was doing something I shouldn't and would appear out of nowhere to ensure I was safe.

Scott was loving and patient, attending every doctor appointment and tracking every pill. You'd think I'd love the attention but instead chafed at being dependent on Scott, unaccustomed to being so vulnerable and needy. Just below the surface, my emotions bubbled like boiling black tar in a cauldron. But over time, they stopped churning on the surface and were buried deep where they became dark, messy, and sticky.

Eventually it came time to return to work. ROMI was winding down and Mich had taken leadership and credit for its success. What did I have to return to? I was unsure of my next move. Scott wasn't. He'd seen me broken in more ways than one over the past months and did <u>not</u> want me to return to Microsoft.

> "Why do you work for a company that doesn't want you in a job that doesn't make you happy? There are so many other companies who would love to hire you."
>
> "But I've worked so hard and am finally learning how to be successful at Microsoft."
>
> "That's what I'm afraid of, Jane. I'm not afraid you'll fail. I'm afraid you'll succeed."

What I didn't tell him was that I didn't have the energy, courage or confidence to start over. What if my next job was the same? Better the devil you know. So I insisted on returning, the sooner the better. Wile E. Coyote. Beep. Beep.

Unable to drive a car or even crutch my way up our steep driveway, Scott took me everywhere I needed to go, even back to Building 34. Each day he reluctantly pulled up to Building 34 and helped me out of the car and through the door, silently shouting his disapproval, before pulling slowly away, only to return hours later at day's end to take me home, just as he'd driven me to/from the airport years ago in Atlanta. He didn't ask and I didn't tell him how work was going. Besides, he knew by the set of my shoulders and the look on my face.

Finally, I was given a walking boot. Freedom! Only something was wrong. It hurt like hell to walk. Back I went to the surgeon, who explained in a condescending tone that I was just a 'slow healer' but that all was as it should be. I should have known better; I've never been described as slow at anything in my friggin life. We tried everything to make the pain go away: TENS machines, muscle stimulation, physical therapy and more surgeries to remove, replace and add screws, thus repeating the cast, crutches, walking-boot cycle. Still, the pain remained.

I was finally referred to Dr H, the revered orthopedic surgeon, and "father of traumatology" at Harborview Medical Center. It was difficult getting an appointment because I wasn't *actually* a trauma patient, although at this point, I'd have jumped in front of a bus to get an appointment with anyone who could help me. Dr. H took X-rays from an angle no one else had done. Even I could see the problem when he popped the X-rays on the light table.

"I can't let you walk out of here without crutches. Your leg is broken; the only thing keeping your knee from your ankle is this metal rod that was never meant to be weight-bearing. You're damn lucky that rod never broke."

Thank God! Relief washed over me as I listened to Dr. H tell me I'd spent the last year walking on a broken leg. I wasn't crazy. And I wasn't a 'slow healer' either, assholes.

Having identified the issue, my 12" rod and all remaining screws were removed and replaced with a shiny new, custom-designed bracket and a brand-new set of 1 ½ inch screws. My X-rays looked like something Jack had built using his erector set. The bones finally healed but the pain remained. My body was rejecting the metal in me, letting me know with each step that the hardware was an unwanted intrusion. The pain only whispered when walking softly, but the firmer my step the greater the protest. Running was out of the question. I could only gingerly step off curbs. There was no room for adventure, no veering from the path, no zigging or zagging, which sucked the zippity doo dah from my day. We tried taking more screws out. More surgery, crutches, physical therapy blah, blah, blah.

Meanwhile, I was trolling for a new position befitting a CVP title. Microsoft probably expected (and hoped) that I'd leave the company to pursue a role elsewhere. That was the plan, only I was physically and mentally unable.

Few people knew the extent of my physical injury. Fewer still knew my leg wasn't the only thing about me that was broken. The pain of carrying on, holding on so tightly for so long, was causing more damage than letting go. I need only look where I'd come from to know I wasn't where I wanted to be. So, I let go only to discover the path I was meant to be on was just ahead.

Choices

"When a great moment knocks on the door of your life, its sound is often no louder than the beating of your heart and it is very easy to miss."
— John O'Donohue

"Turn your face to the sun and the shadows fall behind you."
— Moore Proverb

So there we sat. Neither wanted nor expected to be there. I wondered which Steveb was sitting across from me. The boisterous powerhouse I'd seen tear men to shreds, or the nice guy I'd seen padding round the office in his stocking feet? Both. We had a dilemma that was both business and personal. Both knew I wasn't qualified to be the CVP of a technical, product development team. Yet, I was returning from medical leave with nowhere to go, unwilling to continue working in my prior position, still bruised and broken from the one-two punch of betrayal + busted leg. We were at a crossroad. Who would blink first?

I had talked with several friends and peers, all of whom had given me the same counsel – Microsoft was a big company and would/should keep me in a CVP role until I was back on my feet (literally) and could interview for a C-Level role at another company. They pointed out that I <u>deserved</u> and had <u>earned</u> my position and should **not** give it up. Each advised <u>not</u> to accept a demotion to General Manager because

I'd never get back to a CVP job in title or compensation. Ah yes, the money. I was earning big money as a CVP and not keen to give that up. So there we sat.

I heard about how Windows Vista, the long-awaited next-generation operating system, would soon be launching to replace the beloved Windows XP. I was told how Vista was going to be AMAZING! Vista was going to be BIGGER than XP, BETTER than XP! It was a ROCKET SHIP! Being the US General Manager of Windows Vista would be FUN, a real BLAST, one of the BEST jobs in the company (implying even BETTER than being a CVP!). Yeah, right.

Let's see… I could leave a position with maximum prestige and perks to take a job for less money, less prestige, more risk, managing a declining $1B Windows business where I didn't know the product, customers, partners or team and didn't have a lot of advocates vested in my success. Or not. I'd be crazy to take the demotion to General Manager, right?

On the other hand, I liked the idea of learning how to run a technical business. I smiled at the opportunity to lead a commercial sales and marketing team that was completely different from consumer and online businesses. Yes, the role was a lower-profile position, but perhaps it was one where I could create and lead my team, my way, using my yardstick. Or not. I'd be crazy to take the demotion, right?

I had worked hard, done well and had earned the CVP title, dammit! If I took a step back and accepted the GM role, wouldn't I be admitting defeat? Wouldn't I be letting the Kents win? What about the women who looked up to me? What would it say that another woman didn't make it as a CVP? Would people think I was a loser? Would I think that? Would I? I'd be crazy to take the demotion, right?

I was swirling, stuck in a mental blender where every option, every opinion, every expectation went whirring around and around in my head. It was difficult to think and impossible not to. Scott's disdain for Microsoft made him guarded and protective of me. He saw more in me than I did of myself. My self-image was not reflected in his eyes. Scott said he'd support me if I stayed, but he encouraged me to leave. So I had half-hearted interviews for CMO positions at T-Mobile and Starbucks, but didn't pursue either. I didn't want to walk away from Microsoft with a limp, literally and figuratively, yet didn't see a viable path forward either.

So where was God in all this? I needed help, dammit! Where was that clear sense of peace and presence that had graced me in my youth? MIA. It seemed the invisible hand that had guided me was now slapping me. Instead of a finger to point the way, I was getting flipped a different finger entirely. I needed a visible sign of invisible grace. But I felt nothing, saw nothing, heard nothing but the perpetual ping, ping, pinging in my head. Maybe grace had been purged like so much else over the years?

I went to my knees in church but found no peace or answers there. I needed space for grace so took to the woods. Walking slowly on trails amid towering fir and cedar, the 'should' voices in my head gave way to the 'want' whispers in my heart. In the quiet I heard clearly who and what was important – my family – Scott and my boys. I wasn't letting them down. They had everything they needed. Everything but me. My ego, pride, anger and embarrassment were about me, not about we. My family didn't care about titles. My family cared about me and wanted me to be with them, present and happy.

Wearing a title was wearing me out. My new position would give me the space to turn my focus outward, to my family, to build and support a team based on what I'd learned from Dudley, to be a 'we' again.

John O'Donohue wrote, "When a great moment knocks on the door of your life, its sound is often no louder than the beating of your heart and it is very easy to miss." In the quiet I knew. It was time to let go, to replace fear with trust and to take joy in learning something new again. In the quiet, a holy exchange was made replacing the fear of what if for the grace of whatever. I was being given a chance to get out of my own way, give what I wanted to receive and create a team I wanted to be in. On my own terms. I would be crazy *not* to take the job. Right!

Against everyone's counsel except those who counted, I let go of the CVP title and everything that went with it to take the job as General Manager of the US Windows business. My ego would miss being one of the few CVP women at Microsoft, but it was time to stop using others' yardsticks to measure success and begin to use my own again. Let the shadows fall behind me. I turned my face to the sun, never looked back and never once regretted the decision.

Legacy

"We don't accomplish anything in this world alone... and whatever happens is the result of the whole tapestry of one's life and all the weavings of individual threads from one to another that creates something."

— Sandra Day O'Connor

Throughout my home hang hand-pieced, hand-stitched quilts. Each is beautiful. Each is unique. Each has a story, woven in fabric and color, told stitch by stitch, brought to life through the needle of its maker. The oldest is from 1830, created more than a century before electricity became common. It was created with hundreds of hand-dyed fabric pieces, thousands of stitches, each perfect and meticulously sewn at 12 stitches to the inch using a handmade needle. The design reveals the creative mind and capable hands of the woman who sat quietly before the glow of a fading fire, unaware of the masterpiece taking shape through her hands.

Each quilt is a treasure beyond measure, a gift from the women who brought forth and nurtured life, whose hands and heart fed, clothed, educated, and lifted those before us and remind us of the strength within us still, the strength that is our heritage. It's shameful that so few quilts hang in museums; most can be found haphazardly folded in a dank drawer or in a dark, damp corner of second-hand stores. Unlike a Picasso or Van Gogh, quilts aren't auctioned at Sotheby's, their value unrecognized like so many of the women who have gone before us. But their worth is not worthless; it is instead measured in a currency more precious than coin.

If ever our house caught fire, I'd run right past my diamonds, past my wedding photos (mostly digitized now) and wouldn't slow down to scoop up the dog until after I had my great grandmother's quilt tucked safely under my arm. For a quilt, it's nothing special. But then again, it is not just a quilt. It's an heirloom, a legacy sewn by great grandma Isabelle during moments stolen between giving birth to 18 children on a farm in Nebraska. Of simple log cabin design, the quilt was created using fabric scraps from the 50# bags of flour she transformed into bread, pies and rolls in her wood-fired stove each day. The fabric is now frayed, and the stitches are far from perfect. Pieces of wool stick out here and there from the wool batting she'd hand-carded, courtesy of the farm's sheep.

She created the quilt, one of many, quickly and efficiently, out of necessity, each stitch one closer to keeping her children warm. Did she pray while she sewed, weaving blessing into each stitch? Did she think of the future generations for whom this quilt would become her legacy? Or was her mind on the socks to be darned, the clothes to be mended, this quilt one of many things seeking her needle's attention as she gently placed another log on the fire by which to sew?

Over a hundred years have passed, the quilt now far from the Nebraska farm where it was created, passed from mother to daughter, generation to generation, each year a bit more frayed, a bit more faded. Great Grandma Isabelle to Grandma Tilly to Aunt Marie to me. Not all great grandma's children would live on, but her quilt remains very much alive, pulsing with her quiet strength, patience, tenderness, sorrow, and joy.

Today, my gas fireplace turns on with the flick of a switch. An app regulates the heat in my home. My quilts now adorn more walls than beds, but the stories they hold, the truths they have seen, are needed more now than ever. Feeling the need to honor the great tradition of the women before me, I decided one summer to sew a quilt of my own and went to Vicki, a friend who'd hand-sewn many beautiful quilts including crib quilts for Andy and Jack. I was practically bursting with pride when I told Vicki my intention, but she just stood there, speechless, looking at me as if I had two heads. Maybe I was talking too fast and she didn't understand.

"I...am... going... to... sew...a...quilt," I said slowly and with conviction.

"With a needle?" asked Vicki.

"Uh... I suppose.... yes, and thread too!" I replied, still puffed up with conviction.

"Uh, huh. You? You sure? Really?"

"Yup."

"Oh boy. This should be interesting," said Vicki.

Vicki helped select a pattern, cloth and everything needed to get me started. Her instructions were painfully obvious and unnecessary, I thought, for I was impatient to begin. Not wanting to be presumptuous, I started small and simple. Just a blue and white 9-square baby quilt. Easy-peasy. Hmmm... who knew threading a needle was so hard? And tying those teeny knots on the end of the thread was trickier than it looked. Maybe I needed some coffee first. Yes, I'll have a quick cup of coffee. Perhaps another. Okay now, where was I? Yes, needle threaded and knotted. Check. Here we go. Stitching, stitching, stitching, OUCH! Stitching, stitching OUCH, stitching OUCH! @#?$%!

Where did all this blood come from? Hmmm… maybe I'll go show this to Vicki, just to be sure I'm doing it right.

"Hi… can I show you my quilt?" said I from her doorstep as she looked at me quizzically.

"What quilt? I thought you just started this morning."

"Yes…well… I'm not quite finished," I stammered.

"Let's see what you've got so far…" she said followed by "HA HA HA HA HA HA HA."

This went on quite a while as Vicki alternated between looking at my bandaged fingers and my bloodstained 'quilt.'

"Jane, go to the kitchen and make some wild rice soup for lunch. Give a shout when it's ready."

"Okay," said I with much relief.

I could hear Vicki chuckling as she began to wash the blood out of my quilt. By the time lunch was ready, she had sewn hundreds of tiny, perfect stitches, without any blood on her or the quilt to prove it. That day marked my first and last attempt at sewing, for I was better with a ladle than a needle, we merrily agreed over a delicious bowl of soup. I had always admired Vicki's quilts but now had a new sense of appreciation and awe at her skill, especially when I see my uneven, awkward stitches beside hers.

Today's culture tells me to airbrush my life, to show only the parts of me that are pretty, perfect, plastic. Yet strength and beauty are found in the bits and pieces we hide from others, in the parts of our lives never posted on Instagram. Only when I share what is imperfect in me will you share what is incomplete in you so that together we peel away the veneer of perfectionism to reveal what is real and true, proclaiming all our bits and parts worthy and valuable. Quilts represent to me the chaos of the soul, the days when my worth felt like bits of scraps, unvalued, discarded, just parts and pieces with no rhyme or reason. Surely, I'm not the only one to feel that there is beauty in my bits and pieces, that my scraps are not worthless, despite what others may see at the moment.

I wonder as I admire the quilts adorning my home, what will be *my* legacy? Can words be my needle and actions be my thread? How can I bring together people to weave a living quilt where all bits and pieces are valued and worthy, where talents, humanity and differences are celebrated and lifted, rather than tossed aside or passed over? Can I ignite and unite the hidden dreams, hopes, capabilities and actions of others to create something meaningful, heartening, and beautiful? For it's often the bits we fear to share and the scraps we feel unworthy that become the richest, strongest, most beautiful fabric of our lives. Each has a story woven of pain, fear, strength, resilience, and joy, joined stitch by stitch, integrating our light and shadow, our gifts and gaffs, to become what we are called to be, part of a beautiful whole. Sewn with time, talent, grit and grace, a living quilt of people can leave a legacy of positive change. That is the legacy I devote my life to create. I can only hope my living quilt of words and actions will draw less blood than my attempt with needle and thread.

Rebooting Jane

*"Success is not final, failure is not fatal:
it is the courage to continue that counts."*
— Winston Churchill

*"Courage is being yourself every day
in a world that tells you to be someone else."*
— Christina Lauren

The morning of my new job as General Manager of Windows Commercial, I stood bolted to the floor of my closet trying to decide what to wear. In a face-off with myself, my hand extended, frozen in midair, reaching but not grasping the outfit that I would wear on the first day of my new job. My clothes hung innocently upon their hangers, unaware of the meaning I'd assigned to them, unaware that upon their shoulders hung my identity. Today was a new start. No one knew me. Who would I be?

It was so much easier when I was Janie, wearing a St. Lawrence green plaid Catholic school uniform just like everyone else. But today I was not Janie. Today I was Jane. I was a big girl now, and today I got to choose. Did I want to be like everyone else? It would be much easier and better to blend in, to follow the leader. But I had followed the leader before and been led down a path not right for me.

Many people want to be led by another, to play it safe and let someone else decide what's best, never putting themselves on the front line, believing life is easier that way. Maybe it is easier. I'll never know. I believe in fighting for what I want rather than looking back and wondering about the person I might have become if only. Did I want to belong? Yes. Did I want to fit in? No. I reached past the designer jeans, past the couture shirts and clothes bought for CVP Jane. My hand finally landed upon a tailored blouse and dress slacks that was to become my new uniform. Too boring, eh? Where's the designer labels, polished nails, hair and makeup that shout, "I've arrived! I'm successful!!" you ask? Fuck you! There, I said it. I had finally reclaimed my inner Fuck You. Hello old friend. I was dressing for me, not to fit a role or others' expectations of me, but for me. If I was to be judged by my appearance, at least it would be *my* appearance and not one fashioned by others. For the first time in ages I went to work comfortable in my own skin. They say dress for success. I was dressing for me, and for me, *that* was success.

I arrived before the sun on Monday morning, well before anyone else had turned on the lights or taken note of my return. My new Windows office was in a dark, depressing building that had been a mortuary in its former life. A mortuary. Perfect. Just the place to lay to rest what no longer served me. RIP ego. Goodbye pride.

The Jane who walked into the mortuary that was my office was not the Jane who left Wisconsin to join Microsoft as a CVP only three years earlier. That Jane would not have recognized herself, and if she did, would have wondered why she'd ever exchanged her Wisconsin snowblower for a Washington raincoat and success for the scars of the last few years. No, she'd think, coming to Microsoft had not been a good exchange at all. But the Jane who entered the mortuary that was my office was not the same.

There was no entourage to greet me, no announcement in the *Wall Street Journal, Brandweek* or any other trade rags to herald my arrival. No bullshit, no bother. Just me, stronger, smarter, more resilient… and hopefully, wiser and humbler.

It was still dark as I entered the old, dank building. Nestled amongst a grove of trees, the office smelled damp and musty as though it was being reclaimed by the vegetation surrounding it. It smelled of earth, I decided, taking a deep breath. I liked it. Only in broken earth can a seed germinate. Just as a sequoia requires intense heat for the cone to open and let go of its seed, the fire of adversity had melted enough of my ego to open my heart and let go of expectations, freeing me to begin again.

There was little of the anxiety that typically accompanies new jobs. Few knew or cared I was there. As I walked the halls and sat quietly in my new office, there were no grand expectations, not much to prove. There were no thoughts of promotion, for there would be none. All that remained was a yearning to create something special. I never again wanted to have my ego so connected to my position that when one goes, so goes the other. I wanted to learn from and share all I'd learned – the good and bad – to create a successful team and business, a living quilt made with people of all shapes, colors, talents, and passions. I wanted to lead with courage and conviction, to immerse myself in the goal of creating an environment where the best, the brightest, the most creative were attracted, retained and, most importantly, rose to their full potential. Easy to say, but well done is more difficult than well said.

Within a few hours of arriving, Mauricio, Robert, Elan and the rest of the Windows leadership team gathered in a conference room to greet me. So. *She* was the new boss? Each must have been highly underwhelmed as they introduced themselves and explained what they did while I looked back with a blank stare. They threw so many technical words and acronyms at me that I felt like ducking. Did they know how little I knew about the billion-dollar Windows business for which I'd been entrusted? Could they tell I'd had to look up 'operating system' on HowStuffWorks.com and didn't understand either the stuff or how it worked? I was too stupid to understand *Windows for Dummies* but was smart enough to read the skepticism on my teams' faces.

These first moments were important, as they assessed me and I them. This team hadn't been given much support and I had already decided NOT to fake, bluff or pretend to be something I wasn't. I didn't know about their business, but I would learn. I didn't talk about marketing plans, sales results, scorecards or reviews. I simply made them a promise. I promised not to pretend to know what I didn't, be something I wasn't, if they would teach me what I needed to know. In exchange, I'd learn what was good about them and help make them great, to get and give them what they needed to be successful. That's what I said. What they heard was "blah, blah, blah." They were non-believers and assumed I was as all before me.

Despite the best efforts of their interim leader, this team had been getting all the arrows and none of the accolades for a long time. I met with people each week, always asking them to teach me something new – two important things – one about the business they managed and one thing important to them.

At first, they were reluctant; sharing personally and professionally was new and awkward. Like me, the team had learned to don their armor and be on guard within the halls of Microsoft. But like Dudley, I asked and remembered. I remembered that Jake was from Boulder and had in-depth technical knowledge, Eileen and Jennifer were vendors who ran the programs, Zakia was due in October with her first child and was analytical, Robert loved all sports and knew the Partner community better than any, etc. I learned that like quilts, we were each incomplete pieces, but together created something strong and enduring that would withstand the test of time and the storms that come with it. As I asked, listened and came to understand their strengths and what was as important to them, the team came together and began to rally around one another. Which was good because we soon needed to circle the wagons against the dark clouds forming on the horizon, a shit storm called Vista.

The November 2006 Windows Vista launch that Steveb said would be FUN, a real BLAST, one of the BEST jobs in the company was not. Not fun. Not a blast, real or otherwise. Windows Vista, the long-anticipated, long-overdue, super-hyped, critically important next-generation of flagship Windows XP that promised to revolutionize the way the world worked, was a turd even bigger than Scott Paper. And like Scott Paper, management turned to Marketing to blame and fix. We were Marketing. Within a few weeks of taking the job, before I even knew my job, I was under not-so-friendly fire from my ex-peers, CVPs who demanded to know how we had managed to screw up the launch of Vista (such a GREAT product!) and specifically (using precision questioning) what we were going to do to 'fix it"... the marketing, not the product. Obviously, I had not read *Windows For Dummies* well enough to have the answers.

Many people assume having a certain title means you have the answers and nothing fazes you. Nothing could be further from the truth. No title gives you a 'get out of jail free' card from pain and suffering. We all fall, flail and fail sometimes. In truth, courageous leaders fall, flail and fail more than most so that those who follow don't have to.

Despite the help of my team, I felt overwhelmed as I drank from the Windows fire hose. The team buddy-breathed with me as best they could, but mostly I gulped air and tried to keep my head above water. Each day was like entering a dunk tank filled with icy water. I'd climb upon the perch while balls whizzed by, each ball representing someone or something important that I didn't yet know but needed to learn because I was about to walk into a meeting or present on the person/

topic. I'd start the day feeling prepared and cautiously optimistic, until someone inevitably hit the bull's eye of what I didn't know, sending me into the ice bath of unworthiness. WHAM! Dunk! Dammit!!

Just as I'd scramble out of the water and back onto my perch, it seemed another ball would hit, dunking me once again. No matter how often, each time I hit the water I'd flail about, discombobulated. Dunk, splash, *flail*. Dunk, splash, *flail*. Over and over again.

At first, I fought the dunk. I clung hard to my perch, knuckles white, face grim and determined. I tried to avoid customers, partners and issues, to make myself a smaller target. But I couldn't hide. Efforts to resist the dunk were futile.

I began to dread the dunk. Anticipating the dunk was worse than the dunk itself. I could feel my body stiffen, my throat tighten, adrenaline pumping in anticipation of the inevitable, my mind and body on high alert. The more I projected, the more anxious and exhausted I felt.

Yet with each interaction and each dunk, I would eventually get my feet under me and stand up. I saw people extending hands to help me. In my flailing, I hadn't noticed the steadying hands guiding me to my feet. Educating me. Providing resources. Giving support. Dunk, splash, flail, *stand*. Dunk, splash, flail, *stand*. Over and over again.

I began to embrace the dunk. My focus and effort shifted to standing. The more I resisted and flailed about, the more difficult and longer it took to get my footing. As more effort went to standing, less energy was spent avoiding, fighting, and dreading the dunk. Focusing on things I could control reduced both my anxiety and my fear. Even so, I needed to get to my feet faster, which meant I had to flail less and stand more. Yet, this was all that I knew how to do: try harder, dig deeper, do more. The real lesson was in noticing the hands that reached in to help out. The real growth would come if I could accept and trust that the hands reaching for me would bring me into balance.

I had learned to rely on myself growing up. I would rather fall a hundred times on my own than ask for help once. But I *had* fallen a hundred times. More. My knees were scraped and scarred.

A person can flail but not fail if they focus on the 'l' that separates the two words. The letter '*l*' can stand for lots of things... letting go, leaning in, learning, listening, loving. Take your pick, but pick, because without embracing the '*l*' in f*l*ail, all you get is fail. I wanted to let go, lean in, learn and listen, but fear kept getting in the way. One letter. Just one letter makes all the difference. Turn an M upside down and it becomes W. Me becomes We. Me to We. Isolation to fellowship. Inward to outward. Hurt to help. Rotating just one little letter turns a world upside down, or rather, right side up as my mantra 'If it's to be, it's up to Me' became 'If it's to be, it's up to We.'

I was surrounded by people who knew more, were better at their jobs, than I was. It was a constant battle to keep ego at bay, to remind myself to listen and then force myself to shut up so I could learn. Donning the false mask of bravado that said "I'm invincible" was as much a part of my morning routine as brushing my teeth and combing my hair, applied with my foundation and mascara. But I didn't want to fake it; I wanted to be real and honest, as I'd promised.

Lacking the courage or confidence to remove the mask completely, the real Jane behind the mask was revealed bit by bit. Without exception, every person I shared my vulnerability with, each person I asked for help, did so without reservation, graciously. If they judged and found me lacking, I didn't see it. As I got to know the team and they me, my focus shifted from what I was and wasn't to what they were. Unconcerned about being the best or the smartest left space for me to recognize, appreciate and develop the best in them. As Dudley had done for me.

In time, I stopped trying to hide, stopped making myself a smaller target and began to open myself up to understand the issues and needs of my team, partners and customers. I didn't have all the answers and finally began listening and believing what I so often told others "It's okay not to know. We're not in this alone. We've got this." Instead of putting the mask on each morning, I began to put the OA coin in my pocket that says "Together we can do what we can never do alone." When I felt unworthy and terrified of being found out, I reached for the coin and remembered I didn't have to have all the answers, I just needed the courage to seek the answers from others, for others.

One Person Can ~~Only~~ Do So Much

"I am only one, but I am one.
I cannot do everything but I can do something.
And I will not let what I cannot do interfere with what I can do."
— Edward Hale

Each morning is a do-over, a reset, the chance to make and do right, to laugh more, love more, learn from yesterday, live forward, begin again or just begin. Yup, I'm optimistic first thing in the morning, when the door is still open to promise and possibility. I'd walk the halls, greet people and ask how they and projects were doing. Did folks have what they needed? That's when I'd learn about the barriers and blowhards in their way, slamming shut doors of promise, squashing possibilities. It soon became clear that what the team needed of me wasn't IQ, technical expertise or marketing prowess. They needed courage. It wasn't enough for me to stand up, they needed me to *stand up for them*. What I hadn't yet the courage to do for myself, I did for others.

In the beginning, I didn't know (or care) what was or was not proper protocol. Interpreting 'No' as 'not yet' became the new protocol. I simply did/got what the team needed, often while being told how it can't, shouldn't or won't be done. So I didn't ask, I just did. If a partner needed resources, I secured them. If someone was getting pushed aside, being shot at or being dismissed, I stepped in and spoke up. I was a real pain in the ass. When told a customer had hit a roadblock with Vista and was angry, I called the customer directly and maintained regular calls until their problem was addressed. We recruited other teams to merge resources and solve problems. By the end of the year, our effective team and budget was typically 2x, 3x or more than initially allotted. If it was the right thing to do, the team was given permission to proceed, even if we had no funding, confident we would persuade others to provide resources. Like a dog with a bone, my boss called me Bulldog Boulware for the way I doggedly pursued and would not let go until we had what was needed.

In exchange, the team delivered results. Year after year, Windows' targets were exceeded. The team never let me down, which made me work harder to be worthy of their support and loyalty. Despite the challenges and long hours, the Windows team had top scores for morale and job satisfaction. After having spent so much time flailing, it felt good to be on my feet again, standing strong and standing up for others. My sense of humor and smile returned, which softened my bite but not the fierce way I defended and supported my business. The team went from flying below the radar to being highflyers, receiving a disproportionate number of bonuses and awards. Bulldog Boulware. Woof.

Yet it wasn't the resources, promotions, and bonuses that most cherished most. Yes, those were important and necessary. The things people still remember and remark upon 10+ years after working together were the words written and spoken ... scribbled notes of thanks, emails quickly written to recognize achievements, words of appreciation, encouragement, recognition, understanding and concern genuinely given. And received. I've come to understand that you can't give authentic praise and gratitude to others if you're unwilling to see and receive it in yourself.

Notecards became a Windows team trademark. Within a few days of starting as Windows General Manager, I ordered a large box of personalized notecards with my name and Windows logo. I didn't write much, but each note was specific, personal and heartfelt.

> Dear Eileen, GREAT JOB on creating the new partner training program! The feedback has been fantastic! Matt at Dell specifically called you out for your ongoing support and proactivity! Way to go!
>
> Wole, your demo last week was a home run! You showcased Windows features that met Customer X's specific needs, reflecting how well you listen and know the technology. I learn something new every time I watch one of your demos. I see how hard you work to make it look so easy. You nailed it! Thank you!
>
> Fei – Wow! You really know your stuff! Thanks for being the 'go-to' person for me, the team and others. Your deep, deep understanding of Windows and ability to answer even the hardest technical question is much appreciated! Thanks for being so helpful and willing to share so generously all you know.

Handwritten cards were left on people's desks, sent through interoffice and US mail. I kept notecards and a list of people/achievements in my backpack for when I had a spare moment to jot someone a note and didn't leave for the weekend until each person was recognized. When there are a lot of good people doing lots of good work, you go through a lot of stationery. I went through my first box quickly. Then another. And another.

I began to see the notecards displayed on people's desks, taped to their walls and used as coasters. I was considered a very demanding boss with high expectations and so receiving a handwritten note meant something. It didn't matter if you were a Microsoft Bluebadge, vendor, partner or other – all deserved and received recognition of professional and personal milestones. Soon, the entire Windows team began sending notes of thanks and praise – thanking the sales organization for closing a bid deal, thanking partners for resolving a gnarly problem, thanking customers for their input and commitment, recognizing one another for achievements, milestones, results.

It's easier to congratulate than to correct. Nothing is more cowardly than leaders who haven't the courage to address problems. On my team, my problem was Ethan. Ethan had been on the team for several years before I joined. Each year he was passed over for a promotion, told he wasn't quite ready. Truth is, Ethan was never going to be promoted, which everyone knew but Ethan. He was a great guy. He worked hard. It wasn't a matter of ability or attitude: he knew his job, was committed and had a can-do spirit. Ethan simply wasn't the detail oriented, project manager the job required. He was a big picture, creative guy who wasn't great with numbers and it showed in his work. Ethan didn't have the aptitude for the job he was in. Round hole, square peg.

Everyone isn't good at every job, but everyone is good at something. By keeping Ethan in his role, *I* was failing *him*. I owed it to my employee to have the tough conversation, so, soon after joining my new team, Ethan and I sat down. I tried to be kind, but direct; yet as I spoke, I witnessed a man whom I respected and admired crumble before my eyes, head bowed, shoulders sagging as if he were carrying a burden too heavy to bear. Then his shoulders shook as he began to sob. Ethan knew he was failing. He had been trying harder and harder yet felt more and more defeated each year. His wife had been asking why others were promoted and not him. Despite putting up a brave front, he felt uncomfortable and embarrassed around his peers. It was difficult to witness Ethan's pain, watching confidence and bravado flow from his eyes.

Oh God. What had I done? I felt horrible sitting there, unsure what to do, how to proceed. We talked quietly while I answered a few questions, then left the room to give Ethan time to regroup. When I returned, we transitioned the conversation to areas where he excelled, his dim eyes slowly lighting up as we discussed his interests and strengths. Ethan left the team soon after; it didn't take long to find a new role that played to his strengths. I kept track of Ethan from a distance until our paths crossed a few years later. He approached me with a huge hug and big smile. Ethan was happy. And successful. He said our tough conversation changed the course of his career. In finding a role that played to his strengths, he'd reignited his passion, experienced success, regained his confidence and his life. I had never told anyone about our difficult conversation, but here he was openly thanking me for the day I made him cry. Which brought tears to my eyes.

Despite working in a pressure cooker that made me crispy at times, I really liked my job, loved my team and did my best for both. Yes, I was demanding, difficult, defiant, impatient and stubborn. I was also courageous, authentic, tenacious, smart, loyal and supportive. I tried to enter a room with positive energy, a welcoming smile and a kind word; a kind word releases tension as surely as one cynical comment creates it. One person can do so much. One person can change the direction of a meeting, a team, an outcome by what is said... and isn't. But my bar was high and I didn't suffer fools lightly. People who were positive, learning and trying their best received my best. Woe to those who were negative, ill prepared, or unwilling to help others. They were soon gone. Positive GSDs (Get Stuff Done) people attract the same. Top players hire people better than themselves, while B players hire C players so they can feel superior. If you hire people better than yourself from the beginning, in the end you'll be surrounded by friends you want to be like, not just employees who want to be like you.

Keeping an eye on the entrance of a room, I could look out for the hesitant, the unsure, the outsider entering the room. I knew just what to look for, having so often entered rooms filled with many yet knowing none. All it takes is one person, one quiet gesture – a quick wave, a smile, a nod – to welcome the new and different, to make the invisible visible and bring outsiders in. At Microsoft, the invisible outsiders were often women.

Outside In

*"Your crown has been bought and paid for.
Put it on your head and wear it."*

— Dr Maya Angelou

Most days I believed I had the best job, the best team and the most fun. On the other days I was insecure, was unable to secure funding, the team bickered, and work was a grind. While leading the US launches of Windows Vista, 7, 8 and 10, I'd become fluent in operating system TLAs (three letter acronyms). I could confidently speak entire sentences and have conversations using almost no words found in Webster's dictionary:

"IPsec is integrated with Windows Firewall and supports IPv6, including IKE, AuthIP and NAP."

Once it became clear NAP was network access protection and not a snooze taken after a big meal, I understood the enormous complexity and responsibility of keeping a company's information and people safe. I'd launched Huggies diapers with 'Leak Guards' to help moms avoid diaper blowouts. Now, 10 years later at Microsoft, I was launching Windows with 'Defender' to help corporations avoid hacker exploits. Different words, same crap.

We'd taken the $ billion Windows business to record results. I was proud of the achievement but was most proud of the people who stretched and grew while growing the business, those who became more than what they thought they could or would be. Among these, I was especially proud of the women.

For the first two decades of my career, women in leadership or executive positions were rare. Women leaders were the exception so had to be exceptional professionally yet fit in personally. In the 80s and 90s those who 'made it' typically did so by assuming a persona – cheerleader, little sister/jock, butch, sexy. I wasn't a cheerleader, sexy or butch. That left little sister/jock, which fit me like a golf glove. My presence was non-threatening to the guys and their wives, none of whom gave me a second look. Which I saw as a good thing.

Today, only one in five senior leaders is a woman, despite women earning more bachelor's degrees and MBAs than men and staying in the workforce at the same rate as men. Progress isn't just slow, it's stalled, according to the annual McKinsey Women in the Workplace study of 279 companies employing 13 million employees. MIT found women receive higher performance ratings and are less likely to quit than male employees but are 14% less likely to be promoted than their male colleagues. I don't get it. Not recognizing and utilizing half the workforce is akin to driving using only one hand and making only right hand turns, forever circling around and around and around the same track. No wonder progress is going nowhere.

The Kents believe women aren't as motivated to advance and excel as men. Not true. I was approached almost weekly by women seeking coaching or mentoring. There aren't enough women or people of color at the top to mentor all those trying to get there. At one point, I counted 27 people on my calendar with whom I'd meet before breakfast, for breakfast, over coffee, over lunch, etc. By the end of the day, I was wired and tired from the coffee and discussing the same well-known issues outsiders faced, regardless of title, background or age. There were more seeking my time than I had time to give, so I began mentoring only those who mentored at least five others, which quickly weeded out anyone willing to *take my* time/support but unwilling to *give their* time/support to others. I championed a Career and Professional Development Program targeted to women and minorities, yet open to everyone. Unfortunately, the people who volunteered and attended were seldom the people in the castle tower who held the keys to real change.

There are good reasons many executive women looked the other way when asked to mentor, sponsor, advocate and empower other women. Too busy. Didn't want to play favorites. Didn't know how. True enough, but not good enough. It was relatively easy to find someone willing to be a sage on a stage, or perhaps host an occasional event, but difficult to find mentors for women who didn't have 'high potential' stamped on their foreheads.

I wondered if there was more to it.

Many I mentored, from newbie to the most senior executive, shared similar feelings of inadequacy and imposter syndrome. They often looked, dressed, thought, and sounded different than the many, which made them outsiders. Being an outsider was bad…if it weren't, they wouldn't be on the outside, right? Outsiders received coaching on how to act, sit and speak to 'improve their impact'… to be more like the many… signaling differences were not only different, but not as good, ergo *they* were not as good. In trying to fit in, outsiders reigned in or downplayed unique strengths and capabilities, diminished their impact, diminished themselves. Of course they had imposter syndrome; they were impersonating insiders to fit in, to keep from standing out as an outsider.

Mentees wanted to know my recipe, the secret sauce that made me successful. Most had devoured and could quote leadership and management books, had listened to podcasts and speakers that made success look easy, inevitable. Just follow these simple steps. But following the steps led them to despair. "*They* have it all figured out... *I* couldn't possibly...*if only I* had..." comments reflected their fear, uncertainty, and despair (friggin' FUD).

Mentoring was often as simple as holding a mirror up to reflect the incredible achievements and capabilities outsiders overlooked in themselves. Outsiders knew the answers to their questions better than I but sought my validation because they lacked confidence to trust their own voice. Not surprising I suppose, considering the number of voices telling them to lower their voice. We're quick to assign labels to women. My personal favorite is bitch. Sometimes I need to use a sharp edge to cut through the rigid barriers between me and where I need to go. Men are called strong and elevated while women are labeled a bitch and denigrated for having a sharp edge. Labels are like crowns; others may place a label on my head, but only I chose which label to wear.

Microsoft women continued to dismiss or be dismissed, to downplay achievements, secretly fearing they were not ready or worthy of their role/title. Harvard Business School found women consistently self-promote less than men. Women self-evaluated their performance lower (46 vs 61) despite having the same *or higher* scores than men. Women's promotions often come with a shadow of doubt from the nudge-nudge, wink-wink Kents who imply, but seldom overtly state, an outsider's promotion/position is not earned, but is given due to gender, color, or other bullshit reasons. False whispers become poisonous ear worms.

Some asked how to become a FEARLESS LEADER, like me. Yikes! I used to relish being called fearless. But acting fearless made me feel like a fraud. There is a cowardly lion behind most people's roar. EVERYONE is afraid. I wish there was a secret recipe or How To book to eliminate fear. There isn't. The best I can do is try to be less fear full...to fear less...not be fearless. It's okay to be scared. Fear is a good indicator – am I truly in danger or am I simply outside my comfort zone? Discomfort doesn't kill; it just feels that way sometimes. Tums usually helps.

The pressure to do more, be more, is especially strong in women. No matter how much is done, it's never enough because you're running several races simultaneously - work, parent, partner, friend, family - with no finish line. The pressure didn't go away, it intensified, once I earned the promotion, had the baby, lost the weight, for there was ever more to be done. Even after reaching the top in title, I still felt like an outsider on the inside. The pressure I felt didn't abate until my focus shifted. From thinking of myself as someone who didn't belong, who had to fight the many or change to fit in. Microsoft insiders wanted innovation so long as it occurred the same way it had always had, before outsiders threatened 'when things were good.' But things were never good for outsiders.

Ascending the castle wall is hard. It's even harder to make it to the top tower. It is easy (and justified) for women in the towers to revel in their achievement. But victory isn't reaching the top, it's helping others ascend. Victory is claimed only when women and Dudleys lower the drawbridge and provide rope to enable outsiders below to come inside and up. When we make outsiders insiders versus threats, all will be able to contribute fully and ascend equally. Only then will we finally stop driving around and around in circles and start driving real progress and innovation. That's 'when things will be good' for all.

Doing What 'Can't' Be Done

*"Nothing has ever been achieved
by the person who says 'It can't be done.'"*

— Eleanor Roosevelt

While I'd been getting my legs back under me on Windows, Apple had taken the legs out from under Windows and Microsoft by introducing a tsunami of revolutionary consumer devices like iPad, iPod and MacBook. As if it weren't bad enough that Apple (and Google) devices were gaining the hearts and wallets of consumers, Microsoft began to see iPads and MacBooks infiltrating the enterprise. What? Foul! Microsoft *owned* the enterprise. But like fruit flies, Apple products just showed up and multiplied despite not being on IT's 'approved' PC lists. The guys in the IT department were being overrun by the folks in marketing and sales who purchased Apple tablets without first getting approval of the IT or Purchasing departments. Anarchy! Since Apple didn't run Windows, Word, Excel, etc, this was bad, very bad for Microsoft. Enterprise customers and software sales were Microsoft's bread and butter.

Apple was cool. So was Steve Jobs. Windows PCs were not. Neither was Steve Ballmer. The "I'm a PC" advertising campaign did little to dispel the reality that PCs made by HP, Dell, Lenovo, etc. were dull and quickly losing ground to Apple, who was taking a bigger and bigger bite of PC sales. Microsoft was frustrated that PC makers were not introducing designs that leveraged touch screens and other innovative Windows features to compete with Apple. Instead, PC makers competed against one another for a smaller piece of a smaller pie. So Microsoft did something remarkable and bold. Microsoft designed and introduced their own device called Surface to compete directly with Apple, setting a new standard of excellence for Windows PCs. In doing so, Microsoft leapfrogged Dell, HP, Lenovo, etc. Boy oh boy, did that make the old frogs croak!

It was into this pond I leapt.

Surface was designed to compete against Apple for the hearts and wallets of cool people. Surface was a revolutionary, super-premium product at a super-premium price, so few at Microsoft thought it would appeal to enterprise customers, who were budget constrained, concerned about function over form…and were generally not cool. So when I was approached about forming an organization to compete against Apple in the enterprise, I leapt at the chance. I became the first-ever VP of Windows Devices. There was no precedent at Microsoft for what I'd been tasked to do: create a sales and marketing organization accountable for selling Windows devices including Surface *and* HP *and* Dell *and* Lenovo *and* Asus etc. to commercial customers. Basically, the goal was to keep Apple iPads *out* and get/keep Windows tablets *in* the enterprise. No one had a clue how to do it. Many thought it couldn't be done. We didn't know what it would take, if it was possible or even how to track, measure or reward success. It was my dream job.

I knew no one better at achieving the impossible than Juliana, my business manager and right arm on Windows, who could move mountains or orchestrate a way to tunnel through or around them with organized precision. She was good at everything I was not…and many things I was. Juliana was my first recruit.

Now all we needed was a sales organization. Position descriptions were written en route to the annual sales and marketing conference. I was given 15 minutes on the agenda to talk about the device team I was forming. It didn't' take 15 minutes. I had jotted only a few notes on a scrap of paper. I didn't know much. So that's what I said.

"We don't have everything figured out, but we'll figure it out together. It's probably easier to say what we don't have yet. We have no job titles, no playbook, no supporting infrastructure, no quotas or incentive system. What we have is an opportunity to create a new business and culture where we'll be holding the pen writing the rules. To be successful, candidates must be passionate self-starters who thrive in ambiguity, like running through walls and creating what doesn't yet exist. I promise you will have at least as much fun as frustration. And I promise to have your back. Any questions?" There were none. "Anyone interested in learning more should contact me." More silence.

I felt myself channeling Kathi, the President from Kimberly-Clark who had so often been accused of being rah rah. But passion and enthusiasm were two things I had to offer that were in short supply at Microsoft. I was breathing fire, chewing nails and spitting vinegar and looking for others willing to eat from the same menu. After all, I wasn't recruiting accountants. But I didn't expect salespeople in the room to be interested either. After all, these were super-seasoned, super-successful Microsoft salespeople working in coveted jobs for which they were paid mightily and respected mostly. I was gobsmacked to find myself the belle of the ball with whom all wanted to dance, as salesperson after salesperson reached out to Juliana and me with requests to interview for the new team. Never underestimate the power of passion + opportunity. Together with a handful of people, we scrambled to set up formal interviews and covert meetings until by week's end, we'd filled the majority of key roles on the team.

As expected, the folks in Human Resources worried we were not following protocol and moving too fast, which is what HR is paid to do. I didn't think we were going fast enough, which is what I was paid to do. So many 'top tier' sellers had applied that I was suddenly ruffling the feathers of traditional team leaders who were upset about losing their best salespeople. Passion attracts the passionate. Great attracts greater. Soon my 'top tier' sellers recruited 'top-tier' sellers and in record time, we had ourselves a 'top-tier' device team My approach was simple:

1. Attract and hire people better at what they do than me (this turned out to be easier than expected)

2. Create clear and mutual measures of success (less easy given we didn't know what success looked like or how to measure it)

3. Get the team what they need to be successful (Many, many people provided help and support)

4. Remove barriers in their way - including myself (Bulldog Boulware - check)

5. Recognize and reward justly and generously. (tricky given #2 but doable given #4. Woof.)

We were all set to set the world on fire. But we couldn't get a spark, much less a flame.

Fueled by passion and seeing abundant opportunity everywhere, my device sellers came sprinting from the gate ready to change the world but soon hit wall after wall of resistance from the risk-averse world of corporate IT who generally saw change as a threat. The tech guys liked to evolve rather than innovate, knowing they'd lose their job if something didn't work and receive no glory if it did. Rather than a sprint, the sales cycle became a slog as tech departments took their time doing proofs of concept before purchasing devices. In the meantime, we watched in frustration as Apple whizzed past in the express lane, bypassing the IT tech departments altogether. Not used to failing (and by all measures, we were failing), our lack of sales demoralized the team and validated all who said we couldn't/wouldn't be successful and grumbled about disbanding the team altogether.

Being from Iowa, I likened our team's situation to popping corn on the stove. "My job is to provide the best pan and oil. Your job is to provide the kernels of opportunities. Together, we apply heat and movement. Eventually the kernels of opportunity will pop, slowly at first, but in time the pan will overflow as the reality becomes much greater than the initial opportunity. Trust me. I'm from Iowa and make a lot of popcorn. I know these things." And so I did and so it did.

The first really big sale came from Eric and Pallavi. They sold 60k tablets to Royal Caribbean after teams around the world worked night and day to design apps and tablets that met Royal Caribbean's unique needs for its state-of-the-art, technology-enabled cruise ship. In the end, it was just the first of many, many more sales. Pop. Pop! POP!! Our pan poppeth over. The day the Royal Caribbean deal was announced in the *Wall Street Journal*, Microsoft's stock price shot up. The work of our Surface and Device Team had been noted by Wall Street, signaling Microsoft was finally competing in the hardware game for real and was playing to win. It was just the beginning.

Little was expected of the team yet we delivered big, selling hundreds of thousands of devices into the enterprise. Known as the honey badgers for the fierce way we pursued opportunities and wouldn't give up or be deterred, the team shared strengths, fears and motivation until our stories, loyalty and commitment intertwined. I kept my promise to have the team's back and together we created a new business and a culture that has kept us committed and connected to this day.

In time, the impossible happened. Sales of Surface to enterprise customers exceeded consumer sales! Impossible! Can't be done!! Unconcerned with what couldn't, shouldn't or wouldn't be done, we just did. Each win was celebrated within the extended team and was communicated in updates that converted the non-believers into believers. It took well over a year of hard work, helping hands and perseverance before the team proclaimed success… and for the non-believers to begin claiming credit for the team's success.

Many on my team received well-deserved rewards, awards and promotions. I did not. I'd like to say it didn't matter to me. It did. A little. Several of the women (and men) now lead global sales organizations. *That* matters to me. A lot.

Looking back, I came to Microsoft as a CVP with the pedigree, persona and position that should have been a slam dunk success. Instead I failed, experiencing closed doors and hallways filled with rare air, loneliness, and FUD. Humbled and demoted, I changed course and took two roles unlikely to succeed… only to experience unprecedented success, impact, fellowship and purpose beyond job title or expectations. In the process of letting go and redefining success, success found and redefined me.

Home

"There's no place like home. There's no place like home. There's no place like home."

— Dorothy

When I left behind the CVP role and title, I promised myself I'd be the same Jane at work and home. Almost every manager I knew at Microsoft kept their work/team life and personal lives separate. Or if the two did occasionally intersect, it was a well-orchestrated and somewhat awkward affair. Yet I had experienced how great it was to work with friends and people you care about. For me, work is about people and people are personal. So the doors to my home welcomed all.

Upon arrival, all are met by Frank and Bud, the true hosts of my home. They flank the front door, greeting and providing blessing to all who cross the threshold. Literally. Frank and Bud are statues of St Francis (Frank) and Buddha (Bud) who stand together at the base of a fountain just to the left of our front door. Both are smiling with arms raised to the heavens, welcoming each and every one regardless of faith, heritage, politics, orientation, color or circumstance. Frank and Bud welcome all but intolerance.

Regardless of how busy, unless I was traveling, Scott, Andy, Jack and I ate together each night at a small wood table that was over a century old and magical – it even had a lightning bolt scratched [on] top. Around the magic table Scott, Andy, Jack and I a[te] and discussed something new over dinner. Many of the [ideas] created and lessons I learned over dinner carried over to [work,] vice versa. The boys taught me the importance of asking the right questions, then listening to the answer received, not given. Questions are windows that both open and close. When the boys were little, Scott and I asked Andy and Jack how their day was only to hear an unenthusiastic "okay" in response. Window closed. Instead, we began asking the boys to 'teach me something new' during dinner. Shazam! Window open! Andy and Jack came alive as each took turns sharing something they'd learned/read/saw that day. Finally! It was *their* turn to teach and *our* turn to listen.

Over the years, the 'something new' evolved. In grade school, a great conversation about tongue rolling ability would naturally lead to attempts to touch tongues to noses or elbows (alas, I can do neither). The same conversation in high school led to conversations about genetics and evolution. A simple question, a simple invitation to 'teach me something new' created a window into Andy and Jack's world through which Scott and I learned what sparked their interest and made each come alive.

The same thing happened when applying 'teach me something new' at work. Windows flew open. "What do you think is most important for me to know? What action do you think is needed? What is and isn't working? What didn't I ask that you would have?" Within the team, questions showed respect and strength, not weakness. The only thing experts love more than sharing their expertise is being asked to do so. Only Ego expects to know all despite asking nothing. Whether young or old, around a dinner or conference table, asking to be taught something new unleashes knowledge and generates enthusiasm, replacing the fear of not knowing with curiosity.

~~un~~WORTHY

never forgot how easily and comfortably Dudley, a K-C executive, had brought me into his home for hot dogs, removing any perception that he was different or better than me in any way, despite his title. He made no effort to impress me with his home (it was beautiful) or his car (it was not), effortlessly impressing me far more by what he didn't do or say.

And so, years later, like Dudley, I invited people to gather for simple meals. Scott welcomed all with a glass of wine and the boys set another place at the table, seldom knowing who might be joining us or where the conversation would lead. The house came alive as we said grace and broke bread with gays and straights, old and young, liberals and conservatives of all religions or none at all, people we had known for years or had just met. Our family by blood lived many miles away, but our family by choice gathered close. The boys heard, participated, and absorbed all, the great and the gritty, the funny and the frustrating. As a 9-year-old, my son Jack once laid his head on the table one evening and groaned, "why can't we just have a normal dinner like other people?" after our guest, Jan, informed Jack mid-sentence and mid-bite that she was happily married… to a woman. Without missing a beat, she went back to chewing and the conversation at hand. The initial shock wore off and upon that simple base of honesty and acceptance, Jan and Jack forged a friendship that extends to this day.

All were invited around the table, even people I'd just met at the airport, for I knew what it was like to be away from home night after night, which sounds exciting and fun until you do it so often that even the best meals at the finest restaurants taste of loneliness.

Scott, Andy, Jack and I were constantly humbled and amazed by how much we learned and grew through the years from people sitting around the table. If nothing else, my kids learned there is no 'us' vs 'them.' We are all we. Our table is where people came together without pretense and where friends became family amid a chorus of chaos, clinking, baking, burning, shouting, smiling, grace, griping and laughter until "how did it get so late" was heard, hugs and goodbyes were exchanged, and people again crossed the threshold, taking with them warm memories and leftovers as Frank and Bud silently extended their grace.

Enough

*"An injury isn't just a process of recovery
it's a process of discovery."*

— Conor McGregor

"At the end of pain is success!" Have you ever noticed that this saying always has an exclamation point after the word success, as if declaring as fact that pain magically goes away once success is achieved? If you endure enough pain, success will follow, and all will be well. If only.

My leg had slowed me enough to appreciate things I had taken for granted, to notice the things I had overlooked. But the chronic physical pain in my leg was taking me down, step by step, draining my energy and spirit. So after five years of unsuccessful surgeries and therapy to remove the pain in my leg, after years of walking carefully, Scott and I weighed how much more I could and should lean in versus put up with what I had. Would the end of pain occur after just one more surgery? Or would one more surgery create more pain? I returned to Dr. H, who had diagnosed my broken leg years earlier, for guidance.

Removing all the hardware in my leg – the plates, screws, rods, etc. – was risky. Too risky, he counseled. "Jane, your leg is like Swiss cheese, full of holes from all the different screws put in and taken out of you. The hardware provides needed support. If removed, there may not be enough bone mass or structural strength left to support you. Without the hardware, you may not be able to walk on your leg at all." Oh. Well. Hmmm.

The hardware provided support, but at the cost of pain and limited mobility. At what odds do you risk not walking again – 10%, 20%, 40%, 50%? I didn't even know where to begin to assess the math on this. When it comes to making business decisions, I love numbers. I love to analyze, assess, project, connect, slice and dice until the numbers release their secrets and spill their guts, indicating a clear path forward. But this decision wasn't about the numbers. Like most of the decisions Scott and I made, if we assessed the degree of risk based on the numbers, we would never have married, never left Iowa and not done most of what we did. Our brains told us the numbers weren't in our favor and begged us to listen to the experts whose counsel we had sought. But when experts looked at me, they saw only what was broken and couldn't be fixed. They saw how far I had come, not how far I had yet to go. They wanted me to be satisfied with the something I had, but I yearned for the everything I needed. So while my brain screamed DANGER, my heart softly whispered *courage, faith, trust.*

We met with Dr. H again; he was the only person I trusted to perform the surgery. Again he said he did not recommend the surgery. Bugger. I learned that Dr. H was about to go on an extended holiday. Would I like to schedule my pre-op appointments with his staff while he was out, the scheduler asked? Yes! Yes, I would!

I trusted Dr. H's professional counsel but didn't follow it, for I had long ago discovered that perseverance and passion tipped the scale of probability in my favor. I would rather risk all than live a compromised life that others thought was good enough. A life that's 'good enough' isn't.

It was 6am Monday morning when Dr. H looked up from his clipboard, recognition dawning on his face. "It's *you*," he said with a look of disdain as he realized I'd been scheduled for surgery he'd recommended against. I didn't mind. It wasn't the first time in my life I'd heard those words and seen that expression. I had already been prepped for surgery by his staff and was determined to go forward with the surgery – and was not above begging. In the end, he agreed and the hardware was removed.

A few hours later in post-op, I heard the surgery was successful; the metal had not calcified and was easily removed as if knowing it had done its job but was now hurting the leg it was intended to help. I listened with tears running down my face, for I already knew all that. My leg had told me so. There was no ache emanating from within my bones. The ethereal filaments of perpetual pain binding my body and spirit were gone.

Despite the odds, recovery was quick and complete. Within weeks I was reclaiming ability and confidence, my leg enabling what it had un-abled for the last five years. The support of plates and screws were replaced by the strength, courage, faith and resolve my heart had lent it. From the beginning, the numbers and experts had not been in my favor. In the end, my recovery required discovering the expert voice I trusted and relied on the most – my own – and so tipping the scale of probability in my favor. It's true. Sometimes at the end of pain *is* success!

Correction of Errors

"Your life does not get better by chance; it gets better by change."
— Jim Rohn

On the outside, all was well. My family was flourishing and happy. The device team had gained momentum and recognition. Despite renewed physical mobility, my world became smaller as I spent more time in meetings and business reviews than with customers or partners, and more effort in defending than enabling the team. I couldn't shake a growing sense of disquiet and discontent.

Microsoft was undergoing a cultural shift under the leadership of Kevin Turner, who had been hired by Steve Ballmer to tame Microsoft's wild, wild west ways. Kevin Turner, known as KT, was a seasoned exec hired as Chief Operating Officer to create a culture of fiscal accountability. KT came to Microsoft like a sheriff slinging a big gun and a saddlebag full of business scorecards.

"You manage what you measure," became a popular new saying within Microsoft. The device team was being measured within an inch of our lives. Too big to be treated as a startup that could fly undetected and under the radar, success had put us on the firing line. The scrutiny was understandable given how much the business had grown and how much visibility Wall Street was placing on Surface/Windows tablet sales vs Apple/iPad sales. A battle for the enterprise was underway. There was a lot at stake. But the team was still learning to fly, still building the wings and instrument panel as our plane soared, leaving lots of ways to interpret which direction and how high we were flying.

KT's scorecards measured and assigned green, yellow or red to virtually every activity done by sales and marketing teams. Green was good. Red was not. Those whose sales or marketing targets had become red were quickly shot by the big guns. The professed goal was to create targets that were SMART (specific, measurable, attainable, relevant and time-bound). In reality, goals were set to achieve aggressive targets based more on Wall Street's expectations than market realities.

Soon the culture became so scorecard centric and fear-based that managers would do almost anything to avoid missing their targets, even if it sometimes undermined the business and the people. Those who missed their numbers 'went red' and were dutifully flogged in a Correction of Errors (COE) business review until they were once again 'in the green' and out of the firing line. You could tell which teams were caught in a red Correction of Errors death spiral by their pale pallor and slumped shoulders. Once caught in the grip of a COE, it became a game of survival where people's self-worth and career were on the line. Businesses stuck in the red were guilty until proven innocent and subjected to weekly inquisition, which only ended once you became green or were reassigned to a new job.

When people care more about avoiding failure than achieving success, they stop playing to win and begin playing not to lose. There is no winning a game played not to lose. Mistakes can be milestones from which you build and grow or crushing millstones under which you stumble and fall. Accountability creates confidence while flogging creates fear and casualties. I know, because even though my scorecard was usually green, I began to invest more and more energy in avoiding red and defending results rather than taking risks and celebrating successes.

My top tier sales team began toppling from the time spent logging, reporting and uploading data into a system created by Paul and analyzed by Jason who became so proficient at data slicing and dicing that he was reverently known as The Sword. Juliana took The Sword's information and smooshed it into an Excel spreadsheet, which spit out a graph that was cut and pasted into PowerPoint slides I pored over prior to presenting from the front line.

Correction of Error business reviews occurred monthly if green and weekly if red, starting before 8am and ending past 6pm, with patience and humor waning as the minutes slowly passed. The too small conference room was filled with the smell of taco bar, Sterno and fear as two dozen executives responsible for managing billion-dollar businesses sat glassy eyed and numb, avoiding eye contact in case they got asked a precision question they didn't know how to answer and would throw others under the bus to save themselves. Tensions mounted as chests constricted, anxiously dreading the clock's advance toward the allotted time to plead your case and receive a verdict…a green stay of execution…or RED! Go to COE jail! Do not pass go, do not collect $200. Only this was not a game. Executives torn to shreds in those meetings often did the same to their teams the following day, until everyone felt like confetti… without the celebration.

Perhaps one of the more bizarre but well-intentioned gestures of support I received at Microsoft was being handed a tube of Preparation H just prior to entering a COE review. "It'll reduce the bags and dark circles under your eyes… never show signs of weakness, Jane." Uh… Thanks? It did indeed help the dark circles under my eyes but did not help me see the dark swirl and strain I carried home each day.

It was impossible to spend long days at work scrutinizing and wallowing in what wasn't right, then magically switch gears once home. I know. I tried. My negativity formed a dark cloud that followed me over the threshold, raining toxic thoughts that drowned the good and made it difficult for positivity to get a foothold. Research shows the average person has up to 60,000 thoughts per day and roughly 80%-95% are negative (closer to 100% if in a COE), creating negativity bias.

People experiencing negativity bias:

- remember traumatic experiences better than positive ones
- think about negative things more frequently than positive
- recall insults better than praise
- react more strongly to negative stimuli
- respond more strongly to negative events than to equally positive ones

Check, Check, Check, Check, Check. Ugh.

Scott responded by amplifying the negativity I brought home, creating a nasty swirl that began spiraling out of control despite our best efforts. We became so raw that even the most innocent comment chaffed. Our marriage was going red; we needed a COE... without the firing line. I turned to Karla Obernesser, dear friend, marriage counselor and co-founder of WeDoRelationships. I respected and trusted Karla immensely but didn't want to cross the line from friend to counselor. She told me about Drs John and Julie Gottman, renowned authorities on marriage and creators of the Gottman Method, the world's leading approach to couples therapy. Karla suggested looking for a Gottman Certified Counselor. I looked for the Gottmans. I didn't have far to look. Their practice was in Seattle.

Dr John Gottman is known for conducting 40+ years of research on marital stability. John Gottman can watch a 10-minute conversation between romantic partners and identify patterns of behavior that with 90% accuracy predict divorce in the next six years. So naturally, he wanted to meet with Scott and I before agreeing to counsel us. It was like sitting down beside a very wise, kind, kinda rumpled grandpa wearing a yarmulke in a room filled to the brim with books and papers. But this was no Hallmark movie and John was Dr Gottman, not my grandpa. As we talked, Dr Gottman discreetly assessed and mentally calculated the likely success of our marriage and whether he could help us.

Over the next months, John guided us through the Gottman Method. He exposed us to information and skills we hadn't learned or experienced growing up, like how to overcome gridlock, turn toward vs away, make and receive bids for connection. He helped us recreate a shared sense of meaning. We learned having a 5:1 ratio of positive to negative language can predict successful relationships and that happy couples have a 20:1 ratio of positive to negative expressions when simply conversing. Drs John and Julie Gottman found the four behavioral predictors of divorce or break-up are criticism, defensiveness, contempt and stonewalling. They call these the Four Horsemen of the Apocalypse.

There was much to learn and unlearn. Change is hard, but Scott and I were motivated. We changed horses, became intentional about noting the positive in one another and learned to fight better because our relationship was worth fighting for. In truth, I have worked more and fought harder for my marriage than anything else in my life. Sometimes it felt our relationship hung by a thread. Not a golden thread, mind you, but a natty piece of twine, frayed and grey, at risk of snapping under the weight. When things got too heavy, friends and counseling lightened my spirit, rekindled my commitment, and helped me hang on until I could dispel the darkness of negativity and find my way back to seeing the positive in Scott, others and life. For me, marriage takes a community effort and requires constant care, maintenance and adjustment.

In the process of meeting and getting to know us, John encouraged me to put my thoughts and stories to paper, to write a book. He handed me the business card of his publisher (I think it was his publisher?), telling me to call him when I was ready. I taped that business card to the bottom corner of my PC, where my gaze tends to land. It represents hope, I guess. It's been years since I first taped that card. Over time, the tape starts to curl a bit at the edges. Occasionally, I adhere new tape to the old, so there are now several layers securing that card. But the card stayed stuck. So did our marriage. Without John's encouragement and counseling, I likely wouldn't be married, and you likely wouldn't be reading this book.

Whatever I focus on becomes bigger while everything else recedes. When I focus on errors, I find plenty. A focus on correcting the errors of others is a mistake that put my relationships in the red at home and at work. Conversely, there is a gob of research by the Gottmans, Mayo Clinic, Harvard, National Institute of Health etc on benefits of positivity and a positive mindset, including:

- better relationships
- improved productivity, creativity and engagement
- improved emotional and physical health
- reduced stress; happier and more confident
- attracting positivity and positive people (because it's contagious and likeable!)

Check, Check, Check, Check, Check. Yay!

I couldn't change the culture at Microsoft. Enduring the constant COE focus on what was wrong was exhausting. But resistance is not futile. My team and others made time to laugh, celebrate, support and reinforce the small things that make big differences. By doing small things often, my relationship with Scott and others went from red to green, from a correction of errors to a celebration of successes. In the process, my view changed, my perspective changed, my future changed. I changed. Because life does not get better by chance; it gets better by change. Check.

Time Out

"Taking care of yourself doesn't mean me first, it means me too."
— L.R. Knost

By my calculation, I'd been supporting myself and others for more than 30 years, mostly in 'stretch' leadership roles. But my stretch was sagging like an old pair of underwear that had initially fit well, felt good and moved naturally, but was now a bit frayed and worn around the edges, prone to riding up. I needed a break. I was lucky. I qualified for and was approved for a 10-week sabbatical, enough time to get the snap back in my britches.

I had not taken so much time off work since my teens. Taking a sabbatical seemed a fantasy. Microsoft would *pay* me to *not* work? Inconceivable! I felt giddy and guilty at the same time. While many Microsoft folks go on significant once-in-a-lifetime adventures during their sabbaticals – safaris in Africa, summer in Tuscany, hiking Machu Picchu – I went to Iowa. Then spent the rest of my sabbatical locally, doing normal things in a normal way. I was in heaven experiencing life from my deck instead of my desk. I had meals with friends and family and took walks with Scott as I hadn't in decades. All with no urgent texts pinging, no critical emails waiting, no important reports, presentations or reviews pending.

After a few weeks of checking in with my team "just to see how things were going," I began to realize most texts, emails and reviews weren't urgent, critical or terribly important after all. Huh. I began to forget my phone, leaving it behind when I left the house. Huh? I began to laugh and sing out loud. What? For reasons I couldn't explain, I took pictures of my feet… propped up on the railing of our deck, in the ice-cold water of a mountain stream, at concerts, beside a campfire, in the cool grass. Each day was greeted with the same "Buckle up Buster!" attitude that I had as a young girl. Scott and I held hands; Jack and I hiked. I felt a foot taller, having sloughed the weight of Microsoft temporarily from my shoulders. I remembered what giddy felt like.

Time slowed, days stretched, but the calendar could not be denied. I clipped my Bluebadge onto the clothes I had shunned for the past 10 weeks as my feet trod the familiar path to the office. My tan arm hesitated as it reached for the button that summoned the end of my sabbatical and the elevator that carried me 24 floors back into the anxious arms of Microsoft once again. Deep breath. And another. Okay, let's do this! Doors opened.

Despite proclamations of, "It's so great to have you back! We missed you, Jane!" it seemed both Microsoft and the Device Team carried on just fine without me. Pallavi, my protégé with Wile E. Coyote tendencies, quite enjoyed the novelty of getting blown up and shot at in COEs and was reluctant to hand the stick of dynamite back to me. I looked around at the whirling dervish of activity, at the decisions still swirling and the progress unchanged since I'd been away and wondered if my presence (or absence) mattered or if the hole people make when they leave is simply filled in by another Road Runner, another Wile E. Coyote. Such were my thoughts as I walked into my team meetings and Career and Professional Development and Women's Leadership meetings where Pallavi, Dina, Dana and others had energetically and capably taken hold of the leadership reins. Just as they were meant and supposed to do.

Their confidence and conviction were validating and comforting yet made me pause. Was I really missed, needed or valuable to my team and others? My musings and vulnerabilities were met with laughter as I was told how often the phrase, "What would Jane do?" was bantered about over the past weeks when progress was difficult or people were uncertain. My absence hadn't left a hole, it had created a space. Like seeds that need fertile soil and sun, people were germinating and growing in the soil of opportunity I had tilled and the space I'd created. Once I stepped back and got a bit of perspective, it was easy to see how many seeds planted over the years were bearing fruit and now providing support for other seedlings.

I fought to maintain the perspective I had gained on sabbatical, to work fewer hours, to care less and let go more. I had changed, but of course Microsoft and the needs of the business had not. Soon I was consumed by texts, emails, reports, presentations and reviews that had seemed so unimportant for the past 10 weeks and now seemed urgent, critical and important once again. It wasn't long before thoughts of singing and proclamations of "Buckle up Buster!" receded. The giddy was lost in my giddyup as I hunkered down to work.

I don't know how much longer I might have remained on the Microsoft crazy train but lucky for me, two people derailed me with words so tough yet loving that I jumped from the train at full speed. The first came from Juliana, her head cocked to one side looking thoughtfully, sadly as if she'd lost something important. "Jane, you wouldn't like the person I see you becoming." Ooofh! Big gut punch from a tiny woman. The second happened in September, only a few weeks after returning from sabbatical and after coming home from work feeling excited about the new hires I'd just met, yet stressed and frustrated that I needed to work that evening to prepare for another review meeting in the morning. After explaining as much to Scott, he raised his hands and said,

"STOP! I can't stand it!"

"What?"

"I'm losing you and I can't stand it!"

"What?" I said, finally focusing, raising my eyes to his.

"In 30 years, you've asked my opinion on what you should do, we've discussed what's best for the family, I've given you my help and support. But you've never asked what *I* want you to do for *me*!"

"That's not true… but okay… what do you want?" I stammered, feeling ambushed and defensive. This wasn't fair. *Of course,* I had asked what Scott wanted through the years, hadn't I?!?!

"Jane, I want you to go upstairs and send your boss an email that says you're done, you quit. You're not coming in tomorrow or ever again. Be nice, or not. I don't care! I don't want to share you with Microsoft. I can't stand to lose you again. The Jane I fell in love with returned to me during the time you were on sabbatical. Now I'm losing that Jane all over again. I can't bear to see you leave me."

oh. silence.

"You're blowing this chance and you don't even see it! Jack is in his final year of high school. You could see and do all the things you've missed out on! We can afford for you to retire. Why are you choosing Microsoft over us? Jane, take the next year off and go back to work somewhere else if that's what you want. What *I* want is *you*. Now that I've had you back, I don't want to ever lose you again. I want *you*. That's what *I* want."

silence.

I stood there. Numb. Impenetrable. Mumbled something about how he was not losing me and went upstairs to change out of my work clothes. Nothing more was said when I returned downstairs, but our conversation kept running in a continuous loop, over and over it tumbled in my mind, "you're blowing it…missing out…losing you…want you… "

A few weeks later, I sat in a meeting with a dozen other executives planning our approach to the MYR - midyear review - scheduled for February. The insanity of planning for a meeting that would not occur for another five months seemed ridiculous but typical. We were ramping up and about to enter the review express lane. Vroom. Vroom. I knew what was coming. I'd done ten laps at Microsoft already. This would be my 11th annual review, so I knew how all-consuming and stressful the next few months would be, and how empty my tank would be once I crossed the finish line in five months, only to turn the corner before accelerating again. Scott's voice echoed in my head as his words pierced my heart. "I don't want to lose you again, Jane. I want *you*."

I thought of the many photos of my feet taken while on Sabbatical. Photos depicting where my feet wanted to be now that my leg was healthy. It was not at Microsoft.

I thought of the many jobs and how hard I'd worked to support me and others over the past three decades. I'd done a damn good job. It was enough.

I thought of the teams I'd built and the people I'd mentored and how they were now building and mentoring others. It was good.

I thought of all the people who still needed support. It wasn't enough. It would never be enough. There was more I could do.

I thought of my boys and friends with whom I wanted to spend more time and do more things. I could and would.

I thought of Scott, the struggles, the successes, the years behind and before us. I loved Scott and the life we'd created. I wanted *him*.

I thought of *me*. Of the little girl riding Buster, of the young woman stepping out of forestry and into corporate America and of my ache to step back into the mountains.

I was ready to go to the next part of my life, wherever that journey would take me. It was time.

I texted my boss and arranged a time to meet later that day. It was a short meeting. It took under 30 minutes to tap out of a career spanning 30 years.

I didn't leave because I was afraid I had or would 'blow it' as Scott had warned. I hadn't. Just the opposite. I had a strong marriage and a good family. I'd done a brilliant job, put in my time, done my best to inspire desire, to lift others up, and to help people be better and do more than they thought possible. I had done my best to create a living legacy. I had created a community of people who meant more than a job title, who were committed to making others better, stronger. I wasn't lost and didn't need to be found.

I left because it was time to go to what was next. It had seemed a lifetime ago I'd arrived at Kimberly-Clark wearing a pinstriped suit and floppy bow tie thingy. I'd experienced many roles, many countries, many evenings and weekends and many Dudleys and Kents since I had run out of gas in Chicago on my way to orientation so many years ago. It was time to change lanes gracefully, to exit the Microsoft expressway and enter the Boulware frontage road, to refuel and discover where the next road might lead. It was time to reset my GPS to Jane.

From Boxes to Becoming

"Small steps add up to complete big journeys."
— Matshona Dhliwayo

After weeks of goodbye happy hours, lunches, and coffees, it was my last day as a Bluebadge Softie. I made the final rounds, said the final farewells, and sent my last email, knowing I would not and could not log back in the following day. I had talked of retiring, as people do when they've had a bad day, but still, retirement had come suddenly, sneaking up slowly until it finally pounced.

My farewell email was brief....

> From: Jane Boulware
> Sent: October 13, 2015
> To: Device Newsletter Extended Team
> Subject: THANKS A MILLION – Commercial Managed Hits 1 Million Tablets!

We hit a major milestone this month, having shipped **1 million tablets** to US Commercial Managed customers since the Device team formed in FY14. Wow! I am so proud of what we have achieved together – building from zero a commercial managed Windows tablet business that has kicked iPad and Android butt with wins in every industry, segment, and geography. Thanks a Million!

Today is my last day at Microsoft; I leave you in the super-capable hands of Pallavi S and the Device Leadership Team. The foundation is laid, our momentum is strong, and we have the best team and products in the industry. I will be cheering you on from the bleachers as you take the business to the next million+ devices. It has been an honor.

Onward!

Jane

One million. My team had just sold and shipped their one millionth device, a milestone that seemed inconceivable less than three years ago. Yes, I felt proud of them and of me.

Click. Click. Click. I took my time logging off, typing my last OOF (out of office) message. This time there would be no return date, for I was leaving Microsoft and did not plan on returning to corporate America again. It didn't seem quite real, but the three cardboard boxes at my feet said otherwise.

Three sturdy boxes. Thirty years.

Two boxes were filled with awards and stuff showcasing what I had achieved over the years, boxes that reflected what I did, not who I was. I'd like to say they didn't matter to me but they mattered too much to be chucked or left behind.

That left One. Sturdy. Box.

One box whose contents mattered the most. A white pickle bucket with JANE written boldly across its belly in black marker contained treasures from the first 18 years of my childhood. Treasures from the past 30 years of my career were nestled into one cardboard box with

'THIS SIDE UP' written across its belly. Like Snorty in my pickle bucket of long ago, the memories held in Box One were precious to me.

The Jane bobblehead my team had made for me. She looked like she could tackle the world.

The photobooks. The cards. The jar filled with notes. *"Earn the trust of Jane and you've earned a dynamic champion of your work, your success and your life's passions." "The most phenomenal, inspiring, challenging and compassionate exec I've ever worked for." "Thank you for always having the team's back. It means the world to us!"*

It was quite a box, let me tell you, for in it were years of success and failure, of laughter and disappointment and, most important, of friendship. Box One was light, as happiness tends to be, but felt heavy, as loss always is. Unlike my pickle bucket, these treasures would not be lost, for I'd be carrying the experiences and friendships with me always.

Exiting Microsoft, I gratefully exhaled what was and deeply inhaled what was to be. "Buckle up, Buster!" I said to myself and smiled.

Retired to Inspired

*"The meaning of life is to find your gift.
The purpose of life is to give it away."*
— David Viscott

Surprised by the surge of emotions after leaving Microsoft, I felt like a crash test dummy who'd gone from 100 mph to an abrupt stop while everyone else remained in the fast lane, waving as they zoomed past, calling me a lucky bastard and wishing they were me. It was disorienting. Like a junkie, I missed the hit of adrenaline from being stressed out and in over my head. A friend swore it took her a year to detox after leaving Microsoft, often waking in sweaty anxiety from dreams of scorecards and MBRs. I missed the challenge of building businesses and people.

How can someone be retired and remain passionate and committed? I considered going back to work in corporate America, but it seemed a cop out to do what I knew and resume what I did. Yet there were things left unfinished in my life. After so many years addressing five-alarm fires, the thought of long lazy days filled with nothing to do didn't ding my bell.

Unable and unwilling to slow down, I continued to wake before 6am each morning, filling my calendar with mentoring, consulting and commitments made by and to others, just as I had at Microsoft. I didn't know how NOT to be busy, how NOT to work, having never done so. One sunny afternoon I heard the garage door open and sprang from my chair so Scott would not catch me sitting and doing nothing, as if he would scold me as my father had done years ago. Embarrassed by my actions, I set about learning how to say 'no' to others and 'yes' to myself, even/especially if the yes meant doing nothing more than enjoying a lazy day in my La-Z-Boy.

In time, my time became less filled with appointments, projects, and others. I found a new best friend and she is me. Yes, I still hear voices in my head whispering to do more of this and less of that, but it is becoming easier to shush the voices and put them in the background, like turning on the noise-canceling mode of my earbuds. My own name has moved from last place to among the first in line. I discovered that I am a joy to be with, just ask me. A bit guarded at first, but the more I open up and get to know myself, the more I like me. I'm not certain why I was so afraid to know me deeply, discover who I am. Maybe I was afraid I wouldn't like what I found. But I do. A lot.

My spirit gets younger by the day, and I find myself singing out loud, kayaking in Puget Sound, doing headstands on my paddleboard, hiking in Alaska, snowshoeing in the Cascades, walking in the rain, and golfing with Scott. I'm more often muddy and wet, wearing a ponytail and a smile than groomed and wearing the expensive jewelry that mostly stays locked away. Those who used to ask if I was feeling well now comment on how well I look. Is it the kickass cowboy boots or the sassy gal in them?

It turns out I am not alone in my later-in-life explorations, spiritual and otherwise. I have joined a group of women and mystics whom my sons refer to as my "woo-woo" friends. My woo-woo friends reawaken my faith by challenging it, taking it from something passive to something integral to my thinking and outlook. God finds me where I am, less in the church of my youth and more in nature where I celebrate God in all things living, praying in God's divine cathedral as did St Francis of Assisi.

I stop telling folks I'm retired because it's not true. I am *inspired*, but that's too hard to explain without sounding smug to those slogging through another day of work. Instead, I just say that I've shifted my time and talent from making a living to making a difference, paying forward what I've learned and earned.

That's why profits from this book are donated to Boys & Girls Clubs of America's Youth of the Year scholarships. Clubs provide the people, programs and opportunities that change lives… just as Sister Francis Xavier did for me so many years ago. So yeah, maybe my eyes don't glow like Sr FX, but until my spark sputters, my 'retirement' will be devoted to casting as bright a light as possible before my light burns out.

Mom

You can be a mess and still be a good mom. We are allowed to be both.
— unknown author

My mother's 80th birthday approached in my early days of "retirement." Maybe it was the milestone, or maybe it was because I finally had time to reflect on the past, present and future. As I said, I have no memories of being hugged or kissed as a child, although I suppose I was. Neither do my four brothers or sisters. Having five kids, juliejeffdougjanelinn, in six years makes all but the necessities unnecessary. Madonna Bernadette was the mom who said, "go outside" not "go play" for she had neither learned nor time to play. This is why if asked to name the color of my mom's eyes, I'd have said… sad. Sad and tired, but mostly sad.

Years ago, I took mom under my wing, where she has remained safely nestled. No matter how busy, we always made sure to talk throughout the week and visit throughout the year. Yet in all those years, she had never come to me. For her, airplanes were something to be feared, not flown. But time was slipping away and so was Madonna Bernadette. Finally, mom came to visit. As we sat quietly together on the deck one sunny afternoon, I summoned the courage to ask what it was like to raise five kids so close in age. I asked her to share her favorite memories. Silence. She sat in absolute stillness, looking somewhere I could not see, considering the question. "I can't. I don't know. I never think about it," she quietly stammered. "I've blocked those years out."

I got it. I was sad but not surprised. When things got too much, mom would need time to regroup, relearn coping skills and renew prescriptions, all of which occurred during periodic stays at the state mental hospital in Sioux City, IA. I thought back to one Saturday afternoon as a young girl working at Lou Walsh Motors. Dad and Mom pulled up in the car, rolled down the window, and said they were headed to Sioux City. Did I want to give Mom a hug, Dad asked, as Mom sat in the car looking straight ahead. I looked up from the car I was washing, "No. Goodbye." I answered, unsure when I'd see mom again as they drove away.

I understood why mom chose to tuck away all memories of those years. Opening her heart to a few cherished memories risked opening the floodgates to the bad memories that could drag her under into an abyss of sadness. So all memories were equally locked away. That night, I understood but couldn't stop the tears from soaking into my pillow as I replayed Mom's words over and over in my head. I tried to imagine a darkness so crushing that the joy of raising my two boys could not penetrate. I couldn't. I cried for my mom, in so much pain and guilt that she chose not to remember the years spent raising five beautiful children. And I cried for me. And for Julie, Jeff, Doug and Linn. In many ways, it was the five of us whom mom locked up and left behind in that mental hospital in Sioux City.

So as mom's 80th birthday approached, our conversation on the deck echoed in my head. I knew there was only one gift mom needed for her 80th birthday. Mom needed loving memories.

I sent an email to each of my siblings asking them to share their favorite memories of Mom from their childhood so we could create a memory book for her 80th birthday. I received no response. Nothing. Silence.

Oh boy. This wasn't going to be easy. Linn, the youngest and kindest, was first to come forward. Then Jeff, the pragmatic one, joined in. Doug wrote me a heart-felt, honest letter (in pencil) letting me know that he had no memories of Mom besides ones involving chores. There was nothing he could share that she'd want to read, he insisted. Julie remained. completely. silent.

Okay, okay. Let's, I proposed, share memories of our childhood in general, not just memories of Madonna Bernadette. Ahhhh…that got the creaky wheels turning. Eventually, even Julie the oldest, upon whom much responsibility of raising four siblings fell, came forward with stories and fond memories.

In the months leading to Madonna Bernadette's 80th birthday, my brothers and sisters and I cobbled together memories. I carefully printed each memory onto 6"x6" squares, our childhood captured in slips of colored paper. On the weekend of mom's birthday, we gathered as one. Julie, Jeff, Doug, Linn and I folded and refolded each piece of paper. Did anyone else notice that Julie had the most memories, each folded slowly, carefully, tightly, as if trying to keep the memory contained. Jeff, the engineer, folded corner to corner, neatly, cleanly, and efficiently; the memories were a task to be finished. Doug invited his teen daughter to fold his papers, still reluctant to be too close to them. Linn folded her papers only once, as if the memories didn't want to be contained any longer and were eager to be told. I didn't fold my papers. I scrunched them. For me, the memories were messy with lots of edges that simply couldn't be made two dimensional.

All five of us were in our fifties, with children of our own. Time had softened the sharp edges of our stories. Looking around, we realized Madonna Bernadette had done something special because each of us (and our families) were gathered from across the country to celebrate her. We loved one another, were friends and would do anything for each other. We were good people who had raised good kids using experiences and lessons informed by Madonna Bernadette. Our hearts were full as we dumped the pretty papers into the glass bowl that Linn had decorated with the word "Memories."

Together with our kids, we took Madonna Bernadette to dinner at the only Italian restaurant in Carroll, Iowa. Over spaghetti and chicken alfredo, we removed the pretty papers from the jar one by one, reading each memory aloud. We laughed together. We cried together. At mom's request, a few papers were torn up and not returned to the jar. One by one, one laugh, one tear at a time – the stories healed the cracks in our hearts.

That night, mom remembered. That night, mom heard and witnessed the deep love of her five children and their acknowledgement that she had done the best she could. That we were proud of her and we loved her. That night, I saw my mom's eyes were green.

Mom later told my Aunt Kathy it was the best day of her life.

Youth of the Year

"Start where you are. Use what you have. Do what you can."
— Arthur Ashe

"We rise by lifting others."
— Robert Ingersoll

It's been many years since I served on the board of the Boys & Girls Club in Wisconsin, since Scott and I drove a busload of kids to Lambeau Field. I am still a cheesehead and though the memory of a little boy on the bus is years ago and miles away, I'm still haunted by his whisper *"it's not her day to eat."* So when asked to join the board of Boys & Girls Club of Bellevue (BGCB), I said 'Yes.'

Four days later, my car's GPS announced "You have reached your destination" while pulling into a Boys & Girls Club Youth Center I didn't know existed. It was a dark and gloomy night, as was the building before me. What am I doing at a Youth Center? At 56, I'm no youth and I don't feel centered. Hmmm…. would anyone notice if I ditched and went to McDonalds instead? Suddenly the Club doors burst open, unable to contain the energy of so many kids within, kids of every color and size, laughing, playing music and games, being kids. "Okay, fine. I might as well go inside," I thought, drawn toward the light and laughter. I was surprised and delighted to be greeted by welcoming shouts only to realize the enthusiasm was for the pizza delivery guy entering behind me. Oh. Not bearing food of any kind, I was overlooked and out of place amongst those who had made this place their own.

"You must be Jane. I saw you walk in," said the Youth Director, taking in my wrinkles, long blonde hair, diamond earrings and dress slacks. He steered me away from the pizza table (dammit!) toward a long, rickety table with folding chairs and four adults who looked more like the kids than like me. The five of us were here to judge the Youth of the Year speeches that evening, determining who would receive a coveted scholarship and get to advance to regional competition. I felt the four other judges sizing me up, for I too was being judged. I failed. I failed the 'too' test. I was too rich, too white, too old. *I* couldn't possibly relate to what *they* felt or experienced. Us vs Them all over again.

Despite my warm smile and hello, the conversation and eye contact politely bypassed me. True, I didn't look like, talk like or live like 'them.' Not now. But I had been here before. Years ago, I'd been the one standing before the rickety table, scared and nervous, giving a speech that would earn me a small scholarship. If it weren't for the $320 scholarship I won in high school, in a room just like this one, I might still be working at, versus eating at, McDonalds. I know that even a small scholarship can go a long way, and so understood what this opportunity meant. They might not see me, but I saw them.

I saw the nervous girl on a makeshift stage hiding behind heavy makeup, baggy black clothes and tattoos, her arms more accustomed to handling French fries than holding notecards. In her scared brown eyes I saw mine. She spoke with a distinct accent, yet her voice was mine as she said her name. Alisha. Alisha rocked from foot to foot seeking equilibrium on a stage foreign and frightening, yet remained steady and steadfast in her determination, committed to accomplishing this thing she had set out to do. Tears threatened but did not betray. Her strength was undeniable as she told her story of overcoming and her hope for the future. For Alisha, the road ahead would not be an extension of the path behind. Through the Boys & Girls Club, she was learning to chart a different course to a destination that she, not others, chose.

I leaned in, listening as another teen spoke. And another. And another. The kids' gender, age and race varied, but each wove a story was woven with threads of despair, resilience, hope and action. They were what the little boy on the bus looked like when grown. As I left the Teen Center that night, I silently promised scholarships for Youth of the Year.

Three weeks later, COVID hit. Schools, businesses, and services everywhere were closing. The board of directors met to discuss and vote to close Club doors. The Boys & Girls Clubs of Bellevue was struggling to make payroll, even without COVID. The decision was a no-brainer.

> "The risk!" "The uncertainty!" "There's no money!" All agreed.
> "What would it take to keep the doors open?" The question shifted our energy and conversation.
> "The schools are closed. There's no way to even get kids to the Clubs."
> "But what if we could?" said another.
> "We can find a way. We just haven't yet."
> "We'll do whatever it takes." All agreed.

And so we did. There was no choice. It was indeed a no-brainer. We would keep the doors open for kids who had no place else to go now that schools and all other doors were closed to them. It would only be for a few weeks, we told ourselves.

But as the weeks dragged on, the kids, the Club and the board became more desperate. Without school and its free lunch programs, many had no place to go and nothing to eat.

The kids who came to the Club were those who could least afford to pay. Our revenue was down 95% yet we expanded, opening 7:30am-5:30pm to serve those who needed us most. The Club was sanitized, hands were washed and washed again, temperatures were taken, masks were worn, meals were given, remote learning was initiated. Kids soon looked past the masks and began smiling with their eyes, laughter ringing down the hallways as fear gave way to hope and happiness once more, for anything is possible on a full stomach. The **Boys & Girls Clubs of Bellevue** stayed open, providing services for 75 straight weeks. In total, more than 127,000 meals were provided to kids and their families and $1 million in scholarship and financial aid funds were awarded.

Like the story of the loaves and the fishes, I can't explain how the staff and Club made it through COVID. Day after day, Club staff left the safety of their homes and their own kids to care for others' kids. The Club served the kids, and the Board served the Club. The Board stepped forward and up, over and over, to meet the Club's needs. Those who had, gave and motivated others to give and give and give until there was enough for all. Together we raised enough to keep Club doors open, kids safe and bellies full.

Never was it whispered, *"It's not her day to eat."*

As the threat of COVID receded, some asked when we'd finally be back to normal. Never. You can't go back to what was when you've become awakened to what is. It was clearer than ever there was more than ever to do. A year after joining the Boys and Girls Clubs of Bellevue, I became Chairman of the Board. I didn't really want to or feel qualified, but was asked and able, and so I did. I had to. I had to because I'm no longer the kid seeking the scholarship, I'm the person ensuring the scholarship exists.

I had reached my destination and had a promise to keep.

It's Time

"There's only one thing more precious than our time and that's who we spend it on."

— Leo Christopher

"When I stand before God at the end of my life, I would hope that I would not have a single bit of talent left and could say, 'I used everything you gave me.'"

— Erma Bombeck

I've had a Tiffany & Co clock on my desk for more than 20 years. I really like that clock. I received it while at Kimberly-Clark, my first-ever Tiffany gift. It came in the legendary pale blue box with instructions to bring the clock to a designated Tiffany & Co store whenever the clock stopped running. Of course, there were no Tiffany & Co stores near Neenah, WI so I dutifully schlepped that clock with me to NYC, Chicago, etc. and went through the hassle of finding a store and waiting for the folks there to do their magic to get the clock running again. What a pain in the ass. That's how much I liked the clock. For years I did this. Until recently. Recently, I noticed the clock had stopped again. I rummaged around my desk drawer until I found the teeny tiny screwdriver that I use to tighten my glasses on occasion. I began to unscrew the back of the clock. I unscrewed the little plate inside. Then I saw it. An Energizer battery. WTF.

There was no magic unique to Tiffany & Co. For years I had followed the instructions given, having been told they could do something I could not, when I had the capability all along to keep the clock running. So who do I curse – the bogus instructions or me for following them?

There will always be Kents and Tiffanys instructing what can't, won't and shouldn't be done. Sometimes, the loudest voice limiting and tearing me down is my own. It's my choice. I choose which voice I listen to and act upon – the ones lifting and encouraging onward or tearing down and holding back. Whenever I *compare* my insides with your outsides, I feel unworthy and threatened. But when I *share* my strengths and celebrate yours, we are both stronger. Your strength doesn't threaten me, nor does my strength weaken you. It becomes okay not to know, wise to ask, and human to experience FUD. I am not an imposter when I fail to achieve impossible expectations, twisting myself into a pretzel by attempting to do and please all. All that does is make me crusty and salty.

If I did nothing, pursued nothing, achieved nothing, even then, I would be worthy.

Like you, I am worthy as I am. I didn't have to earn it. I didn't become it. My worth didn't come in a Tiffany's blue box, a graduate degree, a bank statement, or an impressive title. I didn't lose it when I fell off Buster, while bent over the toilet purging, when I succumbed to FUD, got dunked, failed. Kent didn't take it from me nor did Microsoft. Scott didn't give it to me, nor did Dudley, my friends or my kids. It was there all along, waiting to be claimed. It is my birthright. As a child, a student, an adult in every city, country, and company I lived in and worked for, I was worthy. I *am* worthy. I am enough.

Now I know. Maybe I always did, if only a little bit sometimes.

I acknowledge my worth each time I create and use a yardstick for success that measures what is important to me, not you. Each time I hear 'not yet' when others say 'no.' Each time I create a door where others see only walls. Each time I walk through a door and hold it open for others to follow. Each time I extend and lend my own uncertain hand to help steady you. I recognize and honor my worth when I pick myself up and begin again. And again. And again. Because success doesn't mean I don't fail, it means I don't quit.

In the quest to fill my pickle bucket, I've climbed high and breathed rare air… and fallen far and landed hard. At times, my bucket runneth over. Other times it echoed, empty and bottomless. In truth, my worth was never defined by how much I put into my bucket but by how much I took out and shared with others.

Scott recently asked, "I mean this in the most loving way, but do you ever think you're doing too much?" As a sign of how much I have grown, I neither rolled my eyes at the first half of his question nor got defensive at the last half. Instead, I thought about his question during my walk that night. And the next. Huh. "Am I doing too much?" is never something I had seriously asked myself… or been asked. It was a very good question.

Yes, maybe I did/do too much sometimes. But in a world that needs so much, I did what I could and do what I can. When I stand before God at the end of my life, I would hope that I would not have a single bit of talent left and could say, 'I used everything you gave me.' Until the clock of my life ticks its last tock, I will stand up, show up and lift up. It is who I am… or try to be.

Today's culture tells me to airbrush my life, to show only the parts of me that are pretty, perfect, plastic. Yet strength and beauty are found in the bits and pieces we hide from others, in the parts of our lives never posted on Instagram. When I share what is imperfect in me and you share what is incomplete in you, we peel away the veneer of perfectionism to reveal what is real and true, proclaiming all our bits and parts worthy, beautiful and valuable.

Far from perfect yet I acknowledge my worth, beauty and value. It's been a struggle to get here, let me tell you. And I struggle still. So I share what I know and learned in hope you struggle less.

So you know.

So you know you are worthy. Regardless of gender, age, income, race, or title. You are enough. So, wind your own clock and silence the voices that keep you small or dim your flame. Set upon the journey and summon the courage to champion what is good and worthy in yourself and others. Though it seems unclear, you will find your way. There is always a way, even if you have not found it yet. For there is no better way to do great things than to begin and no one more worthy of success than you. It's time.

Epilogue

"The life I touch for good or ill will touch another life, and in turn another, until who knows where the trembling stops or in what far place my touch will be felt."

— Frederick Buechner

As a child, I didn't know the color of Mom's eyes because I never saw them. They were focused elsewhere and always, understandably, busy. We were both still young when I first tucked Mom under my wing for protection and only years later, when considered old by most others, was I able see the world through her eyes, which I learned were green.

In her final years, we spent hours talking of death, purgatory, and heaven. Mom was pretty sure she wasn't going to hell, but heaven seemed a longshot, despite the many rosaries said, novenas prayed, and masses attended. She was placing her bets on purgatory, the Catholic way station between heaven and hell, where exit is earned through the grace of others still living. "Well," I asked Mom, "isn't that the same as life? Maybe we receive grace from love and acts of kindness… and misery from hateful words and actions? Maybe you're in purgatory now and when you die, you'll go straight to heaven, just pass Go and collect your reward."

"JANE!! It doesn't work that way!" she insisted adamantly, fearing a lightning bolt would strike me. Since I was already blaspheming, I decided to push my luck and told her how I planned to finally take her hiking with me after she passed and asked her to send me a sign to let me know she was happy, wherever she was. Again, I heard "JANE!! It doesn't work that way!" Despite her considerable angst, no lightning bolt struck me down, which I took as a positive sign.

I talked to Mom nearly every day through the decades and could tell how she was feeling by the way she said 'hello' when answering the phone, so I was not surprised by her final goodbye. It's impossible to know if she finally passed from cancer, Alzheimer's or something else but all my efforts to shepherd Mom to a peaceful passing were met with strong resistance. I'm not sure if I was a shitty shepherd or she a stubborn sheep. Probably both.

Her passing wasn't pretty, but Madonna Bernadette was laid to rest surrounded by 8 children/spouses, 12 grandkids, 4 great grandkids, brothers, nieces, nephews and many life-long friends, each recalling lively days where her open smile, perpetual wit and sharp tongue were wielded freely. Determined to leave her children an inheritance, Mom squirreled away dollar bills, saved and shoved in an orange, plastic Metamucil canister we discovered in the bowels of the bathroom cabinet. She hadn't much, so each dollar represented something she didn't purchase for herself, but instead wished for us.

Yet we received far more than she could have wished. Did she hear her kids and grandkids laugh, cry and sing from a circle of lawn chairs in my brother's garage following her funeral? Did we not echo family reunions of yesteryear? Surely no choir of heavenly angels sounded more divine (insert lightning bolt here). Although Mom questioned her contribution, if life is measured in love, friendship, faith, hard work and conviction, Madonna Bernadette's impact is long-lasting and lives on in her family and those whose lives she touched.

Mom was finally at peace. Well, not quite.

As promised, when I returned from Iowa, I took Madonna Bernadette hiking in the mountains. On the crest of a favorite trail, I stopped for lunch. I talked and shared the views with Mom, as if she sat beside me, even though I knew "JANE! It doesn't work that way!" Despite the blustery day, a feather slowly, gracefully, landed on my peanut butter and jelly sandwich. It just sat there. I laughed and cried, realizing Mom was no longer under my wing. I was under hers. I guess that's the way it works.

Acknowledgments

It was never my intent to write a book, much less one so personal. I promised to write down some of my stories. That's all. But stories want to be heard and soon there were too many to print, too many people to honor. Thank you to those important stories and people found and not found in these pages. You know who you are.

Family is my favorite word. For me, family starts with my husband, Scott, and sons Andy and Jack. For over four decades, Scott has lived nearly every story with me, never doubting or questioning my worth, anchoring me and our family with faith, support and crazy glue when things cracked. He wasn't sure about me writing this book, but knows I keep my promises. Jack was guardian of my voice throughout the process. There were bitter versions of some stories until Jack said 'That doesn't sound like you, Mom' and he was right. I listened as Jack helped me reflect the light in the darkness, to find my voice through words honest and fair. In the process, I got to know, see, share and receive more of Jack than ever before. I'd write the book again, just for that. Andy gave me the courage and encouragement to continue. He didn't join in the process until it was nearly finished, when I was losing faith and momentum. Andy told me it was great and really resonated with him. Then he called me a few weeks later to talk through a problem he was having, saying this book made him realize I could relate to what he was going through. I melted. And finished the book.

Thank you to...

family by blood and by marriage mentioned directly and indirectly, including Julie Jeff Doug Linn Madonna Ron Audry Jack Marilyn Tammy-Kim Mary Beth Matt Clay – you've scratched your head at my choices sometimes, but you've always been there with support, love, and prayers.

my large, extended family of friends – you've scratched your head at my choices sometimes, but always provide wine, wisdom, support and shenanigans, if not prayers. Special shout out to Eileen & Charlie Kollmeyer, Jennifer Mount, Patti Cockerham, Janneke van den Berkmortel, Joanie Parsons, Sarah Haggard, Lisa Hufford, Paula Pollack for your encouragement and positive nudging throughout the process. Super duper special shout out to Karla Obernesser and Jan Hill who highlighted, underlined, marked up, and made notes page by page, over more than one glass of wine. There aren't enough toasts in the world to express my gratitude.

Dudley Lehman and the many high-integrity leaders like him for doing your best in ways big and small. You make a big difference, even if you don't know or receive credit for it.

Corbin Lewars, my editor. This would still be a bunch of discombobulated stories if not for her rubix-cube capabilities, faith, and friendship.

Julia Pollack for helping with the final push of Worthy's birthing process, providing much-needed expertise and energy when I became tired and cranky. Together with Lyssa at Cedar House Audio, Shiloh Schroeder at Fusion Creative Works and Erin Donley, we delivered a beautiful, strong book.

Jane Boulware for being resilient, courageous, honest, fun and real. I like that you make people scratch their head at your choices sometimes. Even if no one else reads this, you still wrote it. Promise kept.

Made in United States
Troutdale, OR
02/19/2024

17825753R00181